On Hegel's Logic

On Hegel's Logic

Fragments of a Commentary

by
John W. Burbidge

HUMANITIES PRESS
NEW JERSEY

First published in the United States of America in 1981 by
Humanities Press International, Inc.
Atlantic Highlands, N.J. 07716

First paperback reprint 1995

Library of Congress Cataloging in Publication Data
Burbidge, John W., 1936–
   On Hegel's logic.

   Bibliography: p.
   Includes indexes.
   1. Hegel, Georg Wilhelm Friedrich, 1770–1831—Logic.
2. Logic. I. Title.
B2949.L8B87 160 81-6699
ISBN 0–391–03902–4 (pbk) AACR2

Printed in the United States of America

To My Teachers

Preface

In the Introduction to the *Science of Logic*[1] Hegel compares the superficial ease with which a young man mouths a proverb with the wisdom that is enshrined in the same statement made by one who is old and experienced. In the course of passing from one to the other, an individual goes over the thought a number of times, each time discovering a new implication, explicating a term that was vague and general into something precise and detailed.

Such a self-correcting process lies behind the present study. But it would be foolish to assume that it has reached completion. The way in which drafts, which had appeared to be sufficient, dissolved into ambiguity and imprecision requiring rethinking and reconstruction gives evidence against too presumptuous a claim. Yet the fundamental principle of interpretation (derived from Hegel's Psychology and from Paragraphs 79 to 82 of the Encyclopaedia) has been confirmed and strengthened to the point that a self-justification of the process has been achieved. On this basis, I am strongly tempted to make the same claim as Hegel: "I could not pretend that the method which I follow in this system of logic—or rather which this system on its own follows—is not capable of greater completeness, of much elaboration in detail; but at the same time I know that it is the only true method."[2]

In the course of reaching this stage on the pilgrimage to philosophical wisdom I have benefited from many who have taught me both formally and informally over the years. All are intended in the dedication of this volume. But a number need to be mentioned because of their relation to the particular content of this study.

It was Emil Fackenheim who first ignited my interest in Hegel, who introduced me to the mysteries of the *Phenomenology,* and who ten years later supervised a dissertation on the relation between the logic and the philosophy of religion of Hegel and Schelling. Without his inspiration and example, I would have left Hegel behind as a philosopher remembered from an undergraduate education. Under Thomas Langan I had the good fortune to be introduced to the *Science of Logic* for the first time not in translation but in the original German. While embarking on that undertaking I became associated with Klaus Hedwig, with whom I read and discussed·difficult passages, and who over the years has always been ready to debate questions of interpretation. The final version of the following monograph benefited significantly from his very perceptive criticisms of an earlier draft. Jacques D'Hondt, Kenneth Schmitz and Jim Paulin have provided informal encouragement and instruction. The manuscript was first drafted while I was working at the *Centre de Recherche et de Documentation sur Hegel et Marx* at Poitiers, welcomed by the Directeur, M. Planty-Bonjour and the Sécretaire, M. Vadée.

Not only teachers of Hegel should be mentioned, but also teachers in logic and the philosophy of logic: David Savan, Arthur Pap, Alan R. Anderson, and Fred Wilson. Although none of them would particularly agree with what I have done with their instruction, this book would not be as logically precise as it is, were it not for their influence.

Finally there are those of my colleagues and associates at Trent who have provided many invaluable opportunities for discussion and reflection on these themes: David Kettler, Costas Boundas, Karl Rautenkranz, Bill Phelan, Peter Royle, John Hillman, as well as the faculty and students of the Philosophy Colloquium. My secretary, Marian O'Brien, has managed to type these incomprehensible pages not only once, but twice, with barely a mistake. And my wife and family have supported and encouraged the venture throughout a sabbatical year in Poitiers, France, and again during a summer vacation at Montsoreau on the Loire. Indeed it would be hard to imagine the writing of this book without the benefit of French wine, French cheese, and French bread, enjoyed in their company.

Table
of
Contents

Part One

Prolegomena

Introduction

Nothing seems less appropriate than the title of Hegel's most important work. The *Science of Logic* appears to be neither scientific nor about logic.

This judgement filters through the comments of many anglophone interpreters: "I think it is an important fact about Hegel that there is a tremendous amount of arbitrariness in the course that he takes."[1] "In fact most of [the] arguments collapse ignominiously without the underlying premise of ontological necessity."[2] "I think that he did not in all respects completely understand the nature of that dialectical relation between ideas which he had discovered."[3] "The abstract nature of the universal, the disparate character of the contraries, the inadequate grounding of contradiction—each of these is nothing but the persistence of the empirical factor which we tried vainly to dispel in our discussion of opposites."[4]

When one turns from friends to foes, the criticism becomes more strident. "Hegel thought that, if enough was known about a thing to distinguish it from all other things, then all its properties could be inferred by logic. This was a mistake, and from this mistake arose the whole imposing edifice of his system. This illustrates an important truth, namely, that the worse your logic, the more interesting the consequences to which it gives rise."[5] "Hegel's intention is to operate freely with all contradictions. 'All things are contradictory in themselves,' he insists, in order to defend a proposition which means the end not only of all science, but of all rational argument."[6]

Is this assessment justified? Does Hegel fail when measured against his own criteria? To answer these questions will be the task of the following study.

The theme of our approach can be briefly stated. To evaluate Hegel's logic against the conventional standards of formal logic begs the question. For Hegel is asking about the grounds of all logical validity: what justifies the norms that logic imposes on the world—the intuitive transitions, the laws of thought, and the forms of inference? In showing how Hegel responds to this problem, our commentary follows an heretical pathway: we ignore Hegel's suggestion that the logic is a metaphysics. Even though Taylor, Mure, Findlay and McTaggart all claim that the development of the *Logic* demands reference to ontological and empirical material to justify its transitions, we consider its argument to reflect simply the operations of pure thought.[7]

To substantiate the claim that the *Logic* is the science of pure thought, we undertake two preliminary investigations. We clarify what is distinctive about thinking as a psychological operation—what makes it different from other functions of intelligence. Then we indicate how thought may purify itself from relativizing contingencies. These tasks command our attention in the next two chapters. Hegel's psychology provides us with clues to the way in which thinking is generated out of, and distinguished from, the functions of intuition, recollection, imagination and memory. And his theory of language shows how individual idiosyncrasies and cultural prejudices can be transcended.

Our subsequent commentary is deliberately fragmentary. Rather than reviewing every chapter of the *Logic* we will consider only the first section of each of the three books—these being concerned directly with the concepts and categories of intellectual operations. In the first of these sections, "Quality," thinking is presented in its most immediate transitions, namely becoming,alteration and process; in the section on "Essence as Reflection into Self," we examine the laws of thought and the principle of sufficient reason; in "Subjectivity," concepts, judgements and inferences are analyzed.

Seldom are the pure logical categories entertained in abstract isolation as pure meanings. They are used rather to articulate structures and features of the world. Despite the fact that terms such as *being, quality, ground,* and *individual* are concepts, they also characterize what is. Hence it is no wonder that logical patterns are mirrored in systems of metaphysics and epistemology, and that a significant parallel can be discovered between the history of philosophy and logical developments.[8] Although

Hegel makes reference to philosophies and philosophers of the past, however, such material is used simply to illustrate the structure of pure thought. For reasoning, which has been used to justify their philosophical claims and to show their limitations, need not be historically contingent but may be objective and universal. By appealing simply to the history of philosophy, Hegel could not justify his claim to science. Intelligence on its own has to distinguish its concepts clearly and to bring any resulting movement of thought consciously to mind. From the perspective of this intellectual discipline alone will the student see in the history of thought a coherent progress rather than a random succession of discoveries. Hence we shall not pause to discuss Hegel's remarks on possible applications of his discussion either to the history of philosophy, or to nature and world history. Hegel's lectures on these topics can be appropriated on their own. By proposing a purely logical exposition, we will face the more fundamental difficulties in Hegel's philosophy, which are conceptual.

The abstractness of our approach leaves aside much that attracted Hegel's attention. However, our concluding chapters do look at two large areas that ultimately need to be incorporated into a comprehensive philosophical perspective: our experience of the world (which is the subject matter of the *Phenomenology),* and our disciplined reflections on nature and history (which complete the encyclopaedic system).

It is by now evident that this study of Hegel has adopted the principles of Hegelian analysis. Its fundamental premise is that a philosopher is to be allowed to interpret himself. Only when his argument is taken seriously on its own terms can it be effectively assessed in terms of its adequacy or truth. This critical assessment grows out of the concrete internal character of the specific philosophical enterprise.

The last word, then, lies with the reader. Each reflective thinker needs to come to grips with the heart of the matter, struggle with its complexities, and become convinced (or otherwise) of its inherent structure. His own intelligence is sufficient to discern and apply any relevant evaluating criteria. After all, if Hegel's *Logic* is a science, it will justify itself only through such a reference of pure thinking to itself.

2

Representations
and
Thoughts

"The difference between representation and thought is of special importance: because philosophy may be said to do nothing but transform representations into thought."[1] Both representations and thoughts involve intellectual operations. Only the latter, however, can provide content for a philosophical science of logic. Thought, Hegel suggests, relates ideas with a measure of necessity, while representation is continually affected by contingency. Thought is under the constraint of its own deliberate procedures; but representation often responds to external stimuli and unconscious associations. To enter the realm of speculative philosophy, then, one must first transform representations into thoughts.

Such a distinction, when first presented, has the appearance of being a stipulative condition for the Hegelian enterprise. But if it is not justified, other positions are equally possible. *All* mental operations are radically conditioned by contingency, say the empiricists, and the validity of any idea or of any relation will depend on some external consideration such as its correspondence to the actual state of the world. Any mental association, reply the romantics, is the product of that depth within the soul which is in contact with ultimate truth; it only needs interpretation to become a profound revelation of inherent necessity. Each refuses to make a satisfactory distinction: the first imputes contingency to thoughts as well as representations, the second expects to find necessity in the most casual associations.

Hegel reflects on the contingency and necessity of intellectual processes when he distinguishes thought from representation and from intuition. At the same time he shows how they are related—how one prepares the way for another. But this analysis does not lie within the science of logic itself, since the discipline of pure thought is to have already freed itself from the contingency of representations. Rather, since thinking and representing are both operations of the mind, their differences and similarities will be shown only by careful psychological analysis.

Our commentary on Hegel's logic thus requires a preparatory study of his chapter on Psychology.[2] By rendering determinate the character of diverse intellectual operations, we will be able to recognize in them the ground that underlies and justifies the transitions, reflections, and conceptualizations of pure thought. Hegel's claim to an inherent scientific necessity will thereby not be based simply on an appeal to immediate intuition but will be opened up to critical evaluation.

Intuition

The first intellectual operation Hegel considers, namely intuition, displays an important characteristic: although it is an activity of intelligence[3] it does not alter the intuited content; its object is present prior to any distortions resulting from external reflection. The act of intuiting, then, is not complex, but simple and direct. In the immediacy of the moment intellectual activity is united with some determinate content; and once this something is "seen" no further justification is required. The act by itself justifies the validity of the content, and the truth of the content is self-evident for the intuiting agent.[4]

The fact that this intellectual action does not distort suggests that "behind its back," so to speak, and unsuspected in its conscious activity is a process of mediation. For two conditions have to be fulfilled. In the first place, the object must become transparent to the activity of intellect, leaving no impenetrable surd. In the second, the agent must act vis-à-vis the object in such a way that he does not simply fit it into his subjective and contingent whims, but surrenders himself to the object as it is. Intuiting intelligence must unite these two conditions in a simple and single act.

When the object is presented only through contingent sensations or experiences, its essential nature may remain hidden. Kant, for example, argued that sensations are only *appearances* of a thing. His rejection of intellectual intuition is a direct correlate of this claim that the opaque object, as given, resists the penetration of the mind, even when the latter operates according to the demands of strict objectivity.

Alternatively, the subject, conscious of himself as desiring, may seek to appropriate the object into his own world. His contingent interests focus his attention on those features that respond to his particular projects. Subjective activity then introduces an arbitrary selection that prevents the agent from being open to the fundamental characteristics of the object itself. Even though the resistance of the object is overcome and it becomes transparent to the agent's desires, his activity distorts its inherent features and misrepresents its nature.

In his Phenomenology,[5] Hegel outlines the processes through which these two impediments to genuine intuition are overcome. The first involves pushing the Kantian analysis of experience one step further by rendering implicit features explicit. The second traces the actual experiences of the individual who seeks to organize the objective world around his subjective desires.

Kant draws a sharp distinction between an arbitrary association and one that is objectively necessary: the latter is justified by a rule or law.[6] The relation of sufficient condition, however, is not one of temporal succession, but of reason. The "I", as intellectual agent, draws an analogy between the rational principle of sufficient reason and a temporal series.[7] This means that only where "I" can find determining conditions in the content of sensation can "I" conclude that the succession has objective validity. Otherwise "I" have only a contingent, subjective stream of consciousness.

The conditions that justify applying the category of cause are derived neither from the subject nor from the a priori forms of appearance (space and time) but from the given qualitative content of the appearances, which is presented directly by the thing in itself. The "I", then, separates subjective associations from objective relations by distinguishing those aspects of appearances that are introduced by the subject—their spatial and temporal diversity—from those aspects that are intrinsic to the thing as it really is. Having made this distinction, it can then use the latter to infer that objective nature. The thing in itself is no longer opaque, no longer in principle hidden from view. For once space and time's distortions have been annulled, the process of sufficient reasoning reproduces in intelligence the dynamic relation that integrates the many appearances into one object. Intelligence, then, has the same relating structure as the ground of phenomenal experience.[8]

The second impediment is overcome through the processes of self-consciousness. Although desire appropriates objects into the world of the subject, it meets an obstacle when it seeks to appropriate another desiring subject. For the latter on its part is endeavouring to cancel the independence of the former. A struggle results, and the stronger forces the weaker to obey his whims. While the victor can still cater to his own personal interests, the vanquished must limit his actions. He cannot simply appropriate the object; he must struggle with its independence and transform it according to the wishes of the stronger. His egotistic desires are subjected both to the demands of the master and to the resistant characteristics of the object. Pushed beyond his contingent subjectivity he is forced to treat the world as it is, even though he is also acting on it. "This quaking of the single, isolated will," said Hegel, "the feeling of worthlessness of egotism, the habit of obedience, is a necessary moment in the education of all men."[9] The child, for example, disciplined by the stronger will of the parent or teacher, begins to take the subject matter studied with utmost seriousness, and does not simply regard it as the arena for his own arbitrary interests.

Through the two processes of understanding and of disciplined submission, the impediments to intuition are overcome. But these two necessary conditions are not sufficient. For intuition is grounded in an immediate unity of subject intuiting and object intuited. Both processes, then, must come together in one subject who is relating to an objective world. And not only must they be synthetically coexisting; they must be integrated into a single activity.[10] Intuition identifies with the object because in one intellectual process it both reproduces the inherent dynamic of the object and subjugates its own whims to the resisting characteristics of that object. Authentic intuition can be immediate only where this synthesis has crystallized into such a simple unity that its distinct moments have vanished into oblivion.

This unity has collapsed the determinate moments of the mediating process. Intelligence simply finds itself determined; it has thereby a content. But the content is present in its own activity—in feeling. The immediacy of this moment precludes any reflection that would specify its characteristics. Therefore, although intelligence is one with its object in that it feels determined, its activity is only a muffled pulsation.[11] And since no context of relations explicitly determines its character, it is bedevilled by contingent particularity. Its content may be "the most sterling and true" or it may be "the most scanty and most untrue."[12] One or other of the necessary conditions may be lacking, or insufficiently present; the determination may be of something important or trivial. Because the "pulse" is "muffled" it does not present its material unambiguously.

Intelligence does not rest content with this indistinct immediacy. It reacts to the felt fact of being determined and directs its *attention* to what has occured. Various aspects of the original determination are, one after another, brought to consciousness, isolating them in succeeding moments of time. And by thus distinguishing between the attending act and its determinate content, intelligence situates the latter in external space. The intellectual content that was presented in the simple immediacy of a single activity has fallen apart into discrete moments that are related externally by temporal succession and spatial contiguity. The first determination introduced by intelligence to clarify the content of intuition, then, is this crystallization of its external relations—the process of attention. Oblivious to inherent characteristics or implicit context, it simply isolates the given content into discrete moments that are now external to the intellectual activity itself.[13]

Both the moment of immediate feeling and that of attention are, however, the acts of the same mind. Thus, when it directs its attention to these processes instead of to their content, it becomes aware of their essential relation. The immediacy of feeling contains implicitly the moments differentiated by attention; attention can only differentiate because it presupposes the immediacy of feeling. Each is but an abstracted moment of a single process. This unity of feeling's unity and attention's disunity is *intuition* proper.[14]

Several aspects of this analysis of intuition need to be stressed because of their significance for what follows. In the first place, because the immediacy of feeling is itself mediated by the double process of understanding and submission, its determinations are not subjective impositions on an alien object, but instead provide access to characteristics inherent in the subject-matter intuited. This content will be retained through the various processes of recollection, imagination and memory as the material which is progressively appropriated by intelligence. No new material—even that of its own intellectual operations—can become its object unless it both determines the mind as immediate feeling, and enters the focus of attention.

In the second place, although feeling certainly happens in time (and in space)[15] its content is not initially present to intelligence as spatially and temporally determinate. The content acquires such a form *for* intelligence because of the latter's activity in attention. Since this external form is the result of an intellectual initiative, it offers no resistance in principle to being translated into the private time of memory and imagination; and in due course its effects can be annulled when the intellect becomes master not only of the content but also of the form of its activity. This latter implication will be critical for the transition from the association of representations to the necessary development of thought.

Representation: Recollection

Implicit within intuition are the conditions that push intelligence into the processes of representation. For intuition became an explicit unity because attention was paid to the two moments of feeling and attention. But as we have seen, attention isolates aspects of its object by relating them externally in time and/or space. When attention now becomes introspective, it distinguishes the intellectual activity of immediate intuition from the content intuited. This content, as isolated by the mind from its initial context, becomes simply an *image* or impression of the intuited determination.[16]

Image and determining object are now posited as external to each other; their relation becomes arbitrary and contingent for intelligence. If one were to focus simply on this phase he would claim that he has only appearances in the mind, not the essential characteristics of the object in itself. Such a claim, however, ignores the mediating process of attention out of which this moment arises.

Attention as activity is not constant; it focuses on one thing and then on another. The image or impression of some object has its existence for but a fleeting moment, and then disappears. Since, as impression, the intuited content has been appropriated into the subjectivity of the intellect, however, it does not simply vanish into the bare externality of the past. It continues within the mind, even though it is not explicitly present to consciousness. For consciousness as attention is but one aspect of intellectual activity. In its totality intelligence is the conditioned result of all its experiences, even when these experiences are forgotten in the immediacy of the moment. The *subconscious* endures through the varying moments of intuition and of conscious attention, and retains those determinations that, as images and impressions, have been isolated from the objective world. Now, however, they are only implicit. Yet the subconscious is not simply a dark cellar in which each image rests undisturbed in its private niche until summoned. To retain the impression through time, intelligence is active; on the one hand it allows space, content and time to fall apart, on the other it relates past to present. By bringing distinct moments together into a unity, the mind subsumes them under a universal.

The relations created by the subconscious are not, however, based on simple contiguity in space and time. In becoming an image, the content of intuition has been appropriated into the inner time of the subject. Therefore its various moments fall apart and do not retain that original spatio-temporal structure that attention first brought to immediate feeling.

Having dissolved such ties, intelligence is free to relate its moments according to other principles; it can respond to specific determinations in the content itself.[17] The universalizing relations it generates, then, are not arbitrarily imposed on alien particulars, but result from the latter's inherent character.

Thus the subconscious, as a second intellectual activity, provides a counterpart to attention. The one relates; the other distinguishes. The one universalizes; the other particularizes. The one responds to intrinsic characteristics; the other introduces extrinsic relations of space and time.

Attention has allowed the original immediate unity to fall apart into a diverse multiplicity. Since that unity has not been maintained, the subconscious will not automatically reintroduce the original network of relations. In responding to its determinate content it may range far afield. Isolated features from widely different images may be associated because of some vague similarity. In its darkness such activity cannot be controlled. It may generate trivial relations as well as crucial ones. Therefore the subconscious cannot of itself annul the contingencies of attention. Intelligence will require the discriminating focus of consciousness to discern which of the relations thus generated are significant.

This begins to happen through the inherent dynamic of the mind. Just as the discrete products of attention pass into the dark reserve of the subconscious, so the results of the latter's hidden activity come back to mind's attention. A new intuition occurs; attention distinguishes a specific feature; but that characteristic recalls an earlier image and the new intuition is associated with the implicit universality of subconscious recollections. What had disappeared is now presented again. Using a play on words, we can call it a *re-presentation.*[18]

A representation is the synthesis of two moments: an immediate intuition and a subconscious relation. On the one hand it is explicit in intelligence as the object of attention—as something immediate and present. On the other hand, this individuality is recognized as being identical with impressions retained in the dark cellar of the mind. This conjunction simply happens: a new intuition calls up a more general reference. The result, however, is neither the subconscious relation nor the immediate intuition. As a representation it is a conscious object of attention that is nonetheless universal. Because intelligence attends to that universality it can even dispense with the intuition. The mind may thus re-appropriate what is implicit and subconscious without requiring something external.[19]

In the process of recollection, two important changes take place. First, an immediate actuality present to the mind has been transformed into a possibility hidden in the subconscious, a content that can be recalled at will into the actuality of consciousness. Second, the radical individuality of the moment of intuition, specific in space and time, has been reconstituted as a universal under which a number of individual intuitions and impressions can be subsumed. Universals as possibilities thus become the coinage which intelligence can use in its commerce.[20]

Recollection is thus the process by which a particular universal, implicit in the subconscious, can be placed before consciousness. It does not specify the intellectual function which leads from one representation to another. That is the work of imagination.

Representation: Imagination

Earlier, in the transition from intuition to recollection, a single intellectual function underlay two analytically distinct stages: the process was isolated as attention; its content became the image. An analogous shift occurs at this point. The subconscious which identifies a common content in a representation is at the same time a functional process of relating distinct impressions. This becomes explicit in the stream of consciousness, where images and thoughts follow one another. Such an imaginative dynamic simply brings to light relations already generated in the hidden recesses of the mind.

In intuition one thing is next to, or follows, something else. But in the subconscious this original spatio-temporal cohesion has been relaxed. Abstracted qualities now provide the intellect with other types of association; two different impressions may follow one another in consciousness simply because they share a single feature in common. The range of intellectual connections between representations thereby expands. For example, whereas the representation of a rose leads to the representation of a thorn, through mental association it may lead instead to the thought of blood, or of a red velvet dress, or of a June evening on the banks of the Neckar.

Whereas a recollected representation connected intuitions and impressions into a simple unity, now, through *reproductive imagination,* the mind ranges through a number of representations, both concrete and abstract, with one calling another to mind. Such associations, even though they presuppose the intellectual activity of isolating and relating, nonetheless simply happen. They are not yet a conscious possession of intelligence. Therefore the mind is subject to the contingencies of the unknown.

Once intelligence pays attention to this relating process, however, it may no longer allow it simply to happen. It may itself initiate the transition to a new idea. This deliberate move to a different image establishes the latter as something more than a novel and contingent thought; it introduces a conscious and deliberate reference to the relating universal—to the common content upon which the transition is based. The resulting idea is the product of *phantasy,* which generates symbols, allegories and poetic allusions. A symbol serves two roles; it has an immediately significant content and has a universal meaning as well. Because this double character leaves its interpretation ambiguous, the symbol does not yet enable intelligence to master its own operations.

Phantasy does not require words or external signs. It generates a deliberate modification in the stream of consciousness. Even though symbolizing and allegorizing creativity will achieve its most articulate expression in speech, phantasy remains a necessary condition for, and is in principle prior to, the appearance of language. For here the hidden dynamic of the subconscious begins to emerge, and intelligence acquires a cognitive capacity with regard to its own functions. It "re-cognizes."[21]

However, symbolic representations generated within the stream of consciousness do not have an independent existence toward which intelligence can direct its discerning attention. They vanish before their specific character can be noted. But since creative imagination is not limited to pure subjectivity, it can choose something objective and existent as the final term in its creative transition. This object, insofar as it is external, escapes the transience of pure consciousness; but as the result of the mind's own initiative, it re-presents the very dynamic inherent in intelligence.

This new object of attention is a *sign.* In it, the immediate content of a given existent is cancelled as irrelevant, and the mind concentrates on the connecting relation. This universal, which is represented only synthetically in the allegorical symbol, is now present as a simple unity.[22]

If the sign simply pictures the universal in a concrete symbol, there is a danger that the mind will focus on the specific features of the illustration and forget that a universal is represented. Therefore even in the most effective sign the relation between the external reality and what it represents is completely arbitrary; this contingent relation frees the mind to focus on the signified universal rather than tying it to the particular features of the actual sign.

Universality is not a single specific thing. It relates particulars and does so as dynamic activity. When a sign is made visible in space, however, it is given a static existence that continues unchanged through time. This may mislead intelligence into thinking that the universal meaning signified is not a relating activity but is rather an independent and unalterable thing. The most effective sign, then, is one which, although objective and explicit, nonetheless has that objective existence cancelled as it passes away in time. In this way, intelligence does not assume that, having expressed its processes in a sign, it can simply contemplate its product, allowing its activity to disappear from sight. Rather, the mind must maintain its dynamic, namely by rearticulating the sign and by moving once again beyond the sign to its meaning.

Sound is an objective reality, which can be produced by the mind, but which also disappears in time. When a sound is made explicit and articulate to crystallize specific meanings, it becomes speech; and speech which systematically relates words to each other is language. In oral language, then, the hidden activity of the subconscious, which transforms intuition into impressions, impressions into representations, and representations into networks of associations, itself becomes present to intelligence as an intuition, and this because it has indeed acquired explicit, objective existence.

The structure of this process provides a good illustration of the Hegelian dialectic. The mind acts to create relations; these are externalized in signs; the signs disappear; the mind must therefore reconstitute the meaning in its own activity; and this in turn becomes the basis for a new expression. Because the sign disappears, intelligence continues to be active. Because the sign is re-expressed, its activity continues to be objective and intuitable. This interaction ensures that the mind directs its attention to its own processes and not to an isolated, static form.

The work of imagination, which started by simply making visible a subconscious process, and which then created symbols and allegories, reaches its limits when it creates a name to signify the meaning present in intellect. When the name disappears, all that imagination can do is to create a new name, synthesizing a new external reality with its meaning. If even a single particular association between a name and its meaning is to be retained by the mind, a new operation is required: memory.[23]

Representation: Memory

Memory reproduces the earlier activity of recollection. There a single image or impression disappears into the subconscious, to be recalled as a universal representation. Here a transient, single sign is transformed into a universal. Its reappearance in the mind recalls out of the subconscious its earlier creation and use. What is re-presented, then, is not simply the image of the sign but the whole dynamic in which imagination produces signs and in which signs refer to their meaning. In this way not only images and impressions become the content of representation but also names that stand for thoughts. Memory is this capacity to retain and recall names.

Names represent the original content of intuition, for they signify the associating activity of the mind; and these associations were subconscious responses to concrete features present in immediate feeling. Indeed, attention introduced externalizing, individualizing relations of space and time, and these were retained in specific images and impressions. But because names signify the *relations* and not the *terms related,* the spatio-temporal contingency introduced by attention is superceded, leaving only the original subject matter, now universalized. Intuition as well as impression fall away; memory can retain simply a sequence of names.

Names refer not only to the mind's original content but also to its mediating activity; this inner, hidden dynamic has thus become externalized in distinct terms. When, in turn, names disappear into the subconscious to be later recalled in memory, their specific distinctness is re-appropriated. The mind thereby acquires explicit terms to refer to its own implicit dynamic. Just as in recollection an immediate intuition could be dispensed with for representations, so visible symbols and allegorical sounds are no longer necessary. Intelligence can move from one name to another within its own consciousness.

Since nothing else remains, names will be associated only on the basis of their meanings. These include the whole complex of relations which intelligence has used to reach the level of explicit universals. By relating these specific meanings, the mind can construct a series of names, reenacting the synthetic activity of creative imagination or phantasy.

Reproductive memory still relies on an act of reference. Intelligence constantly acts to maintain the synthesis—referring the meaning to the name, and seeking an appropriate name for the meaning. Name and meaning have not yet become integrated in an indivisible unity. Were this to occur, the association of names would not refer to an independent realm of meaning. Names would become words and nothing other than words would either compose the mind's content or justify its activity. The residual synthesis in reproductive memory would be dissolved into a single thought.

The synthesis in reproductive memory is not yet a unity, for it still requires the act of referring. The relation between meaning and name as yet remains implicit and is not yet integrated into the conscious content of intelligence. While the earlier relations of imagination, however, became explicit by becoming externalized and distinct in a sign, such a procedure will not suffice here. As Plato saw in the *Parmenides,* whenever a third, relating term is isolated, a new problem is posed: how is this third to be related to its two extremes? Success will come, and the synthesis will be crystallized into a unity, only if the distinctions that separate meaning and name are dissolved.[24]

Meaning is intellectual activity, now signified; names, now reappropriated, are the specific content of the mind. Both, then, are the property of intelligence itself. If it can develop a type of *activity* which is simply concerned with *names* and nothing else, it will have removed any need to refer from name to activity.

This happens in *mechanical memory.* The mind runs through a series of names in an ordered sequence without having to consider any range of independent meaning. The sequence itself is sufficient.

An illustration of this process may be helpful. When teaching a new language, tapes are frequently used. A model sentence is presented and the student is asked to substitute words or phrases employing the appropriate grammatical adjustments. At first he thinks about the meaning of the question posed, translating it into his first language and then retranslating the answer. Competence begins to develop when he responds mechanically without the reflective detour. Indeed, the amount of time left for answers eventually allows only an immediate reaction. As the student expands this ability to relate words to words without referring to their meaning, he expands his mastery of the new language, and indeed begins to think using its categories. The ability to react mechanically becomes, paradoxically, an important step on the way towards thinking in the learned language.[25]

The fact that mechanical learning is important as a means for learning a foreign language suggests that it is also used in learning one's own. Indeed, in an early essay from his secondary school years at Stuttgart, Hegel himself suggests this: "From our youth on we learn the current body of words and signs for ideas, and they remain in our head ineffective and unused. Only gradually, through experience, do we come to know our treasure, and to think something with the words."[26] Mechanical memory, then, is not simply rote learning or memorizing by heart, but also the ability to ramble on more or less coherently "without thinking." Intelligence's activity simply connects word to word following conventions that have been thoroughly appropriated. Once this simple unity between sign and activity is achieved, the mind can, in pure thought, turn its critical attention to the flow of words. But it is mechanical memory that has crystallized the synthesis of word and meaning into a simple unity.[27]

Thinking

At this point let us pause to review the intellectual processes analyzed so far. Attention isolates distinct moments, but does so by means of space and time externally introduced. The subconscious relates different things, but remains hidden in the dark recesses of the mind. Through imagination, these relations are not left in obscurity but acquire more distinct forms as symbols and signs. Then, through memory, the complex synthesis of sign and signified relation is collapsed into a unity. Whereas recollection *internalizes* intuitions, imagination *externalizes* the inner recesses of the subconscious; memory integrates both.[28] Through all three the mind re-presents its possessions to itself. But when the words that represent this internal activity become at the same time its only content, intelligence is free to move beyond the contingency of representations. For the contrary activities of distinguishing and relating have now come together. By means of words strung together in thoughtless speech, relations are distinguished, and distinctions are related; universals are particularized, and particulars are universalized; inherent characteristics are articulated in the temporal flow of speech, and a sequence of time is integrated into a single act of comprehension.

When the mind then turns its attention to this treasury, already appropriated, it can come to know what it already is. It can *re-cognize itself*—its content and its activity—as the integrating and relating agent. For it is the mind itself, incorporating all these many moments into a single unity, that is *the* universal, under which all others are subsumed. In knowing itself, intelligence sets in context all its activities from immediate feeling to mechanical memory, and thereby can comprehend the significance of all its determinate existence. Determinations, simply "given" in the instant of feeling are recognized to be constituent moments of a living and dynamic intellectual existence. What had simply "happened" to the mind, then, is no longer an arbitrary whim of fate that could have been otherwise. As intelligence incorporates into its own life what was originally contingent the latter proves to be a necessary condition of what the mind, in due course, became. By becoming conscious of this dynamic, intelligence heeds the Socratic imperative: "Know thyself." "It knows that what is *thought, is,* and that what *is* only *is* insofar as it is thought";—for its own sake.[29]

When it begins to focus on the content of mechanical memory, however, thinking is only formally concerned with the functions of intelligence. The words that memory has made into enduring categories appear to self-consciousness as independent givens that pure thought can manipulate and organize. This raw material must be reappropriated into the mind's own dynamic so that the discrepancy between form and content is overcome. This involves a three-fold process, one that reproduces the earlier subconscious acts of distinguishing, relating and integrating.

In thought, recollected representations and words are first of all isolated by formal understanding; as each term is considered independently it is transformed into a *category* of thought. Ambiguities and confusions are stripped away. Thus purged of contingent and irrelevant associations, the mind's intellectual content becomes pure thought, true to its own nature.

Because the categories thus isolated still need to be distinguished from each other, this act of rendering precise pushes further. Discerning judgement analyzes each category to determine the constituents of its meaning—breaking it apart into its diverse elements.

These are then related to each other through a formal process of inference. Conceptual analysis concludes with the formal synthesis of its component terms, showing how they have been integrated.

This operation, characteristic of analytical thought, fails to take account of the underlying ground of the initial categories. They are not simply given, i.e. presented to intelligence by mechanical memory. As we have seen, their meaning reflects the relation between sign and signified—between name and the subconscious act of relating universality. When intelligence acknowledges that it is not thinking alien categories, but rather comprehending its own inherent life, thought begins to explain the analytically isolated categories in terms of subconscious processes acting in response to the original determination of intuition. The conscious interaction between felt content, intellectual operation, and universal term constitutes the very act of conceiving; and this underlies all concepts.[30] Moreover, by relating concepts to each other as subordinate species of more comprehensive genera, judgement explains the conceived terms within the broader context of the mind's intellectual resources.

A discrepancy remains between the activity of thinking and the content of its thought. The final achievement of pure thought consists in recognizing that it is the very process of explaining which determines the content, both as understood category and as judged subordination. This activity of inferring completely embodies the content of intelligence. All alien differentiations are dissolved; all residual contingency is overcome;

and the inherent necessity that underlies all the operations of intelligence is made explicit.[31]

The processes of thought—conceiving, judging and inferring—explicitly reappropriate the content and activity of intelligence. The simple determination of immediate feeling was isolated by attention and abstraction; it was then distinguished from, and related to, other such determinations in the subconscious activity of intelligence. But such processes were contingent in as much as they were uncontrolled. Trivial differences and similarities could be given crucial significance, and inherent features overlooked; the unconscious activity of association could confuse distinct moments. The initial contingency of intuition by which it can be the "most sterling and true" or the "more scanty and untrue"[32] is only transcended when its import is explicitly brought to consciousness and there clearly isolated, when its differences and relations (both internal and external) are precisely articulated. In this way intelligence becomes master of its own processes.

Representation and Thought

Hegel's distinction between representation and thought is not absolute. Inasmuch as a representation is still conditioned by the mind's subconscious activity, it is not something that has been clearly conceived. As a universalized impression, as an abstracted quality, or as an association based on contiguity or likeness, it presupposes an intellectual operation that is hidden and hence contingent; it could be haphazard and irrelevant, or on the other hand be crucially significant. By contrast, thought renders explicit the basic content of the intellect in its discrete moments, purges it of irrelevant associations, and discovers, in the determinate character of each moment, both its distinction from other moments and the continuity that connects it to them. It is not on the basis of content, then, that representations are distinguished from thoughts. Even though the former may be images or pictures, they may also be ideas.[33] The difference lies in the way each enters the range of conscious attention. Whereas some aspect of every representation is simply "given," as a positive *datum* of the subconscious,[34] thought articulates all its conditions, thereby rendering its intellectual operation transparent. Unlike the strict empiricist, Hegel claims that thinking renders explicit a connection inherent in the content being thought, a connection that is not simply the product of experienced conjunctions in space or time. And unlike the romantic, he sharply differentiates contingent associations from relations that follow from inherent features. The thinking that comprehends its own operations distinguishes representations from thoughts.

Pure reason and pure thought are not abstract ideal entities, existing totally isolated from all normal experience; they are functions of intelligence. When in philosophical reflection intelligence turns its attention to the categories of thought, it renders explicit its own implicit activity. It abstracts from distinctions and relations that reflect only contingent or particular points of view; spatial conjunction and temporal contiguity are no longer confused with relations inherent in the content of thought.

By setting aside the determinate intuitions and images it relates, the mind may focus on the intellectual acts of distinguishing and relating in themselves. This becomes the particular subject matter of logic. Thought isolates a relation in a concept; by this very act it passes over to another category; this transition is then itself given a name and becomes an object of thought, leading in turn to something else. Logic simply makes clear how the intellectual relations of intelligence are themselves related. In other words, "the method is the consciousness of the inner self-movement of logic's content."[35] Through this self-knowledge of its own content, thinking becomes systematic, and logic becomes the science of pure thought.

In proposing to use the preceding psychological analysis to interpret the *Science of Logic* we are prey to the charge of psychologism—of making the validity of logical reasoning simply contingent on subjective mental operations. Ultimately this charge can only be answered by an analysis of the development of self-conscious knowledge through experience—a task undertaken by Hegel in the *Phenomenology* and considered below in Chapter 13. But we can make an initial response by considering more carefully the role that language plays in the transition from imagination to memory, and from memory to thought, to see how the subject is able to transcend his own relativism. Let us therefore consider some problems of language.

Problems
of
Language

For Hegel, intelligence becomes the master of its own operations when words are integrated with the meanings they signify. On the one hand a verbal sign renders explicit what was implicit in the subconscious; on the other, through familiar, routine use, the mind employs words without reference to an independent meaning. Thus the discrepancy between a word and its import is dissolved. Words categorize mental impressions and operations; grammatical conventions structure intellectual associations; the flow of speech integrates them into a pattern of continuity. Thought becomes articulate when it uses language to bring its own processes explicitly to its attention.[1] "We only know our thoughts, only have definite, actual thoughts, when we give them the form of objectivity, of a being distinct from our own implicit subjectivity, in other words, when we give them an explicit, external character. At the same time, this external objectivity bears the stamp of that inner dynamic. The articulated sound, the *word,* alone is such an internalized externality."[2] The pure thought of logic, therefore, uses the vocabulary and grammatical conventions of ordinary language.

Hegel's chapter on Psychology, however, leaves an unexplained gap between the intellectual function of imagination, which produces signs, and that of memory, which by synthesizing sign and meaning, uses the vocabulary of conventional speech. For the remembering individual does not simply internalize the private language his imagination has arbitrarily created. Rather he appropriates the terminology and grammatical structures that have become current in his cultural environment. Indeed the more objective structures of public language appear to be necessary for the subsequent transition to logical thought. After all, it is the cultural context that maintains a relatively consistent meaning for specific words. By preventing the individual from simply reinterpreting the visible or oral form in accordance with a momentary subjective whim, it reinforces retentive memory, the function that "elevates the *single* synthesis to a universal, i.e. permanent, synthesis, in which word and meaning are for it objectively united."[3]

This poses a problem. Intelligence can become master of its operations only if it reappropriates the words that directly signify its own activity. But the vocabulary and grammar of conventional speech are not the creation of the individual, and therefore are not the immediate product of his sign-producing imagination. If the mind remembers according to such external categories it may well be relying on structures and forms that are not intrinsic to itself.[4] Public conventions may distort and misrepresent private intentions. If the individual uses the former, his attention may be directed away from the latter and he will be prevented from achieving intellectual self-knowledge.

Hegel cannot afford to gloss over this critical tension between sign-making imagination and retentive memory. On the one hand he must show how the public structures of conventional speech can be used without distortion by an individual intelligence to signify his own private meaning. On the other hand, the objective universality of language must provide an appropriate means for annulling the effects of subjective contingencies due to momentary whims and peculiar perspectives. Ordinary language must both express unambiguously, and transcend, individual meanings.

Even if this first dilemma is satisfactorily resolved, a second problem remains. Hegel prefers the use of oral speech because visible signs inadequately represent mental processes. Spoken language, however, is always the vernacular of a particular culture and of a particular people. Indeed Hegel rejoices in the use of German because its categories "appear in the form of substantives and verbs," and because "some of its words even possess the further peculiarity of having not only different but opposite meanings so that one cannot fail to recognize a speculative spirit of the language in them."[5] In this it compares favourably with other modern tongues. For both its grammatical structure and its vocabulary are uniquely appropriate for thinking through the dialectical relation between categories and their speculative significance.

Thus Hegel relies on word-plays, etymologies, and meanings that are peculiarly German. For instance, in the *Science of Logic* he points out that *"Aufheben"* means "to preserve, to maintain, and equally . . . to cause to cease, to put an end to"[6]; and when he writes "the truth of being is essence,"[7] he plays on the German *Wesen* (essence) related to the past participle of the verb *sein* (to be). Similarly, *Urteil* (judgement) means, by its etymology, original partition.[8] In the previous chapter we noted his puns on *Erinnerung* ('recollection' and 'internalizing') and *Vorstellen* ('to represent' and 'to place before').[9] In a letter of 1805 to J. H. Voss he writes: "Luther has made the Bible speak German; you, Homer—the greatest present that can be given to a people; for a people is barbarous, and does not consider the excellent things it knows as its own property until it gets to know them in its own language; if you would forget these two examples, I should like to say of my own aspirations that I shall try to teach philosophy to speak German."[10] His concern, then, was to render philosophy more German.

However, Hegel also develops this point more generally. Not only Luther but also the Italian poets, Dante, Boccaccio and Petrarch, are cited to justify the assertion that "It is not until a thing is expressed in my mother tongue that it becomes my possession."[11] And when Hegel was invited to teach at a university in Holland, he replied: "With regard to the language in which one usually gives lectures at Dutch universities, this would have to be in Latin, at least initially. If custom permits a deviation from this, I would soon endeavour to express myself in the vernacular; for I hold it to be essential for the thorough mastering of a discipline, that one possess it in his mother tongue."[12] The general principle is enunciated in his lectures on the history of philosophy: "In speech, man is productive; it is the first externality that he gives himself, the simplest form of existence which he reaches in consciousness. What man represents to himself, he inwardly places before himself as spoken. This first form is broken up and rendered foreign if man [uses] an alien tongue to express or conceive to himself what represents his highest interest. [When one uses his mother tongue] this breach with the first emergence into consciousness is accordingly removed; to be at home with one's own possessions, to speak and think in one's own language belongs to the form of liberty."[13]

These references are polemical, combatting the scholastic tendency to use Latin as the universal language of scholarship. But if their positive import is taken seriously, a significant difficulty is raised for the Hegelian endeavour. The grammar and vocabulary of each language has been conditioned by the contingent features of its history and geography. Because each nation has its unique tradition, the connotations and associations of terms are culturally specific. If thought is to be integrated with one's mother tongue, it will be affected by such contingencies. Rather than transcending particular expressions and establishing an inherent logical necessity, then, it will articulate a relative world view. Thought will simply reflect the peculiar perspective of its own language.

Hegel wanted to avoid any such final surrender to partial perspectives. His frequent use of "absolute" as noun and adjective is an indication that, in philosophy, individual and cultural relativism is to be transcended and structures inherent in nature and history made evident. But if philosophy is the science of thought, if thought operates with the categories of language, and if language is nonetheless culturally specific, such an attempt appears doomed to fail. Hegel is thus faced with a dilemma. Either the universal structures of thought transcend language so that thought and word fall apart and he is condemned to the fate of Sisyphus "never quite succeeding in expressing all he means even to himself," always pointing beyond language to the ineffable[14]; or thought is inextricably bound to language and is thus culturally relative, never achieving the absolute truth of philosophical wisdom.[15]

This dilemma poses a problem not simply for Hegel's own endeavours, but also for any translator or commentator. The English language has its own vocabulary and grammatical tradition. While its Anglo-Saxon roots provide words that have Germanic cousins, the Latin influence has been maintained both through its academic heritage and through the introduction of French in 1066. A history of maritime trade, of proficient engineering, and of active political debate has created a wide range of associations and connotations. And its grammatical style rejects the more elaborate constructions of German or Latin. The vernacular thus formed is what the Anglophone must use if he is to repatriate philosophy and make it his own possession—if he is to become fully master of his thoughts. How, then, can he transform Hegel's Germanic expressions into fluent English prose?

Does he search on the one hand for some ultimate realm of meaning, located, like Plato's ideas, in a sphere beyond language? In that case he will have to leave the specific, concrete arguments of Hegel's analysis behind, and endeavour to express the inexpressible in conventional English. Hegel's German will be used as a ladder to that which is beyond language—a ladder that can then be kicked away. For from the light of a pure intellectual vision he can turn directly to the idioms of his mother tongue. Or must he take account of every subtlety in the language used, retaining the specific sense of each term? Then he will be forced to educate his reader in German at the same time that he introduces him to Hegelian thoughts.[16] German words will be retained ('*Dasein*'); artificial new words created ('sublated'); hyphenated constructions introduced ('being-for-self'). Because such terminology violates common usage, the writer *and* the reader find that they are prevented from thinking. For word and meaning have become dislocated psychologically. The freedom that comes from mastery of the categories of thought is surrendered to new conventions, arbitrarily introduced in English, that must be continuously called to mind.

Paradoxically, in recognizing that, for Hegel, the words of language and the categories of thought have been integrated, the interpreter disrupts that very unity. Either he does justice to their unity in Hegel's German, in which case he forfeits it in the translation, or he achieves their identity in his own text at the expense of dissociating Hegel's meaning from its expression.[17]

The problem posed by the relation between languages is analogous to that posed in the individual's appropriation of a common vernacular. In each case a particular with its specific difference is to be related to a universal; and in each case the relation cannot be achieved simply by subsuming the less under the more general. Rather, it is a question of integrating human experience in such a way that the universal does justice to the specific features of the particular. For the necessity of pure thought cannot be achieved if the factors that introduce differences are left to wield a subconscious and uncontrolled influence. Their effects must be brought explicitly to the mind's attention and purged of distorting contingencies. Just as personal meanings need to be integrated with common speech so cultural distinctions need to be incorporated into universal thought.

What was missing from the analysis provided in the previous chapter was the relation between an individual intelligence and its society. That discussion simply examined intellectual functions, not social relations involving practical action. If the transition from individual sign-making fantasy to the memory of conventional speech is to be philosophically valid, however, some intermediate process must be presupposed. What function mediates between the individual and his culture, between person and people?

The answer to this question is provided in Hegel's lectures on the Philosophy of Spirit given at Jena in 1803-4.[18] In this material Hegel discusses language, along with memory, as one of the first objective forms of consciousness.[19] But he returns to it later when talking about the nation or people. Indeed, using vocabulary borrowed from Schelling (and later rejected), he calls the earlier moments of speech, work and family "potencies [which] are on the whole ideal; they acquire existence only in a people; language *exists* only as the language of a people, as indeed do understanding and reason."[20] In other words, while the individual consciousness can take its signs and, through memory, make them into language, this capacity is only realized in a social context. Although Hegel here relates individual capability and social reality, he does not move directly from one to the other; in between is a lengthy discussion of the process called recognition. When one acknowledges and is acknowledged by another, the individual consciousness surrenders his exclusive pre-occupation with himself. Indeed this mutual activity constitutes a more universal context for his particular action. Because his individuality is transcended, a new totality is produced, "the spirit of a people."[21] It is the process of recognition, or mutual acknowledgement, then, that provides the transition between individual consciousness and the spirit of a society.

This early text suggests that the concept of recognition is central to Hegel's philosophy of spirit,[22] and of particular importance for the analysis of linguistic operations. When we turn back to the *Encyclopaedia* to see if this suggestion is confirmed we are not disappointed. Prior to the "Psychology," in the chapter on "Phenomenology" Hegel introduces recognition under the "Life and Death Struggle."[23] A comment from Hegel's Berlin lectures, added by the editors, is significant: "To prevent any possible misunderstanding with regard to [the struggle to the death] we must here remark that the fight for recognition pushed to the extreme here indicated can only occur in the natural state, where men exist only as single, separate individuals; but it is absent in civil society and the State because here the recognition for which the combatants fought already exists."[24] The medium of recognition that is lacking in the state of nature is, significantly enough, specified in the Jena material as language: "Neither can demonstrate [that the one consciousness is an actual totality] to the other by means of words, protestations, threats or promise; for language is only the ideal existence of consciousness. Here, however, they are actual, absolutely opposed, absolutely isolated from each other; and their relation is solely practical, solely actual. The mediating moment of their recognition must itself be actual. Therefore they must mutilate each other."[25] When someone cannot mediate his self-conscious insistence on unrestrained freedom to an opponent through speech, his only recourse is to overt action—even physical combat.

We are here presented, then, with a significant relation between the process of recognition and language. On the one hand, recognition mediates between the individual consciousness and its social context—between sign-making fantasy and the reproductive memory which uses a common tongue. On the other hand, a common language provides in a society the means of recognition. Other than in the state of nature, language and recognition presuppose each other.

The few short paragraphs of the *Encyclopaedia* on the life and death struggle reproduce a discussion from the *Phenomenology of Spirit*. The first two pages of the chapter on "Lordship and Bondage" offer a "detailed exposition of the concept" of recognition.[26] A consideration of this passage will clarify how recognition serves to resolve the dilemmas posed by language.

Recognition involves at least two individuals—one who acknowledges and one who is acknowledged—in a context where the one is conscious of the other. But this dynamic relation is intrinsically complex, for there are here several distinct processes to be integrated in a single act. Any analysis, therefore, must both distinguish the various moments while maintaining their integration.[27]

In the first place recognition involves the awareness of similarity. The acknowledging individual, both self-conscious and conscious of the other, discovers that he is the same as the individual acknowledged. Features that characterize his own intrinsic nature are presented to him as something external. He thus learns that he is simply an instance of a more general universal. The consciousness of this fact has two implications: on the one hand he has lost any sense of his own individuality; on the other the individuality of the other is equally annulled. In the moment of universality, each individual loses his specific identity in the awareness of a common essence.

In the second place, the individual reacts against this loss of himself. To preserve his uniqueness he must cancel that which is common and reaffirm his own distinctness. Where language is not present this process requires physical struggle. Through language one can deny any suggestion that his thoughts, attitudes and interests are like those of his antagonist, and back it up with threats. This effort to maintain one's own particular character by denying the common universal essence has in turn a number of implications: first one individual suppresses the independence of the other in order to make his own independence unique; second, because he had only become aware of his own intrinsic nature through the other, he suppresses at the same time this explicit consciousness of himself. Having ignored the other, he is prevented from achieving any precise self-conscious awareness, and so loses genuine independence.

The moment of universality simply recognized the similarity of self and other; the moment of particularity simply denied that similarity. But the denial presupposes that which is denied, and is effective only if the similarity remains implicitly present. When this relation between the implicit affirmation of similarity and its explicit denial is brought to consciousness, the individual becomes aware of himself *as* an individual—as combining a universal nature and a particularizing difference. Thus, recognition goes beyond simple universality and simple particularity to individuality. This also has its implications. On the one hand, because the negative force of the denial is reduced from an absolute to a relative, the individual becomes aware of himself as similar to the other even in the difference. He then becomes explicitly self-conscious. On the other hand, because he becomes aware of the other as different even in the similarity, he becomes conscious of the uniqueness of the other, and hence grants him freedom.

The one individual would not have initially recognized his basic identity with the other, if the response of the other had not been the same as his own. Likewise the implicit universality entailed in the moment of denial would not have been noticed if the other had not rejected the preliminary identification in the same way. In other words, the final recognition of identity despite differences and of difference inherent in identity is the activity as much of the one as of the other. When one becomes conscious of the other as active, he becomes conscious of himself as active. What is common in the difference is the double structure of a universal affirmation and a particular denial, both of which are acts of a subject. In becoming conscious of himself and of the other as objective, independent individuals, each becomes conscious of himself and the other as subjective agents, actively in relation.

Recognition is a mutual activity; it locates the reality of self-consciousness neither in the material concreteness of each physical body nor in the particular one-sided volition of an isolated individual. Self-consciousness is a dynamic reality that binds together individuals even as each individual becomes aware of his own uniqueness. Because the reality of self-consciousness is nothing other than this dynamic movement of self-awareness, it is not material but spiritual. For Hegel, spirit is the energy or "play of forces" in which the concrete material moments do not simply interact but are aware of their interaction. "They recognize themselves as mutually recognizing one another."[28]

Hegel's discussion of the process of recognition shows how individuals enter into social relations and how they become explicitly and self-consciously individual through those relations. As a general analysis it can subsume various species of intersubjective interaction: physical struggle, civil society, and linguistic communication. Therefore Hegel's solution to our earlier dilemmas involves an application of this particular concept.

Our first problem concerned the transition from an individual's producing a sign to his remembering the conventional signs of a culture; this transition involves two distinct manoeuvres—the use of the same sign, and its reference to a shared meaning. With regard to the first, each individual recognizes, in the moment of universality, that others also can produce signs. In the moment of particularity he affirms his right to generate his own symbols. In the moment of articulated individuality he recognizes that this will to uniqueness is common to all; therefore public conventions may be used to articulate private meanings. After all, the relation between a sign and its meaning is arbitrary and not intrinsic;[29] and commonly used sounds or letters can serve just as well as private creations. Thus conventional signs become the names retained in memory.

As names and words replace physical violence in the struggle for recognition they become a formal means of interaction. Then the three-fold dynamic recurs, this time in relation to the intended content. First, the individual assumes that everybody means the same thing by the same sign. Second, he denies this loss of individuality by affirming that his personal meaning is unique and therefore ineffable.[30] Third, since his denial uses the conventions of speech it shows that universals can serve to distinguish particular meanings, and that particular meanings can only be expressed by means of a vocabulary of universal terms. As this self-conscious use of conventional language expands, the individual discriminates ever more clearly between his own unique contribution and the common meaning, while rendering their interconnection more precise. In this way names and words become the concrete existence of the intersubjective reality called spirit.[31]

When intelligence moves from memory to pure thought and brings explicitly to consciousness its associations and abstractions, it uses categories that are found in the words of ordinary language. Understanding conceives a concept by removing from it contingent associations. For this task of discrimination, it has available specific resources from its social context. Ordinary language itself is used to distinguish common meanings from those that are uniquely personal, thus isolating the intellectual processes that are universal and necessary. Because thought can become conscious of the dynamic of interpersonal relations as well as its own intuiting and representing activity it can transcend the limitations of its particular contingent subjectivity.[32]

Our second problem concerns the relation between a specific vernacular and universal thought. Here there are no individual selves, but only cultures and traditions. Each culture acquires a particular identity through a network of relations that binds its members together. Because its spirit is distinct from any one individual or group, it exists as real only when language builds bridges of communication. Therefore a culture cannot become conscious of its own identity in an abstract or impersonal realm. Individuals, whose intellectual maturity is itself the product of social interaction, bring this dynamic explicitly to consciousness. In this way, as its members reflect on the relationships that bind them together and in particular on the structures of linguistic communication, a culture becomes an explicit, individual and self-conscious entity, clearly distinguished from other cultures.

But self-conscious individuality is the result only of a process of recognition[33]; hence, in the relations between particular cultures, the dynamic which integrates an individual and his social environment is reproduced. Since language is the objective reality of spirit, it becomes the formal means by which cultures interact. At first, members of a culture simply assume that all men understand their language. Disabused of this illusion, they reject those whose speech is unintelligible. Only when they recognize that others have used a common sign-producing ability to create distinct words and grammatical structures, and that therefore specific linguistic conventions are but species of a generic human capacity, do they become explicitly conscious of the distinctive and defining characteristics of their own language. Indeed those learned men who articulate the self-conscious identity of their own tradition do so because of their contact with the grammar and vocabulary of alien cultures.[34]

The process through which the distinctive forms of various languages are recognized is then repeated in relation to their context or meaning. At first men assume that other languages have words to signify precisely the same representations and ideas that are expressed in their mother tongue—that they share the same values and perspectives. Then they draw a sharp contrast between their own virtues and alien vices. Finally, they realize that each culture has used its own peculiar forms to articulate common human experience, and that the universal concern to master nature and to create a society is distinctively conditioned by a particular geography and history. A culture becomes explicitly conscious of its own identity; at the same time it recognizes the distinctive individuality of other cultures. And because it can set everything in the context of human activity and human experience, it becomes aware of the fundamental structure of human life itself. Specific awareness of differences as relative is the means by which a non-relative comprehension of the truth can be achieved. "Since Spirit is common to all peoples, and as long as their [specific] cultural formation is presupposed, the diversity can simply turn on the relations within a single subject matter of a genus and its determinations or species."[35]

In the move from individual to society, subjective and personal particularity is transcended in the objective and public universality of language. In the present situation, the particular is objective and public (in grammar and word use), while the universal as pure thought is subjective and personal. But set in context by bilingual individuals, linguistic differences can be used to discern a shared reality, precisely because of its dynamic interaction with the specific characteristics of each culture. For the reflective individual, then, the vernacular both embodies universal truth in a distinctive, particular form, and provides a unique perspective on human culture and experience. Because, as bilingual, he acquires the ability to use language more precisely, he thinks more effectively. In using words as categories he appreciates both their strengths and the limitations of their particular context; in forming judgements and inferences according to the conventions of grammar he distinguishes contingent forms from essential relations. "He who has mastered a language and at the same time has a comparative knowledge of other languages, he alone can make contact with the spirit and culture of a people through the grammar of its language; the same rules and forms now have a substantial, living value." Thus, although he uses a specific language as the medium of thought, he is able to transcend its particular limitations and move toward the explicitly universal. "Through grammar he can recognize the expression of spirit as such, that is logic."[36]

If the preceding analysis does justice to Hegel's thought, it helps to explain an important passage on the relation between philosophical language and common speech in the *Science of Logic:*

Philosophy has the right to select from the language of common life which is made for the world of representations such expressions as *seem to approximate* to the determinations of the concept. There cannot be any question of *demonstrating* for a word selected from the language of common life that in common life, too, one associates with it the same concept for which philosophy employs it; for common life has no concepts, but only representations, and to recognize the concept in what is else a mere representation is philosophy itself. It must suffice, therefore, if representation, in the use of its expressions that are employed for philosophical determinations, has some vague idea of their distinctive meaning; just as it may be the case that in these expressions one recognizes nuances of representation that are more closely related to the corresponding concepts."[37]

The task of philosophy as the discipline of pure thought is not simply to respond to common usage. Rather by becoming consciously aware of how a specific setting affects intellectual operations, both subconscious and conscious, it sets relativizing tendencies in context and thereby renders determinate both the universal categories and the structures of relations. This transition to the non-relative or absolute universal is achieved by becoming explicitly conscious of particular conditions—the process Hegel calls recognition.[38] In appropriating a common language the individual transcends his own limitations; in learning alien tongues he moves beyond cultural relativism. Philosophy can sit in judgement on ordinary language because it sets its own vernacular in the context of a more universal comprehension of human culture.[39] Therefore it can discriminate between the inherently universal validity of thought and the relative expressions of subjective psychology. The purging of contingencies through the self-conscious use of language, then, provides us with a preliminary response to the charge of psychologism. The inherent validity of the logical transitions and hence their metaphysical character follow from their comprehensive universality.[40]

The process of discrimination, however, takes place within a specific language. There is no supra-linguistic realm of thought. Using a particular set of categories and grammatical structures, the philosopher distinguishes the essential universal concept from the contingent forms of its representation. To be sure, the more a language can articulate this double process of recognition, the more appropriate it is for the discipline of pure thought.[41] But this provides no justification for disrupting a less flexible vernacular by introducing imported vocabulary and alien constructions. It is more important to use the integration of word and meaning already achieved in the idiom of one's own tongue than to disrupt that association in quest of a perfect form for philosophical expression.

From this perspective the lot of the translator and non-German interpreter of Hegel is transformed. Earlier he appeared to be condemned to an impossible task: either he would maintain the identification of language and thought achieved by Hegel while dispensing with it himself; or he would have to break it apart in Hegel's German to achieve it in his own prose. Now, however, we see that differences in vocabulary and grammar provide him with the most appropriate tools for transcending the specifics of Hegel's expressions. Because he is not bound to a single language he can recognize how arbitrary and contingent conventions can nonetheless articulate the necessity of conceptual relations. And thus he is free to express this logical necessity in his mother tongue.[42] Aware of the relativizing influence of grammar and vocabulary he is able to counteract it explicitly.

But what about the reader of a translation or commentary; if he is not bilingual, is he capable of only a less than adequate comprehension of Hegel's philosophy? Not necessarily. The greater the variety of translations and commentaries, the more their specific differences can suggest the comprehensive universality of thought. Becoming aware of why the diversities are contingent will make clear what is intrinsic and necessary. Thus although it is no virtue to be tied to a single convention,[43] neither is it a virtue to be arbitrarily idiosyncratic. Only if he can presuppose conscientious discipline on the part of each translator will the reader be able to treat a particular work as a means for appropriating the universality of Hegelian thought.

This has been the principle used in the present study. While I have cited standard English translations wherever possible, I have not been bound to them. They were modified wherever it appeared to be necessary in light of my understanding of Hegel and of conventional English.[44] Moreover, I have proposed new ways of expressing Hegelian concepts and transitions where a clear and more natural phrase avoided an awkward Germanism.

As one begins to discern the idiosyncracies in any particular philosophy, translation, or interpretation one can get beyond the relativism of that view and, through the diversity of language, articulate consciously the necessity which is the mark of logical truth. "Language has penetrated into whatever becomes for man *something inner*—becomes, that is, an idea, something which he makes his very own;—and what man transforms to language contains—concealed, or mixed up with other things, or worked out to clearness—a category. So natural to man," says Hegel, "is logic—indeed, logic is itself just man's peculiar nature."[45]

Part Two

Thinking

Being

The Beginning

"Logic is to be understood as the system of pure reason, as the realm of pure thought."[1]

Pure thought we have now defined as the sphere of intellectual relations, purged of spatio-temporal, subjective and cultural contingencies. As a science, logic articulates the relations between these relations: in rendering a concept precise, thought moves to a related category; this movement in turn is named, and itself becomes a new concept. If logic is to become a system, however, it must start, not from just any concept, but from one that is not itself the product of a process. This poses a paradoxical problem. The primitive concept is to be immediate and not the determinate result of inferential transitions. Yet it is the name for an intellectual relation, presupposing terms to be related.

In recognizing this problem, Hegel contrasts the immediacy of the logical beginning within the context of free, self-contained thinking with the mediation by which consciousness progressively overcomes its partiality to achieve the comprehensive universality of pure knowing.[2] Since we have postponed to the end of our commentary consideration of the epistemological claim that in pure self-contained thought what we are certain of is true, and what is true is being thought with certainty, our contrast can only be between *pure* thinking and *conditioned* associations of the mind. In the process of dissolving and transcending mental conjunctions based on contiguity in space and time, intelligence has isolated relations that are intellectual rather than externally contingent. Through the self-conscious use of language, the imaginative constructions of subjective egos or of cultural traditions are recognized as relative and, to that extent, irrelevant to a purely logical science. Any intellectual relation that is conditioned by distinctive moments in personal or social history is to be left aside in the abstract discipline of pure thought.

Yet once the relativizing conditions have been dissolved away in pure self-knowledge, we are left with simple intellectual relations that are not in themselves determinate. We have no reason or ground for characterizing them in any specific way, since such a reason or ground would involve a logical, and not simply a psychological mediation. From this perspective of pure intellectual relations, "the scientific beginning remains immanent; there is nothing to do but to contemplate, that is rather to say, by setting aside all reflections and all opinions otherwise held, just to absorb *what is there before us.*"[3]

What we have is simply intellectual relating; all reference to terms has been dissolved in the self-purifying process of self-conscious thought. Even to refer to it as immediacy is to introduce a reflective contrast with mediation. It simply *is*. In other words the verb "to be" fills the requirement quite precisely: as a verb it expresses a relating; it can be used with any subject whatsoever; and it is incomplete and points toward the need for further determination—although not itself determined it is open to determinations. English, however, does not easily use the infinitive as a substantive. For the category involved in the verb "to be" it has instead the gerund *being*.[4]

The category *being* as thus defined is not at all specific. Therefore it does not distinguish between that which *is* a unicorn, that which *is* the number three, that which *is* the rock of Gibraltar, or that which *is* the current rate of exchange. What all such things have in common, and what enables intelligence to relate them all in a single sentence is that they *are*.[5]

Being is thus the most primitive category of the logical science. It lacks any determination by which thought can distinguish one thing or idea from another. But at the same time it articulates a comprehensive relation that is immediately common to all things or ideas.[6]

Being

Pure thought begins its operations by rendering its concepts precise. Only thus will it be able to understand what is involved in a concept and in this way become aware of the developing network of relations it involves. When it contemplates its primary concept, however, thought is faced with a difficulty. How can it define *being*? For definition requires some specific contrast with something else. Because this concept is taken to be immediate it can be compared only with itself, for there is nothing else to which thought can relate it. *Being* is equivalent only to itself. This positive assertion, though, does not distinguish it from anything to which it is unequal, for all specific determinations have been excluded. When it considers this, its most primitive category, then, thought finds nothing there to think. It is pure thinking without any content. But *nothing* certainly is not the same thing as *being*. In thinking the concept *being,* then, a new concept, *nothing,* has emerged. There has been no explicit inference here. The second thought simply and immediately comes to mind.

The situation is not remedied when thought appeals to intuition, that original intellectual activity out of which it is derived. What is the characteristic feature *being* which all determinations of feeling have? What would it be like to intuit being? When all specific determinations are removed, there is nothing left to be intuited. Once again thought has moved to thinking *nothing*. Every effort of understanding to render precise what is involved in the category *being* leads it to another category, *nothing*.[7]

The new category becomes the focus of attention. Understanding is to define it more clearly and distinguish it from other concepts. But the only other concept it yet has for comparison is *being;* and thought finds that anything it uses to define *nothing* is also used to define *being*. Is it simply equality with itself? *Being* can also be defined that way. Is it "complete emptiness, absence of all determination and content"? That was what *being,* as prior to all determination, turned out to be. Is it undifferentiated within itself? Being also "would not be held fast in its purity if it contained any determination or content which could be distinguished in it or by which it could be distinguished from another."[8] The only difference that could possibly remain is that *being* represents that feature which *every* thing has, and which enables it to be thought at all, whereas nothing is *no* thing. However in that very moment of reflection the latter has been thought; it makes sense to say that one intuits nothing. Therefore that category is present in our thoughts and applied to our intuitions, in which case it "is", at least in the sense that a unicorn "is".[9] It is a function of pure, though empty, intuiting and thinking. In the effort to clarify precisely what is involved in the category *nothing,* then, thought finds that it is left with exactly the same definition as it had for *being*. It moves once again to thinking *being*.[10]

The understanding, asked to clarify its terms, has found that it cannot hold the two categories *being* and *nothing* in isolation. Indeed that which defines the one defines the other. From the standpoint of careful, precise thought there is no explicit distinction between them.[11] Yet they are not the same category. For one moved from thinking *being* to thinking *nothing* and from thinking *nothing* to thinking *being*. That movement itself indicates that they are different. Indeed this difference is intended to be absolute: between that which is true of *every* thing and that which is true of *no* thing. Understanding wanted to hold them as discrete abstractions. But the inevitable movement of thought brought them into relation, showing that they could not be so distinguished. The isolation of understanding has been broken down dialectically by the very act of forcing the understanding to be thorough-going in its analysis. The only way the difference can be maintained is through reference to the process of thought itself. For it alone indicates that they are not simply identical.[12] If we bring to attention this intellectual process and signify it with a word, we will have a new category of thought.

Reason considers the process by which the thought of *being* moved over to the thought of *nothing* and vice versa. Through this movement the two are united. But this unity is not static; it is a transition, a passing over, a *becoming*. In *becoming* the two earlier moments are distinguished from each other, yet intrinsically related.[13] We have here a new type of logical move. Dialectically thought passed from *being* over to *nothing* and from *nothing* over to *being*. By directing its attention to this act of relating, thought thinks synthetically (or speculatively) the two moments in their relation. This leads to a category of a different order that includes the first two categories as related moments.[14]

The category *becoming* has as components of its connotation the two previous categories of *being* and *nothing,* the unity of their descriptive definitions, and their intended contrast or opposition. *Being* and *nothing* have been shown to lack any characteristic that would differentiate one from the other in thought; therefore they are the same, and cannot be separated. But this demonstration resulted from a movement of thought from one to the other; therefore they are distinct. Speculative thought has brought the two aspects together. From this perspective their differences no longer isolate them into independent categories. Any independence is dissolved.[15] Yet as moments they are retained. Speculative thought has as its task the clarification of this synthetic relationship of unity and difference.

The earlier discussion showed that *being* is the same as *nothing,* and that *nothing* is the same as *being*. These transitions indicated a basic identity. Each is the unity of *being* and *nothing*. Yet they are distinguished in that one moment is primary and the other derived. *Being* is taken in its immediacy, but then becomes *nothing; nothing* is taken immediately, but then becomes *being.* There are, then, two different processes of becoming. One moves from *being* to *nothing;* the other moves from *nothing* to *being.* For the first we use the term *perishing,* for the second, *genesis.* These two new categories define the process of *becoming* more precisely.

The two relations, *genesis* and *perishing,* are both moments of the overall category of *becoming.* Within the structure of pure thought, however, they are not isolated. *Being* perishes and becomes *nothing,* but that *perishing* has as its result a new *genesis* for *nothing* becomes *being.* Similarly, *nothing* generates *being,* but *being* in turn perishes and becomes *nothing.* The two movements are not external to each other, simply opposed as involving contrary directions. *Perishing* dissolves into a new process of *genesis,* and *genesis* dissolves into the process of *perishing.* As each completes its movement, it is itself transformed into its opposite.

The double process of *genesis* and *perishing* renders explicit that synthesis of *being* and *nothing* implicit in *becoming.* But in the dynamic of thought the two movements cannot be held apart in strict isolation. Each collapses into its opposite. This circle, then, becomes simply one movement, one circular act of thought, and the synthesis becomes a simple unity.[16] In other words the double process by which *being* vanishes into *nothing* and *nothing* vanishes into *being* itself vanishes and leaves a tranquil but comprehensive result.[17]

In its concern for clarity the understanding would reject such a confusion of terms. But it finds that it cannot avoid falling into difficulty. For *becoming* is a self-contradictory concept. On the one hand, because *being* disappears into *nothing* and *nothing* disappears into *being* it holds that *being* and *nothing* are the same. But only if *being* and *nothing* are different can there be any process—any becoming at all. As both uniting its two constituent concepts and holding them in strict opposition, *becoming* is self-contradictory and therefore cannot be understood clearly.

The understanding holds that self-contradictory concepts are false, and to that extent amount to nothing. But this conclusion would simply start the process again, for *nothing* would become *being,* and *becoming* would be reconstituted.[18] Therefore the resolution of self-contradiction will not come by holding stubbornly to the earlier category, but by moving to a new perspective in which the two moments are no longer simply opposites but are subcontraries of a more inclusive category. As an intellectual concept this category must be. But it is not pure *being* since it integrates *being* with *nothing;* it is rendered determinate by this contrast.

Because the process of mediation has collapsed into a unity this new simple concept is an *immediate* content of thought, even though it is the result of mediation. It is *being* which is yet determinate. German has the term "Dasein" to signify this category. In English it can best be expressed by using the indefinite article "a" with the gerund "being". The indefinite article suggests that it is not absolutely indeterminate but is in some way limited by a nothing out of which it comes and to which it may return. For this new category of thought, then, we will use the expression *a being:*[19] the restless dynamic of *becoming* is dissolved into the simple, tranquil concept of *a being.*

The Moments of Logical Thought

With the move to *a being* intelligence completes a unit of the thinking process. The new category is a simple unity for thought, not requiring the delicate balancing act present in *becoming,* nor explicitly abstracting a moment of a larger whole, as in *genesis* and *perishing.* In the transition, then, from the immediate concept *being* to the new immediate concept *a being,* intelligence has passed through all the various logical operations. These can thus be distinguished in a preliminary way.[20]

At first thought simply focuses its attention. Since attention individuates, relations can only be thought explicitly if they are signified by a single term. When this term is retained in consciousness over a period of time, it is segregated from the process of imagination that produced it, and thought can thus concentrate on the relation as a single, isolated category. It is this focusing capacity of intelligence that enables thought to rise above the "booming, buzzing confusion" of its own stream of consciousness. Instead of an endless, indeterminate play of forces, it distinguishes terms and categories.

Attention at the level of pure thought is called understanding. It abstracts a particular category from its context and clarifies its specific meaning. In the unit of thought already discussed, the understanding first isolated *being* as the proper beginning, and later sought to define *nothing.* Similarly the new concept *a being* can be thought without reference to any other term. Therefore the understanding will abstract it from the intellectual transitions out of which it arises and take it as a single, isolatable concept.[21]

When the understanding clarifies a concept, however, it initiates a movement in the mind. From *being* thought moves to *nothing;* from *nothing* it returns to *being*. At this point two alternatives are open to intelligence. It can continue to focus its attention on the two distinct terms and ignore that process by which it moves from one to the other; the understanding can refuse to surrender the precise clarity of isolated categories. When it has to acknowledge the fact that *being* and *nothing* cannot be clearly distinguished, however, it sees that they constitute a contradiction. The whole process is rejected as invalid, since the two are supposed to be different, but have turned out to be the same. Such a self-contradiction appeared in the previous discussion when the analysis of *being* showed it to be identical with *nothing,* and vice versa.

In rejecting self-contradictions the understanding does not surrender itself to an absolute void. In its place it sets another concept, presumed to be more acceptable. This transition to a new concept will be arbitrary unless it results in some way from the foregoing process of thinking. This leads to the second alternative present to intelligence.[22]

This takes seriously the act of movement. Understanding does not rest content with simply contemplating a concept. It seeks to define it carefully and precisely, ruling out all possible misapprehensions. This critical activity isolates the concept, not simply through attention, but through the mediating activity of thought itself. In the end it exposes the fact that the original concept is untenable—that it cannot be isolated without contradiction. *Being* is in fact *nothing; nothing* is in fact *being.* This mediating process Hegel calls dialectic. It reproduces that style of argument enshrined in Plato's early dialogues where Socrates takes a concept presented by one or another of his contemporaries and shows that it cannot be defined without contradiction. While it is a type of intellectual activity different from attention, it is not alien to understanding. Rather, dialectic simply asks understanding to clarify its terms, and forces it to think through the consequences of this clarification to their ultimate limit.[23] A dialectical movement, however, is strictly negative. It shows that the strict isolation of understood categories is not tenable—that it leads to conclusions contrary to what is intended.

At this point, thought may bring the two alternatives together. Because the understanding cannot accept a contradiction, it seeks a new concept. Because concepts signify intellectual acts of relating, this new concept can represent the very process of dialectical thought by which the contradiction became evident. In this move, intelligence reflects on what it itself has done. As if looking in a mirror, it considers both the original category and the dialectical result as intrinsically related. Hegel calls this speculative reason. This name not only suggests the proposing of a new theory or idea that was not present before; it also makes an implicit pun: the word "speculate" is derived from the Latin *speculum,* mirror.

One could call the introduction of speculative reason a move to a higher order. Then *becoming* would be the "meta-theory" that sets the two previous concepts, *being* and *nothing,* in context. It does not follow directly from the earlier dialectic but is introduced when intelligence reflects on what it has done. As a synthesis something new is added; the new concept does not follow analytically from the preceding terms.

It does, however, set them in context. Instead of being isolated, they are taken as related in thought. By reflecting on the relation between the two terms intelligence gives a positive sense to the negative thrust of the dialectic. Given the perspective of *becoming,* for example, thought returns to the earlier concepts (*being* and *nothing*) and finds that the relation which at first appeared as a contradiction is in fact a structure of mutual implication. Speculative reason thus becomes the middle term by which the new category is shown to be an analytic consequence of the earlier logical development.[24]

To illustrate: At first intelligence simply holds together *being* and *nothing* because dialectic has shown them to be inseparable—there is no reason to distinguish them. Having surrendered the concern to hold them in isolation, intelligence no longer finds their unity to be a contradiction, but rather discerns two positive transitions: *perishing* and *genesis.* Thought thus has for its content a totality that includes the double process, as well as the original concepts of *being* and *nothing,* as analytically distinguishable moments.

As a moment in an integrated structure, the *being* that perishes is no different from the result that is generated; hence a unity is achieved. The mediation integrates the various moments into a single concept, now called *a being.* This can become the object of understanding's attention—taken as simple and immediate.[25]

Five moments can be distinguished in this process. First, understanding distinguishes and isolates a concept. Second, dialectic shows that any precise definition involves a contradiction. Third, intelligence looks at the relation which synthesizes the opposites. Fourth, it shows the positive character of that relation by rendering explicit the mediating process.[26] Finally, it integrates the whole structure into a simple unity. Speculative reason, although a third operation after understanding and dialectic, itself involves three distinct acts: synthesis, mediation and integration.

Using the first unit of the logic as illustration, we have clarified the various aspects of logical thought. Since each new concept is but the name for a preceding act of relating, however, these are no universal and formal structures that can be applied to an indifferent content. Rather, understanding, dialectic and speculation are simply names for characteristic ways in which intelligence acts. The actions themselves are always concrete and specific, rendered determinate by the terms related. To show how these logical operations work in a slightly more complex context we extend our analysis to the next unit of the logic. Beginning with *a being* we will follow the workings of intelligence until we come to another concept that is simple and self-contained: an immediate object of attention. Then we will leave the logic of simple transitions and move to the level of reflection, where thought renders its presuppositions and what they imply explicit.

5

A Being

A Being

1. As a simple unity, the category *a being* is present to thought. The previous process of understanding, of relating, and of inferring has dissolved and vanished from the focus of attention. The concept is simply there—immediate and isolated from all relations.[1]

Because the logician can recall the earlier process of mediation, however, he is aware that *a being* retains pure *being* only as one aspect of its meaning, and that *non-being*[2] is also present as its indefinite determination. But this external reflection is not sufficient to justify the logical necessity of any transition. Such a move, to be inherently valid, must follow from simply understanding the concept in its pure immediacy.[3]

A being is not the same as *being*. While the article is indefinite and therefore vague in its reference, it yet delimits the sense of the gerund. *A being* is in some way more specific. To render this new concept precise, then, understanding distinguishes the lack of logical determination in pure *being* from the (as yet imprecise) determination in *a being*.

2. Dialectical questioning endeavours to make clear the character of the determination. Is the determination something different from its being? No, is the reply, for such a discrimination is in no way intended; the determination is rather the determinate way in which its being is present. Is the determination that which distinguishes one being from another? No, because the relation of one to another involves a complexity in no way

involved in the indefinite sense of *a being*. The determination is simply the way a being is—how it is qualified. In answer to these questions of dialectic, then, thought passes over to a new, distinct category: *quality*.

This new term, however, is equally indeterminate. All that can be said is that *quality* is the way a being is. As a positive characteristic it defines *a being's* reality. But it is not simply identical with the earlier category. It is the result of a one-sided concern with the specific determination involved in *a being*. As determination it negates the pure indeterminacy of *being*. Despite the fact that it defines the reality of *a being,* then, it also introduces a certain restriction—a certain negativity.[4]

3. When dialectic thus follows through with the implication of the terms isolated by understanding, it clarifies a double relation between the two categories: *a being* is both the same as, and yet different from, its *quality*. The difference, however, is not really significant. While *quality* distinguishes *a being* from *being* it is not in fact different from that indeterminate characteristic suggested in the indefinite article. Thought passes over from *a being* to its being *qualified* only to pass back again. Speculative reason considers this total process and affirms that what is being thought is *a qualified being*.[5] Even that phrase retains an element of difference that needs to be dissolved. The more appropriate term for the reconstituted identity is *something*.

Something is more complex than *a being*. It refers to the determinate quality "some" and the basic reality "thing" but integrates them into a unity. Therefore it negates the difference between them. In this synthetic act of integrating *a being* and its *quality,* speculative reason negates the negation. By transcending the differences made explicit by dialectical thought it reconstitutes a unity, more specific than the original simple concept.[6]

In this concept thought discovers an active process of relating. Something *is,* but it is also *qualified*. Intelligence moves from one to the other. *Becoming,* as transition, is thus involved implicitly in its meaning.

Attention turns to that process of relating. It is not simply the case that *a being* is qualified immediately; it becomes qualified; a movement of thought is involved. But this distinguishes between what it was before, and what it becomes. The first is *something;* the second is qualified, but in some way different from the first. It is something *else,* an *other*. *Something* becomes *something else* as it changes. The process of becoming is here rendered more specific as change.[7]

Speculative reason brought the two terms, *a being* and its *quality* together into the concept *something*. To establish the validity of this synthesis it rendered explicit the mediating process by which the one leads to the other. But instead of achieving a unity it produced the exact opposite. The analysis of the process has resulted in distinguishing two contrasting moments: *something* and *something else.* Thought no longer has a simple concept, but wavers between two. The negative moment, implicit in *a being,* has now become explicit. Intelligence will be able to reconstitute a simple unity only by developing much more thoroughly that negative determination.

An important new transition has been introduced, not as a sixth stage, but as an alternative form of the fifth. When speculative reason synthetically combines two concepts it may find on examination that the relation is one of integration and that the two collapse into a simple unity. On the other hand, however, the relation may not be integration, but something else, which still leaves the movement of thought incomplete.[8] Because the synthesis breaks apart into a more radical contrast, understanding has a more complex set of meanings to isolate and clarify.

Something or Other

1. The first task of understanding is to clarify the difference between the two terms. Both, however, are *something,* for the *other* is *something* else. At the same time each is *other* than its contrary. The two terms can be used indifferently for one or the other and it is only because thought, as an external agent, holds them apart that it can distinguish them. When dialectic forces understanding to make clear the difference between the two terms now present they turn out to be identical.

The understanding cannot allow this distortion of what it intends. Even though the two terms cannot be defined so as to be distinguished, they are yet different. It is this relation of difference that is to be the object of attention. What does it mean *to be other*?[9] As *being* it is similar to itself and can be isolated. As *other* it refers to something which it is not. Yet because it is isolated by understanding there is nothing else to which it can be related. It can only *be* other in itself by *becoming* other than itself. The two terms are mediated by a transition—a becoming other, or change. But when it changes, what *is other* becomes simply *other,* or what it was originally. Therefore even in the process of change *being other* remains identical with itself. As self-identical it is *a being.* But it is a being *qualified* by the fact that the *negative* force of becoming-other is *cancelled.* As a qualified being, therefore, it is *something.*

Now, however, *something* continues through change; in the process of *becoming other* it remains identical with itself. The *other* which it becomes is the same as itself even though, as *other,* it is not the same as itself. The contrast between *something* and *other* becomes a contrast inherent in *something* itself. In its own being otherness is implicitly present; it is not simply introduced from outside by an alien intellectual activity. We can call this *being other-directed.*[10]

2. Once dialectic distinguishes the moment of *being other-directed,* however, it discerns a contrasting moment: what something is outside of that movement—in itself or inherently. Therefore we have a new pair of contraries to replace *something* and *other: being other-directed* and *being in itself. Being in itself,* however, can be defined only by contrast with *being other-directed.* Even though it is supposed to express the simple positive quality of *something,* it has this determinate meaning because any relating movement is explicitly excluded. Neither can the concept *being other-directed* be isolated. It presupposes that which, outside the movement, is in itself. Dialectic shows that each term is rendered precise only by being contrasted with the other; the two are contraries. Although distinct moments they have an intrinsic relation that can become the focus of speculative reason.

3. The transition from *being in itself* to *being other-directed* and vice-versa happens within the process of thinking the constituent moments of *something.*[11] In one movement the thought of that which is *related to another* passes over to what it is *in itself.* Something is *determinate* with respect to its inherent being. In the other movement, the thought of *being in itself* passes over to the thought of its relation to another. Something is *determined* by its being other-directed. Further reflection, however, shows that even this distinction between *determinate* and *determined* cannot be maintained.[12] Each process mediates the other. For when something is determinate, it has been determined. Equally, when something is determined, it becomes determinate. In both, the determining activity of thought renders the concept determinate. This single determining process can be called *determination.*

As a single category, *determination* integrates the double process in which the thought of *something* passes over to the thought of *other.* Thus it renders precise the transition in which thought distinguishes. In the move from *something* to *other* this act of determining was only implicitly present. Now the distinction has become an explicit, independent category. It is, however, logically incomplete; it is a *determination* of *something.* Like *quality* it is one-sided. A relation to its substantive being is assumed, but not specifically expressed. This incompleteness will become explicit as thought proceeds.

Determination, Constitution and Limit

1. Understanding clarifies the new concept. A *determination* is not an alien feature applied to something simply because it is in relation; it is what something is *in itself*. In becoming determinate, something fulfills its determination.[13] What is implicit becomes explicit; what is inherent becomes the way it is determined.

2. Such inherent determinations of something can be distinguished by thought from others that are extrinsic and contingent. The latter are circumstantial, constituted not by the thing in itself but through its contact with something else. If, to render our terms precise, we limit the term *determination* to inherent features of something, there is an inevitable transition of thought to these other features that could be called its *constitution* (or *modification*).[14] Thus the *determinations* of something render determinate its implicit being; its *constitution* reflects contingent and changeable relations. In so far as something changes while remaining the same the change takes place in this relatively superficial area of its *constitution*.

Dialectic shows, however, that the two terms cannot be held in strict isolation. After all, when something becomes determined, it submits to a process of change. In other words, *determinations* are *constituted* by the process. Similarly, something can accept modifications while remaining intrinsically unaffected because it *determines* how far these *constituting* modifications can go. Each process of becoming determinate contains the other, as a moment within its own meaning.

In this dialectic, the category of *change* reappears, not as that which something undergoes, but as its inherent dynamic. While being modified, something determines its constitution; through a process of alteration it constitutes its own determinations. The passive mood is transformed into the active: *Something* is no longer changed; rather, the process of change both *constitutes* and *determines* itself. The two moments mutually determine each other.

This has an important implication that needs to be made explicit. *Constituting* can proceed within this dynamic only to the extent that the determination allows; *determining* can only be achieved through a constituting process. Each marks the *limit* of the other's activity. And if either goes beyond this *limit,* the determinate *something* is changed, and becomes something *else*. The double process in which *something* changes while remaining the same can thus be characterized by the single term *limiting*.

3. Speculative reason considers this result of dialectical reflection. *Something* is a self-identical process of change; its determinate *limit* prevents the introduction of changes that would destroy its specific qualities and would make it into something else. At first, then, *limit* simply renders determinate the point beyond which something cannot go without becoming other. *Limit* indicates where something is NOT to be.

But we have already noted that *limit* is also the way in which the dynamic of change is rendered determinate. It characterizes *something's* own determining activity. Therefore something is *qualified* by means of its limit, and becomes what it IS. The relation, *limit*, defines what something is as well as what it is not.

Mediating reflection endeavours to make this qualification clear. It distinguishes *limit* (as determining *quality*) from *something* (as the *being* qualified). The former is other than the latter, and can be isolated by understanding.

Abstracted from the *limit* that renders it determinate, the concept *something* is left simply with its being.[15] But that can equally be said of any *other* that may be on the far side of the *limit*. Lacking any specific qualities (which would be limiting) both are no more than simply somethings-in-general. Only *limit* can serve to differentiate them.

Yet the limit is their mutual boundary for it is the point of transition where one becomes the other. Paradoxically then, this cannot keep them apart in strict isolation either. The *limit* that distinguishes them also identifies them through a single relation.

There is here a restless movement of thought. *Something* in itself is simply *a being*. But since it cannot then be distinguished from anything else it is determined by its *limit*. This *limit*, however, does not simply separate it from, but is held in common with, the *other* as their mutual point of contact. Therefore to isolate the pure concept, thought must return to that which is other than the limit, to *something* simply as *a being*. This incessant intellectual somersault is signified by the concept *finite*. Finitude refers to *a being* that is *limited* and a *limit* that applies to *a being*. Thought thus brings together into an uneasy synthesis the various concepts that have so far appeared in its immediate transitions. *Limit* integrates *quality, determination* and *constitution*, while *a being* underlies *something* in all its senses. In *finitude* that diversity is crystallized into the two contrary components of a single category.

Finitude

1. Because it contains both *a being* and *limit, finite* is a complex category. It affirms that *a being* is *limited* and that the *limit* is inherent in *a being*. The implications of this restless tension in thought have to be explored.

Understanding takes the initiative; the concept *finite* is isolated to define it clearly. Inherent in the finite is that it comes to an end, that it perishes. But because the concept is isolated, thought is prevented from moving to any concept genuinely different, such as *infinite*. For it is essential to the meaning of *finitude* that it cannot pass over into *infinity*. But this entails a paradoxical consequence: the finitude of the finite is itself limitless—it does *not* come to an end.[16] The *finite,* which is essentially limited, is still essentially unlimited. How these two contradictory predicates can both be applied requires further reflection.

2. When it first appeared, *limit* simply distinguished *something* from its *other;* it consisted of the way in which thought isolated the distinction, common to both *determination* and *constitution.* Now, however, the *limit* is not indifferent to something's *being,* as though simply indicating where it stops; rather, as an ineradicable limit, it *prevents* that being from going further. It is a *limitation,* thwarting every effort to reach beyond. This resistance, however, suggests that the inherent *being* would go further if it were not thus impeded. What *something* is in itself *ought* to be more than what it is; but it cannot be more because of the restraining *limitation.* When finite's *limit* gets defined more precisely as *limitation,* then, its being becomes an *ought. Ought* both expresses its positive reality and its negative inability to breach the barrier.

Understanding's insistence that the *finite* cannot be dissolved into the infinite requires that *limitation* be explicitly involved in the concept. The *ought* appears only because we reflect on the consequences of that claim. But further dialectical consideration shows that *ought* itself is limited, and therefore essentially finite. For "what ought to be *is,* and at the same time *is not.* If it *were,* we could not say that it merely *ought to be.*"[17] It is limited by this failure. The *ought* therefore contains both moments of the finite: it is the way something reacts against its limitation, and yet it contains this limitation within itself. In this category the two moments of the finite—its *limit* and its *being*—are integrated.

The *limitation* as the inherent qualification of the finite's *being* prevents it from becoming what it *ought* to be. *Ought,* however, is its *being* as qualified by the *limitation.* The category *finite* is explicitly this relation between the two terms. Both refer to its *being* and its *limit.* But the two terms do not dissolve into a unity, for they are opposed to each other. The *ought* struggles against its *limitation;* the limitation *resists* any such pressure.

3. This contradiction cannot be maintained in thought. Rather, the two moments alternate. The *finite* has an absolute limitation: it perishes. It cannot disappear into the infinite, for then the *limitation* would have dissolved, and the simple *ought* would remain. Nor can it disappear into *nothing,* for then the *ought* would have dissolved, and the simple *limitation* would remain.[18] Since each requires the other, the *finite* can fulfil its finitude and come to an end only by becoming another *finite* in which both moments are again present. The new *finite* will in turn perish . . . and so on to infinity. Only through this ongoing alternation, in which the passing away of one finite simply originates another, can *finitude* be maintained as perpetual and indissolvable. An endless transition mediates between the *limitation* and the *ought.*

This alternating movement between *limitation* (as the perishing of one finite) and *ought* (as the genesis of a new one) goes on in thought. Intelligence can focus on this mediating relation within which the two contradictory moments become subcontraries; and this *is* an intellectual activity—it shares in the reality of being. But it is other than finite. It is, therefore, *infinite.*

Infinity

1. Understanding isolates the concept of *infinity.* One might think that this cannot be done—that *infinite* includes its contrast with *finitude* and is thus a double category like *something-other.* But this category appeared, not as one side of a relation, but as the act of relating itself. It names the process of passing beyond, a thought process whereby one *finite* comes to its *limit* and a new *finite* appears. As a distinguishable process it can become a single concept.

2. However thought does not stay with this isolation; dialectical reason asks the understanding to define its terms. First, the *infinite* is *a being;* by means of this term thought conceives a determinate act of becoming present in the intellect. Second, it has been isolated by the understanding as the process of passing beyond the *finite.* But this means that it is the reverse of *finitude;* for in passing beyond, it disregards any *limitation* and transforms the *ought* into an *is.* To render the category of the *infinite* precise, then, understanding must set it over against the *finite.* The latter has not dissolved; it remains as the explicit contrast that defines and thus limits *infinity.*

The two categories of *infinite* and *finite* are not related simply as *something* and *other*. They are explicitly contrasted with each other. The *finite* is essentially limited and resists any impulse to become *infinite*. The *infinite* is what the *finite* ought to be but cannot become because of its limitation. By removing the *finite's* restriction it negates the negation.

An act of negation, however, presupposes that which it negates. Just as the first negation of negation, *something*, required something *else* to negate, so *infinite* requires as part of its precise definition its opposite—the limited *finite*. It is the non-finite. As such it has no precise limit, no precise determination. It is an indeterminate emptiness—a simple beyond.

Hegel refers to this concept, thus rendered precise, as a "bad" infinite. As simple beyond, it cannot become finite. It is confronted by a barrier beyond which it cannot go. This has a paradoxical result; defined by its opposition to finitude, this *infinite* is itself a *limited being*. This concept is "bad," because it is finite; thought has not isolated the pure moment of *infinity*.

When dialectical reason reflects on this implication, it finds a significant parallel between the two terms, *finite,* and *infinite*. In the first place, the limit which distinguishes them is common to both: what makes the *infinite* not the *finite* is also what makes the *finite* not the *infinite*. That is, the limitation which prevents the *finite* from becoming more is precisely the same limitation which prevents the *infinite* from including the *finite*. But in the second place both acquire a positive meaning when they constitute themselves independently of this limit. The *finite* is not simply other than the *infinite*. It maintains its own determinate being as inherently transitory. Similarly the *infinite* is not simply other than the *finite*. It is that which is simply beyond, which is independent of any finite being. In the third place, however, the positive character of each is maintained because its opposite is presupposed. The *finite* is maintained as such despite its tendency to pass away—despite any process that may dissolve its limitation. The *infinite* is thought as a simple beyond because it excludes any temptation to provide more precise determinations that might become limitations. Both concepts are defined by the limit; both have an inherent determination independent of the limit, and both maintain this determination in explicit opposition to the limit. To this extent they are similar. And since the limit of each is the other, each requires its contrary to be clearly defined. They are inseparable, yet qualitatively distinct.

When dialectical reason, then, clarifies the concept *finite*, it finds itself thinking *infinite* as its opposite. When it defines *infinite*, it requires *finite*.

Such transitions do not appear to follow from the connotations of the concepts themselves; they are acts, externally introduced by the subconscious, and reflect the inability of intelligence to comprehend its subject matter. Because thought cannot define the *finite* in isolation it moves beyond the limitation of that term and contrasts it with *infinite*. But the latter can be clarified only with reference to its opposite *finite*. Each effort to reach a complete definition finds itself moving on to the other term. The process continues *ad infinitum*.

This progress to infinity reflects a contradiction inherent in the effort to think each term: a positive determination can only be maintained by contrasting it with a constituting limit that it shares with the other. To avoid contradiction thought maintains the qualitative difference of the two. But this means that it simply runs back and forth from one to the other. Only because they follow each other and are not held together in a synthetic unity is contradiction avoided.[19]

Infinite progress is a perpetual *ought*. It is conditioned by the inherent characteristic of the *finite*. A definite result ought to be achieved by thought if it is to have a precise definition of either *finite* or *infinite,* but it never does. A limitation always appears.

While the *infinity* of the simple beyond is finite because it is limited externally by its contrast with determinate beings, the infinity of *infinite progress* has limitation as a part of its own dynamic—a perpetual *ought to be* that is never achieved. This perennial *ought* is its response to a perennial *limitation.* Thus this *infinite* is qualitatively the same as the *finite.* Dialectical reflection started by assuming that the concept *infinite* could be isolated and defined positively. It discovers instead that it always returns, not only to a finite concept, but also to a concept of the *finite.* Its intention is never achieved.

3. At this point speculative reason enters. Dialectic has shown that, in being *limited* and in being simply an *ought,* the *finite* and the *infinite* are the same. This became concretely present in intelligence as the dynamic of the *infinite progress.* This process itself must be brought explicitly to consciousness so that thought can be clear why the two terms that are supposed to be opposites turn out to be identical. Only then will it be able to determine precisely the connotation of each.

In this process, thought goes beyond one concept to its contrary: from the *finite* to the *infinite,* and from the *infinite* to the *finite.* This suggests that implicit in each is a relation to its opposite. Whenever intelligence tries to conceive one clearly and precisely, the other inevitably appears.

Understanding rejects this claim: they are distinct moments and are

related only by an *and;* any so-called implicit relation is an external impu-
tation of arbitrary thought. But in "infinite and finite," the understanding
sets them beside each other and takes the infinite as only one side; thereby
it is limited. Therefore it is a finite infinite. Similarly *finite* is a positive
independent concept; it has the permanence and internal completeness
which *infinite* should have, and is thus an infinite finite. Even in the effort
to hold them apart, the understanding is inevitably forced to express their
implicit conjunction. Whether the two terms are considered as moments
of an infinite progress or as absolutely independent, the same result
appears: they are conjoined to each other.

The unity of the two terms, *finite* and *infinite,* a unity characteristic of
both, is yet inherently different in each. On the one hand the *infinite* is
primary, with *finitude* differentiated from it; but this differentiation
constitutes its determining and defining limit; it is a "finitized infinite."
On the other hand, when the *finite* is defined[20] as not what it ought to be, it
is thereby made permanent, becoming an "infinitized finite." Once again
understanding resists such an implication. In itself, the *infinite* ought not
become finite; in itself the limitation of the *finite* resists any move to transform it into the infinite. But paradoxically in this defensive manoeuvre
each has already become its opposite. For the *ought* of the *infinite* is a sign
that it has become finite; and the resistance of the *finite* to complete annihi-
lation indicates that it has become infinite and unlimited. Only when
understanding does not consider these inherent implications of its own
claims can it maintain that the terms are absolutely separate.

Since concepts are signs for the dynamic activity of intelligence, they
signify both the abstractions of understanding and their dialectical implications. By becoming self-consciously aware of their setting within the
functions of intelligence, however, thought transforms itself from understanding into speculative reason. It then recognizes that the relations are
inherent in the terms.

Having brought the context of thought explicitly to attention, intelligence discovers that each constituent concept is a dynamic activity—a
process of negating its own negation. The *finite* is essentially limited, and
doomed to perish. But thought must go beyond this limit if it is to render
explicit its essential finitude. Going beyond is a part of its connotation.
But what is not limited by a limit is *infinite*. The concept *finite* can be
thought precisely only if its essential limitation is cancelled as a limitation,
whereby its negation is negated.

Similarly the *infinite* is the opposite of the finite, is an empty beyond.
But in this definition it is limited by the *finite* which it cannot become. As

limited, it is itself *finite,* and so the opposition cannot be maintained. Once again the negation is negated in the very act of rendering the concept precise.

Each moment negates its defining limit and becomes its opposite; yet each has an independent, positive connotation. By comparing them, thought can see both their relation and their difference. The concept of *infinite progress,* however, says more. It relates them in their differences and differentiates them in their relation.

At first this appears as a simple sequence: one follows the other. As such the overarching context of the infinite progress appears to be an external synthesis. The unity of the two moments is not yet explicit. But when we consider the sequence itself, we discover that it follows from the inherent characteristics of each of its terms. The *finite* is considered; thought goes beyond its limitation to the *infinite;* the emptiness of the *infinite* requires a limitation that makes it *finite.* The movement is circular; thought simply comes back to where it began. Although the *finite* disappears into the *infinite,* it reappears from the *infinite.* "In its beyond it has only found itself again."[21] Similarly the *infinite* beyond becomes *finite* when it is limited by the *finite.* This limitation, however, ought not to be present, and thought moves beyond it again to the *infinite.* Once again thought moves in a circle. Infinite progress is this double process by which intelligence returns to both original concepts, having in the interim thought their opposites. The two terms are no longer simple concepts, immediately present in thought. They are the results of, and are thus defined by, this circuit of intelligence.

A difference still remains. One can start the circle either from the *finite* or from the *infinite.* On reflection, this difference turns out to be a matter of indifference. One begins with *finite;* one moves on to the *infinite;* the latter can be either the process of mediation *or* a new beginning; one moves on again to the *finite;* it can be a result, a process of mediation, or indeed another beginning; and so on. Because the final term is the same as the first term, one does not really advance to a new concept. But because it is the result of mediation, it includes the other within it and thus embodies the unity of the two terms. As isolated, each is *finite;* as the result of the process of thought, each becomes *infinite.*

With regard to the negating of negation in *something,* the *other* which resulted was different from any concept previously defined. Here, however, that which is *other* is the same as that out of which *something* comes.[22] This infinite process is not, then, a linear progression. It is a circle in which each process of mediation mediates the starting point for the other. It both posits a contrast between *infinite* and *finite,* and dissolves any difference.

Once before we saw this circular movement in thought. In the atemporal process of *becoming,* the *being* which was generated could be identified with the *being* that perished. The double movement of *perishing* and *genesis* became a circle—a single intellectual process. As such it collapsed into a simple unity.

Here again we have such a move. The double process of mediation creates a circle, a circle that can be called the *true infinite.* As infinite, it constitutes both the *finite* and the *bad infinite* even while dissolving their differences. It therefore does not require any term to render its meaning precise; it defines and determines itself. As simply equal with itself, it is *being;* as determinate it is *a being;* and as positively determined by its own distinguishing and relating process it is a reality—a *qualified something.*[23]

4. Just as the process of *becoming,* as a circle complete in itself, collapsed into a single, immediate concept, so here the process of the true infinite can collapse in thought into a simple category. It is a being that is related to itself. Because the negative moment of determination and limitation is not simply implicit but explicitly posited and transcended, it is self-contained being, *being for its own sake.*[24] This, then, becomes a new immediate concept that can lead to further reflection.

The Process of Thinking

By resolving its restless dynamic into the immediate concept, *being for the sake of itself,* thought has completed another unit of the logic. But this unit is significantly more complex than the earlier move from *being* to *a being.* The latter involved only five operations: understanding, dialectic, synthesis, mediation, and speculative unity. In the former, however, each operation is itself a complex of secondary developments. On the most general level we can see a parallel between the large transitions and the five operations. To qualify something is the activity of understanding. Determining its limits to the point of tension between what it ought to be and its limitation is dialectic. The two are synthesized in simple *infinity;* that relation is mediated in the interplay between *finitude* and *infinity* and integrated in *being for its own sake.* [The complexity in the section between *something* and *finitude* suggests, however, that dialectic is not a simple operation. It involves changing (both externally and internally), determining and defining.]

At the same time every one of these transitions involves the five operations. Within each (namely, *a being, otherness, determination, finitude and infinity),* the understanding isolates a given concept, while dialectical thought examines its implications. Inevitably a paradox arises: what was supposed to be different is shown to be identical; and the simple and self-identical involves a contradiction. To resolve the dilemma, speculative reason turns its attention to the intellectual transitions that have thus become explicit. This relating is analyzed to clarify its mediating structure, and then is signified by, and integrated into, a new concept.

In moving from the first unit of the *Logic* to the second, logical transitions become more determinate. From *being* to *a being* the movement of thought is a "going over" or *becoming.* From *a being* to *infinite* it becomes *change*—a process that allows a contrast between what moves and what does not. In the next chapter it will be *repulsion* and *attraction.* At each stage thought's transitions become more specific and determinate. "Thus instead of three objects or 'categories' we have obtained rather three processes [that is, becoming, change and relation] . . . . To think is only this passage from one contradiction to another, from the negation of the objects to the negation of the processes that constitute them. To think exists only as denying."[25]

Within the first book of Hegel's *Logic* we have begun to discover the nature of its necessity. By pausing to make some metalogical observations we have suggested what is essential to the argument. The contrast between the logical content and the metalogical reflection, however, leaves an element of contingency in the analysis. Necessity will be adequately comprehended when the logical categories considered are not *being* and *change* but the reflective process of thought itself. This composes the content of the second book of the *Science of Logic,* which is Essence, or the theory of reflection.

Part Three

Reflecting

Seeming

Essence

In the logic of *being,* thinking simply passed from one concept or category over to another. When trying to understand *being* intelligence found itself thinking *nothing; being other directed* passed into *being in itself; determination* into *constitution; limitation* into *ought.* These simple transitions, categorized as *becoming,* happened immediately.

In commenting on those processes, however, we introduced a meta-logical reflection that could recognize how one term inherently referred to the next, and vice versa.[1] By making this explicit, we showed that transitions to more complicated concepts are not contingent, but are in some way determined by preceding thoughts.

As Hegel develops the logic, this implicit reference of one concept to another begins to become more explicitly expressed in their connotation. Thus at the end of the section on *quantity, ratio* becomes the basis for *measuring. Measuring* in turn introduces an explicit act of relating, for it brings together two realities, indifferent to each other. This conjunction is recognized as valid, however, only if each term allows for, and indeed encourages, the association. Since mutual reference is now an inherent characteristic of the concept, one passes beyond simple immediacy. Central to the thinking of each term is its relation to a counterpart. What is present immediately in the term is set in context so that its essence can be discerned. The German term for essence, *Wesen,* captures this; for it is the root of the past participle of "to be," *gewesen.* "Essence is past—but timelessly past—being."[2]

Understanding isolates the immediate concept, *essence.* It can be distinguished as a self-contained category because thought has dissolved the immediacy of simple being, and then has taken this act of dissolution for its content.

As an intellectual act, *essence* is immediate and present in the intellect: it is *a being.* Thought, however, distinguishes it from the other *being* whose immediacy was dissolved. Since the understanding's isolating activity ignores the process by which the new concept appeared, these two concepts are related in thought simply as *something* and *something else.* Intelligence passed from one over to the other; *being* was replaced by *essence.*

Dialectical reason turns its attention to this relation. *Essence* is the dissolution of *being.* The movement of thought goes in only one direction; it cannot be reversed. Therefore *being* is the *inessential* in contrast to the *essential.* Understanding insists in reply that the two terms are self-contained, each with its own inherent character;[3] they are qualified beings. The contrast between *essential* and *inessential,* then, is not inherent in the meaning of *being* and *essence,* but results only from the fact that thought considers both terms at the same time. Since it is independent of the two concepts and external to them, dialectic has introduced a third perspective. It could just as well have maintained that *being* (as starting point) is *essential,* and *essence* (as result) is *inessential.*

Speculative reason takes a closer look at this debate. *Essence* was called *essential* because in it the immediacy of *being* was dissolved. This meant that it was simply different from *being.* But in dissolving this immediacy it did not become something else. Indeed, it was *being* itself that initiated the intellectual movement of its dissolution; and *essence* does nothing but signify the process by which the concept of *being* cancels its own immediacy in thought. It is the negative movement of dissolution. To define its meaning clearly, then, it is necessary to consider that *being* which cancels or dissolves itself, the being that seems to be a nonentity. This dynamic, inherent in being, can be called *seeming.*[4]

Seeming

The term *seeming* refers to that aspect of *being* which is not retained in *essence,* i.e. which is inherently vacuous. It has, however, a character of its own, immediately present in thought, by which it is differentiated from *essence.* What makes it *inessential* is not *its being,* for essence also is a being; rather is it inessential because the moment of its immediacy is vacuous and a nonentity. *Seeming* refers to what is immediate but not *a being*. Its only positive feature, its immediacy, is dependent on something else. But, paradoxically, this means that, thus isolated by thought from *a being, seeming* is not itself immediate but mediated.

Seeming, as that in *being* which is independent of *essence,* does not become *essence.* But dialectical reflection discovers that the very determinations which are to distinguish it from *essence* are nevertheless determinations of *essence* itself. *Seeming* is defined as the immediacy of non-being, or as non-being in its immediacy. The two moments of its meaning are: its *non-being* and its *immediacy.* However, *essence* also is non-being; as the dissolution of *being,* its meaning can only be defined using this contrast. In addition, it is immediate; for it signifies a self-identical process present in thought. Therefore the definition of *essence* could equally be the immediacy of non-being, or non-being as immediate.[5] Supposed to be other than *essence, seeming* has the same defining characteristics.

Speculative reason considers the paradox that has appeared. In contrast to what the understanding first supposed, *essence* is not a simple concept that can be isolated in the way *a being* can be isolated. *Essence* signifies a much more complex process of thought: in dissolving, or negating, what is immediately given, it remains identical with itself.[6] It is therefore the self-contained synthesis of a thorough-going negativity and a persistent immediacy. Even while dissolving it is immediately present; and although it is immediately present, it dissolves itself. It is nothing other than this negative self-relation.

If *essence* is a self-contained process, *seeming* is a contrary moment that is not self-contained. Its implicit insufficiency as something vacuous leads to its own dissolution. Indeed this negative relation to its own lack constitutes its immediacy. The category *seeming,* then, is not a simple, given concept, but an activity of self-relating negativity.

The two concepts, *essence* and *seeming,* can be distinguished as negative self-relation and self-relating negativity. This pair of double terms is reminiscent of the language used in explicating the category *infinite,* with its "finitized infinite" and "infinitized finite." As with the earlier term, these contrasting moments dissolve into each other. For the concept, *seeming,* by dissolving its own negativity, simply reaffirms itself as negative. It becomes a self-contained relation. Both moments, self-contained relation to itself (its immediacy) and self-dissolving negativity (its vacuous non-being), disappear into each other in an infinite cycle. This cyclical movement of thought, however, is precisely the connotation signified by the term *essence*. When set within the context of a speculative analysis, the category *seeming* refers not simply to the isolatable residue of *essence,* but to essence itself. *Essence* means that which seems to be a seeming, which shows itself to be a show.

This produces an important shift in the meaning of *seeming*.[7] It started as that which was left behind, when *being* was dissolved into *essence*. Now its connotation has inverted; it is the way *being* shows its *essence*. *Essence* is not the concluding term of a movement of thought, but the movement itself; and *seeming* is simply evidence of this process. When something is taken to be a *seeming,* then, thought has already determined its *essence* because both moments—vacuous and immediate—have been related to each other.

In this discussion of *essence* we started by taking it as a simple category, distinguished from *being*. To clarify this contrast, we introduced the concept *seeming*. On more careful consideration, however, this distinction does not hold. For both *seeming* and *essence* signify the same activity—a self-relating negativity which is equally a negative self-relation. In this process thought dissolves an immediate in order to reconstitute it as immediate.

In the previous chapter, thought passed from one concept to another in a transition named *becoming*. Here, however, the intellectual movement becomes much more complex. When dialectic seeks to define the concepts of *essence,* thought does not simply introduce another term as an immediate contrast: *quality* for *a being; constitution* for *determination; ought* for *limitation*. Rather the original concept already contains reference to its opposite in its isolated meaning: *essence* is explicitly not simple *being; seeming* is explicitly not *essence*. The negative ''not'' is an *essential* part of their positive definitions, referring to what is *inessential*.[8] Mediating speculation, then, does not simply pass over from one positive idea to another. Rather it bounces back and forth from one to the other. For each can only be defined by its contrasting relation to the other. *Seeming* directs thought to *essence; essence* needs *seeming* to distinguish it from *being*. This circular process of thought which, having distinguished the two moments, must still relate them is called *reflection*.[9] Its own immediacy as act is derived from the mutual repulsion through which each concept distinguishes itself from its dialectical counterpart while passing over into it.

This new development can be expressed by saying that *becoming* passes from *being* (by way of *nothing*) to *being;* whereas *reflection* moves from *nothing* to *nothing*. The former starts from a simple concept which is

In essence being what the non-entity is not, then it regards the negativity of the past and has a positive side

present, and in a negative transition moves over to another simple concept. The latter, however, starts from a concept that is already recognized as a non-entity, in some sense vacuous; it dissolves, or negates this vacuity; and the result is another concept that is not simple and positive, but rather is essentially determined by this negative process. It is what the first non-entity is not. *Becoming* passes over from *a being* to *something else*. *Reflection* takes what is nothing (as an indication of what that nothing is not) and it dissolves the simple transition of *becoming* by maintaining the reference of one term to the other. Thus although dissolved by the activity of thought each is yet retained as related to the counterpart which it is not.[10] Because the immediate transitions of thinking are themselves negative, and each subsequent negation renders the process more abstract, *reflection* will require a careful, but complicated, analysis. In this way, however, the inherent necessity of pure thinking will begin to become explicit.

Reflection as Such

Reflection is a process that starts from nothing—from a concept that shows itself to be a non-entity.[11] And its action with regard to that nothing is to dissolve it in thought. In other words, thought's negative activity responds to its own negative definition of the original term. By thus relating negatively to its own negativity, the process can collapse into a simple immediacy that becomes an isolated concept: *reflection as such*.[12] On the one hand it is equivalent to itself, and therefore immediate; but on the other it is a process that is absolute in its negativity; hence its starting point, its process, and its result are all negatively defined.

Dialectic shows that the immediacy of this concept cannot be derived from any one of the three negative moments in isolation but only from their synthesis: The result is *not* the starting point. It therefore embodies the dissolving activity of thought. But the starting point itself is a non-entity. Therefore the result is not a non-entity. The two negatives make a positive, not as immediately given, but as the result of an intellectual transition. The result is *posited* as immediate.[13] In the context of the previous discussion, for example, essence is posited when *seeming* is taken as *seeming*.

Dialectic pushes further. When something is dissolved as a non-entity, an immediate is posited. But the activity of thought that dissolves (i.e. *reflection as such*), begins from that which is taken as a non-entity. By cancelling its negative character it hopes to establish a positive content that is only implicit. This means, then, that in beginning to reflect, thought already *presupposes*[14] the immediacy which will be posited. In taking its starting point *as* a non-entity it presumes that there is an immediacy that can be discovered if that negativity (which is a mediating process) is itself negated.

In light of these dialectical conclusions, speculative reason considers the double intellectual activity of positing and presupposing. In the process of positing its conclusion, reflection discovers what it presupposes. This discovery itself, however, involves dissolving the negative character of its own activity so that the immediate that results can be thought *as* what was presupposed. In *reflection as such,* then, there are three processes of cancelling a negative determination. The negativity of the result is cancelled in positing; the negativity of the starting point is cancelled in presupposing; and the negativity of the dissolving process itself is cancelled in taking the posited result as presupposed. It is this self-cancelling process of reflection that enables thought to render *essence* distinct. The whole negative structure of reflection itself is taken to be nothing but a *seeming.*

Essence, then, is posited as presupposed, that is, as preceding reflection; all that reflection adds is to think it explicitly. This act of rendering the *essence* explicit, however, includes the recognition that its own reflective activity is to be disregarded as insignificant. Indeed, "disregard" is too mild a term; it must be repelled as absolutely irrelevant to *essence.* The presupposed *essence* is to be completely indifferent to the activity of reflection, and the latter is recognized by self-reflective thought as its own addition, external to *essence* and quite inessential.

Within its own intellectual activity and without reference to anything else, intelligence has here distinguished its process from that which is to be independent of that process. That distinction is a part of the meanings of the terms as they are thought. Thus nothing actually independent of thought is involved. Hegel is making explicit the fact that we *think* of relations as external even though this thinking is an integrating intellectual process. The thought of relations as external, however, is quite different from their actually being external. The latter contrast is not a logical contrast.[15]

External Reflection

We started by taking *reflection* simply in itself, isolated from any relations. As non-relative it was considered absolutely. Now, however, we have a concept of *reflection* that is relative. It is external to that about which it reflects. The understanding defines this category of *external reflection* as having a double character. On the one hand it has a given that is presupposed. On the other hand, the explicit process of *reflection* is alien to this given. It is an activity that is aware of its own limitations. When contrasted with the given, it is inessential.

To render clear for dialectical thought the nature of this external relation, the characteristics of its two moments need to be made precise. First, the given is presupposed. In itself it is to be simply immediate being. Its role as reflective presupposition is added and accidental, not essential. Second, *reflection* is external. As mediating reflection it requires a starting point that is a non-entity. Since the starting point to which it refers has been thought as an immediate being, however, it becomes a basis for reflection only because thought arbitrarily determines it negatively.

In *external reflection,* then, the positive moment of immediacy is referred simply to the premise taken as a given; the negative moment of reflection is referred to the activity of thought. Since the immediate given is to exclude any relation to something else, it is not allowed to submit even to an implicit process of change. All transitions are introduced from one side only, from the negativity of *reflection.* This sharp distinction between the immediate as positive and the relating process as negative defines the way the externality of this relation is thought. Yet the two are related to each other in a single concept.

Speculative reason looks at this relation more closely. What does the activity of external reflection involve? It takes an immediate as a presupposition, thus introducing a specific determination. But at the same time it must invalidate this act of taking, or positing, so that, through reflection, its premise will in fact be thought as immediate and not as determined. In beginning to reflect, then, intelligence does not start with a simple immediate. Far from being simple, its immediacy as beginning is posited by the very activity with which reason begins to reflect. Implicit in the immediacy of the premise is the mediating activity of reflection. The relation, then, is not simply a function of self-negating reflection, but is also intrinsic to the presupposition as positive and immediate.

This relation needs to be rendered more explicit. The immediacy of the premise is not simply an expression of its *being*. It is a determinate quality, specifically posited by thought. In other words its quality as immediate is the way it is determined. Equally, *reflection* is not simply the negative process of inessential thought. It takes the initiative to determine the positive quality of its premise.

With this we render *reflection* more determinate. At first it starts from that which is nothing in itself—a nonentity—and by dissolving its illusory character posits as its conclusion what the premise is not. Then it presupposes an independent, immediately given being, which, as essential, is to be distinguished from inessential thought. Now it determines its own starting point. In place of *positing reflection* and *external reflection* we have *determining reflection.*

Determining Reflection

Determining reflection integrates features of the two previous moments. Like *external reflection* it starts with an immediate being. But it posits or determines the way this being is to be thought. Since this act of "determining how" is original with the act of reflecting, it has no independent presupposition, and thus resembles *reflection as such.*

At first the "determining how" is posited as immediately given, and can be distinguished from the mediating act of *reflection.* It can also be distinguished from the *being* that is to be the presupposition of *reflection,* for it is the way that *being* is determined. It stands, then, between the two. As posited, it is not *a being* as such; as immediate it is not *reflection* as such. As determination, however, it adds a more specific character to this being; and it is used by reflective thought to determine what is essential.

Because the act that posits the determination is other than the act that reflects on it, the former is presupposed by the latter and taken to be external to it. In other words, to "determine how" *a being* is to be thought is to presuppose (in the manner of *external reflection*). In both cases reflection precludes any negative aspect of its own reflective activity from entering into the immediacy of what is posited. But whereas in *external reflection* thought began with a being taken to be external, in this process an initial positing or determining act of intelligence is itself isolated from its subsequent reflective consideration. This double activity determines the structure of *determining reflection:* whatever is posited is a *determination of reflection* in both senses: reflection determines it, and it determines reflection.

Dialectic explores both sides of this double relation: *determination* and *being* on one hand; *determination* and *reflection* on the other. In the previous chapter we had occasion to refer to *determinations.* There a *determination* was the way *something* was determined, a transitory aspect of its *being.* Intelligence moved on to other concepts: *limit, finite* and *limitation.* A *determination of reflection,* however, is explicitly isolated from the transitions of reflective thought. Therefore it continues as self-identical throughout the process. And since it is not a transitory moment, it remains common to the *essence* that results from reflection as well as to the immediate *being* presupposed. But since the act of determining is external to the act of reflecting, they are not integrated into a single, comprehensive intellectual activity. Therefore there may be a number of *determinations of reflection,* each isolated as self-identical by thought. Because their identity is derived from the act of positing alone, and then maintained throughout reflection, neither are they related to each other, nor do they reject each other as incompatible. They are simply essentials, whose determinateness has been permanently fixed, and they "appear as free essentialities floating in the void."[16]

This has a paradoxical consequence. The mediating concept (namely, of *determinations of reflection*) does not integrate the activity of thought with the essence it thinks; instead the exact opposite has happened. Reflection falls apart into a number of distinct acts, and essence becomes simply a number of essentials. The negative moment of distinguishing, which is only implicit in *essence's* contrast with *being,* now gains the upper hand.

Speculative thought turns to this mediating concept to comprehend its paradoxical intellectual dynamic. In the term *determinations of reflection* two acts are involved. On the one hand, intelligence acts to determine or to posit, an act distinguished from *reflection* by the activity of thought itself. The determinations thereby acquire a specific identity which they retain because thought then dissolves and forgets its original positing activity. Thus, although intellectually posited, the determinations are constituted as immediate and independent, and hence as other than the reflective process. On the other hand, intelligence *reflects.* To do so, thought maintains the determinations and uses them to reach the essential result. They are therefore central to the reflective process as such.

These two intellectual activities, determining and reflecting, are quite distinct. Determining establishes the self-identical independence of the *determinations;* reflecting then incorporates them into a dynamic process. Yet they are both functions of the same intelligence. The two, then, are not simply indifferent to each other. Something like a love-hate relationship enables them to remain distinct within a single intellectual dynamic. Each rejects the other: the act of determining gives to each essential its own identity so that it will be independent of the changing dynamic of reflection; and the act of reflecting considers the determinations as external givens—positive characteristics not affected by its own negative and dissolving activity. Yet each requires the other: the determinations are posited only because they will be used by reflection to determine what is essential, and reflection can fulfill its operation only by presupposing the determinations. They are objective criteria which, when clearly distinguished, also apply to the intellectual process of formulating them as criteria. It is this self-referential structure that complicates their analysis.

Yet because intelligence both distinguishes absolutely and relates intrinsically and does so in the same act (the act of determining reflection and reflective determination), the *determinations of reflection* integrate the two conceptual realms of external *being* and *reflective* thought. As common to both they are the *essentials;* anything else will be inessential.[17]

The Essentials

Identity[1]

What makes a *determination of reflection* essential? A determination of reflection shows itself to be essential because it persists. What it is in the presupposed being is equivalent to what it is in the discerned essence. Throughout the process of reflection it remains *self-identical*.

This *identity*, however, is not simply characteristic of the object of thought. It is also the criterion reflection itself uses. What is found to be self-identical through reflection is essential.

As a determination of reflection, *identity* is to be used to define what is essential. Therefore dialectic applies the term self-reflexively to itself to distinguish reflection's inessential additions from what is essential. In the previous chapter we identified *being* as that which is equivalent to itself. This characteristic was simply the positive feature of anything that is. The category of *identity,* however, is more complex. It is an equivalence to itself that is maintained through a process of change. This being resists dissolution, and persists throughout the reflecting dynamic. Thus *identity* can be identified only because the process of reflection, while dissolving its presupposition, at the same time annuls this very dissolving activity. Even as a difference begins to appear, it disappears. In the concept of *identity* the moment of change is introduced only to be dismissed as creating no *essential* difference. The moment of difference is posited as a nonentity which is vacuous because it has not been identified.

Thus *identity* has, as one aspect of its connotation, the moment of difference. This difference, however, is not identified. It is any difference.

Within the connotation of *identity,* difference as such—anything that is not *identity*—is excluded and thus not present.

Speculative reason considers this difference that external reflection has introduced and recognizes that difference as such[2] has been identified as a moment within the meaning of *identity*—and that it is thereby essential. To identify pure *identity* any and every difference must be rejected. Because *difference* has thus been identified in this concept as the non-identical that continues to be excluded, it is given a self-identical character by thought.

The concept *identity,* then, has a paradoxical character. It can only be thought because it identifies the moment of non-identity as something to be absolutely rejected. But this means that, throughout the reflective process, it gives whatever it considers non-identical a self-identical character, making it essential. No longer a simple positive concept, *identity* can only be thought by an intellectual activity that differentiates what it is not from what it is, and identifies that *not* to be inextricably entwined with what it is. This *not* or moment of *pure difference* is an *essential determination* of its meaning.

Difference

Understanding isolates the simple moment of *difference* as such. Thus isolated difference is present in thought as relating only to itself; it is the single word "not," crystallized into a category. In the transition from *something* to *other,* and in *being other,* negativity is present, but as *a being*—as embodied in a positive. Therefore it is not pure. Here, by contrast, the negative thrust is completely isolated.

Dialectic uses this determination of reflection self-reflexively to differentiate thought's operations from what is essential: *"difference* is not." *Not* does not here signify pure *nothing,* for it is a determination of *difference;* a relation is yet implicit. The concept can be isolated, then, only by being related to itself: *"Difference* is not *difference;"* it is simply different from itself. But what has been identified as "not difference" is *identity:* yet *difference* is to be differentiated from *identity.* The dialectical run-around can be stopped only if some reference to the previous determination of reflection is introduced. *Difference* is not pure differentiation, isolated from any other conceptual context, but it is *different* from *identity.* *Identity* is an essential constituent of its meaning.

Speculative reason considers this double character that external reflection has introduced: the concept *difference* is *differentiated* from *identity.*

The two constituent terms of the definition are independent of each other, yet both are essential. Although externally related to each other, *identity* and *difference* are brought together into one determination of reflection. The term that signifies this synthesis is *diversity*.

Diversity

The concept *diversity* follows from the two previous categories. *Identity* falls apart into *diversity* because, having excluded *difference* from its meaning, it cannot identify this, its unavoidable contrary. *Difference* develops into *diversity* because it is explicitly differentiated from *identity*. What is *diverse* is different in a way independent of any identification, and at the same time is identified in a way that is irrelevant to any differentiation. The two aspects of the the definition, *identity* and *difference,* have simply been brought together by an external reflection. Any identity or difference between them is a matter of indifference.[3] The two are thus diverse vis-à-vis each other; and the category applies, self-reflexively, to the internal relation between its constituent moments.[4]

Dialectic self-reflectively considers how this result is determined. Because *identity* in *diversity* is indifferent to any *difference* and vice-versa, these two diverse aspects of its meaning are brought together into a single concept through a "third": the act of external reflection. The nature of this external relation is to be more clearly defined.

In the first place, because each term is to have its own independent meaning, the two are mutually indifferent one to the other. There is no inherent reason why they should be associated. Therefore when they are brought together into a single intellectual perspective, an external identity is imposed on them. This external identification is quite distinct from the simple concept of *identity* originally defined.

In the second place, however, the two terms are not simply collapsed into a uniform concept. Rather, as diverse, they are distinct one from another in thought. Because of their mutual indifference this distinction is not inherent, but is also posited by external reflection. Once again, external differentiation is quite distinct from the simple concept of *difference* originally defined.

An identity that is not inherent but is introduced externally by thought is called *likeness*; and an external difference is *unlikeness*. In the concept of *diversity,* then, external reflection actively postulates a likeness and an unlikeness between its diverse moments—in this case *identity* and *difference*. This reflective activity of intelligence is called *comparing*.

Speculative reason then turns its attention to the process of external reflection. *Comparison* first considers likenesses, then passes on to thinking unlikenesses, and vice-versa. The transition from one activity to the other is different from the actual comparison and added to it. For comparing posits either an external identity or an external difference; the movement back and forth from one act to the other is independent of both. This means that the two moments, *likeness* and *unlikeness* are themselves indifferent to each other. Any relation between them is introduced by the reflective transition that acts as an independent "third." Their indifference is expressed in qualifying prepositions: "insofar as," "from the side of" and "with respect to." In itself each moment is simply related to itself: the like are alike, the unlike are unlike and that is all there is to it.

If the two are thought in this absolute isolation, however, *comparison* becomes impossible. For it requires both relations, positing an external difference and equally an external identity. Abstracted from this context, *unlikeness* collapses into pure differentiating, and *likeness* is reduced to simply identifying. Only by moving back and forth from one to its contrary does *comparison* take place; and as we have seen, reflection needs *comparison* to determine *diversity*.

The necessity of this relation between the two moments of an act of *comparison*, however, is not to be found in the *diversity* compared. If things are *alike*, it is a matter of indifference whether they are *unlike* in themselves or not. Moreover, their *unlikeness* cannot lead to any inference, positive or negative, regarding their *likeness*. In other words the necessary association of *like* and *unlike* in one intellectual activity is not inherent in the *diversity* that is being compared, but is required only by the *reflective* act of comparing.

Comparison, then, takes a *likeness* it finds and an *unlikeness* it finds, but must necessarily oppose these two determinations to each other. The contrast is essential for external reflection, but is not essential for its conceptual object. The introduction of a posited contrast is called *opposition,* which signifies the moment of transition that is essential in *comparison*.

Opposition

The simple "not" of *difference* becomes fully explicit in the concept of *opposition*. While "not" identified *difference,* and also differentiated it from *identity,* these two operations were indifferent to each other. Now, however, in one intellectual act the two are identified as differentiated.

Opposition is a single activity of thought that takes an external diversity and introduces an explicit contrast. It opposes the like to the unlike even though in themselves those two relations are indifferent to each other.

Dialectical reflection tries to determine what is essential in this definition by differentiating it from what thought introduces. The two categories, *likeness* and *unlikeness,* signify the two moments that are opposed to each other by external reflection. Taken on its own, however, the concept *like* can be identified only by differentiating it from *unlike,* and vice-versa. Quite apart from any reflective addition, each opposes the other.

This has an implication for the concept of *opposition.* Understanding took *likeness* in itself to be indifferent to *unlikeness;* the opposition resulted from the fact that both were included in one intellectual act. But careful reflective determination has shown that *like* is not indifferent to *unlike,* nor vice-versa. The "not" of opposition is also in the conceptual object and is not simply the result of external reflection.

This leads to a shift in the meaning of the two opposing moments of the concept *opposition.* That which is not only alike, but is also differentiated from what is unlike is called the *positive;* likewise, that which, even though *unlike,* nonetheless includes its contrast with *likeness,* is *negative.* Each of these terms includes its opposition to the other.

The reflective act of opposing experiences a related shift in meaning For no longer can it be said to introduce the opposition between *likeness* and *unlikeness.* Rather it determines that what it posited as *like* has indeed been presupposed as like, and what it opposed to *like* was indeed presupposed as unlike. This similarity and dissimilarity was not an innovation of external comparison, but was present essentially, only to be discerned by an inessential reflection. When this reflection reflects on itself, however, it discovers that it is not totally irrelevant; for it operates differently with respect to the two moments in its conceptual object. It identifies a *likeness* that is unlike *unlikeness*, and it differentiates an *unlikeness* that is unlike *likeness*. The first of these operations determines *positively*, the second *negatively*. But since the *likeness* could have been differentiated from *unlikeness*, and, *unlikeness* identified as not *likeness*, what is determined *positively* as well as what is determined *negatively* could have been reversed. Because each term essentially opposes the other, the reflective "third" that was to introduce the opposition dissolves into irrelevance. Indifferently it specifies one as *positive* and the other as *negative.*

Speculative reason reflects on this intellectual operation that dialectic has discerned. The reflective aspect of determining is no longer a simple identification or differentiation, nor is it comparison. It only determines its conceptual object *positively* and *negatively*. This single determining act can be called the *positive-and-negative*.[5] Within it reflection distinguishes three moments.

In the first place, this name signifies the activity of reflection. In a single act thought mediates between the opposites; and the mediation is nothing but an act of opposition. From this perspective one side is not essentially positive nor the other negative, but they are simply related both positively and negatively one to another. The reflective activity of thought, then, brings them together in a double way. On the one hand it posits both sides because each is essential to the other. But on the other hand it differentiates each side from the other to determine it as something on its own account. The *positive-and-negative* determination introduced by reflection is this double activity that both posits positively and differentiates negatively.

In the second place, thought reflects on the externality of its own processes. The *positive-and-negative* determination is indifferent both to the opposition inherent in the conceptual object, and to the inherent characteristics of its two terms. Which is called *positive* and which *negative* is immaterial and only a function of external reflection. The names could just as well have been reversed.

In the third place, the determination *positive-and-negative* is not simply posited by thought and therefore indifferent to the subject matter. Rather each of the terms is constituted both positively and negatively.[6] Thus what was to be an external unity, within which the two were to be related, now becomes a part of the essential constitution of each. *Positive-and-negative* then is *the* determination of reflection. For it is not simply a category of thought determining the way a being is to be thought so that its essence can become evident. It is also the way the constituent moments of reflection are themselves essentially determined. Applied self-reflexively, this category determines its own essence.

Its self-reflexive complexity needs to be spelled out more clearly. a) *Positive-and-negative* is a synthetic relation. In it the simple opposition of the terms can be distinguished from their simple conjunction; yet both connections are united in one complex operation. Since *opposition* is negativity and *conjunction* is positivity, their unity is just as much a *positive-and-negative*. b) But more is involved. For the two terms are essentially both identified positively and differentiated negatively. Not only is this relation self-reflexively characterized as *positive-and-negative,* therefore, but each of its terms have the same determination. c) To make it more complex yet, the synthetic relation is both positively and negatively related to its terms. For conjunction positively relates terms negatively determined, and opposition negatively contrasts terms positively identified. The single concept *positive-and-negative* determines itself in all of these self-reflexive ways.

The context of such complexity, however, serves to clarify the two original terms: *positive* and *negative*. For they have now acquired specific and independent meanings that are not simply matters of arbitrary application. The *positive* is *posited* by the relating act but as that which, in itself, is *not* dependent on the act of positing. And it is thought as independent of the opposition even while it is only thought within the opposition. Thus, despite its being essentially determined as *positive,* so that its negative relation to the other is to remain inessential, the reference to the other does not disappear into just nothing at all, nor into a bare determination, but becomes something independent. What essentially determines the *positive* in itself, then, is that it *negatively* excludes its *negative* correlate from itself.

Similarly, the *negative* can be more clearly defined. Like *positive* it is not only posited, but is thought as though it were not posited; it is to be the *negative,* self-contained in itself. To this extent it is positive. But as *negative* it is not, like *positive,* to be independent of opposition and purely self-contained; for it explicitly negates its relation to something else. Since the other of the *negative* is the *positive*—a self-contained being—this means that it excludes itself, as *positive,* from itself. It therefore persists *as* that which is opposed to itself, whereas the *positive* has dissolved its opposing determination into its self-contained being. On its own, then, the *negative* contains the total dynamic of opposition.

With this clarification of the two terms the reflective relation *positive-and-negative* is not only implicitly *positive* or *negative;* for it introduces *conjunction* and *opposition* , *identification* and *differentiation* into the consideration of its conceptual object. In fact, each of these determinations on its own is constituted by its self-contained meaning. Were one to consider each only in itself, abstracted from all relation—even from its relation to reflecting thought itself—one might think that, if *positive* or *negative* were not explicitly posited by such a third, and not thereby opposed to its contrary, each would collapse into an immediate thought: pure *being* or *non-being*. We have seen, however, that each moment essentially requires its reference to the other. Only because this is inherent can they be conjoined in *positive-and-negative* by external reflection. In fact, what reflection introduces is not their synthesis, but the abstractness of determining something as positive quite apart from its reference to a negative, or as inherently negative quite apart from its reference to a positive.[7] What is essential about either *positive* or *negative* taken in itself is that *being opposed* not simply is introduced by comparison, nor is an inessential moment of its meaning, but is its peculiar determination. Since this exclusion of the other is explicit within the connotation of *positive* as well as *negative,* each side of *opposition* is on its own essentially determined as *opposed.*

Contradiction

1. The concepts *identity* and *difference* are independent determinations. In *diversity* they are brought together by an externally indifferent reflection. In *opposition,* they mutually exclude each other within a single reflective act. Their conjunction has now become self-contained in a single essential determination.

As this clarifying process of thought proceeds, the two terms involved here become more precisely determined. At first they are simply *identity* and *difference,* then *likeness* and *unlikeness,* finally *positive* and *negative.* At the end of the previous section these last two terms acquired an even more specific sense. Each is independently defined as essentially excluding the other, and this exclusion of its other has become the determining constituent of its own meaning. As both containing and excluding itself and its opposite, each term (*positive* and *negative*) inherently embodies the total structure of *opposition.* No longer introduced by external reflection, *opposition* constitutes a self-contained, independent dynamic. When *opposition* is thus immediate and not generated by a "third," it becomes *contradiction.*

In relating the contrary terms, *difference* and *identity,* the single category *difference* is already implicitly a contradiction. But contradiction only becomes explicit when *difference* becomes defined as exclusion, and when the terms that exclude each other still need to include each other. By excluding what they include they thereby exclude themselves.

To make this abstract description clearer, we will consider the two independent determinations of reflection: *positive* and *negative.* To determine what is essential in their meaning, these terms must be applied self-reflexively.

Positive is posited by reflection as that which is like itself. It is not related to another but is present simply on its own. This means that in its meaning the original act of positing is not only dissolved, but excluded, since *being posited* entails *being related.* In thinking this concept, then, thought proposes it, then maintains it explicitly as that which it has not proposed. But the act of excluding, essential for maintaining its independent meaning, is negative; the *negative,* however, is the other that is to be excluded. Here is the contradiction. *Positive* signifies the simple self-identity of the reflection that excludes even as it posits. But what it excludes is its own excluding act. It is self-excluding.

A similar result follows for the *negative.* It is *unlikeness,* isolated by reflection from the act of comparison, and posited as *negative.* If it were simply the thought of the negative that appeared immediately in intelligence,[8] it would be a simple qualitative determination. But it does not simply appear; it is posited by an act of reflection. It is therefore not an immediate transition, but it is maintained as self-identical throughout an intellectual process. This identical relation with itself is its essential positivity. Yet, because it is denial that has become self-reflexive, it refuses to become anything positive. Therefore this conceptual process explicitly excludes itself.

The term *positive* is self-contradictory, but only implicitly. As the *act* of exclusion it does not require that the self-exclusive character become explicit. With the term *negative,* however, the contradiction is unmistakable. It is pure opposition, opposing even itself.

2. Self-reflexive dialectic shows that thought cannot maintain such a concept, for any effort to think a contradiction dissolves itself. This does not happen because understanding has simply refused to consider such an absurdity. After all, the contradiction only became apparent because intelligence had already thought it. The act of self-excluding reflection was present before the signifying term "contradiction" could be applied.

The act signified, however, is not simple. It is a movement, a transition. Intelligence focuses on *positive* or *negative* as an independent category, but finds that it shifts back and forth from *positive* independence to *negative* exclusion. Neither moment can be maintained; each disappears only to be replaced by its excluded opposite. *Positive* passes over to *negative* and vice-versa. The very effort to think each term dissolves its self-sufficient independence, and it disappears into what it was to exclude.[9] As each disappears into what is explicitly excluded there is simply nothing left.

This negative dissipation of *contradiction* is not the only result. For the act signified also posits, as self-contained and independent, that which is to be excluded. When the negative process of excluding collapses into an empty cipher, then, the positive act that would establish the other category as independent goes aground as well. This doubly destructive dialectic, inherent in determining the concept precisely, lies behind understanding's rejection of the self-contradictory as being false.

This destructive process needs to be considered more closely. We have already seen that reflection posited the *positive* and *negative* as opposites. They were different moments of its activity that were thought to be external yet, as posited in a single act of thought, not completely independent. However, their being opposed to each other meant that they excluded each other in themselves. Since this mutual exclusion is independent of the act of reflection, the latter can be dissolved as irrelevant to the meaning of the two distinct terms. They thereby become self-contained categories; because each explicitly excludes the other, each posits its own independence. But paradoxically this means that its independence is not itself independent—each requires the other which is excluded. When, like Baron Munchhausen, it tries to pull itself up by its own bootstraps, it simply falls to the ground. The effort to constitute its own identity without relying on the other collapses like a house of cards.

Such comments refer only to the formal structure of positing and opposing. We should also reflect on the content of the act of opposing itself: reflection that excludes. It is, in itself, self-contained activity, the positing of opposites. But it equally dissolves its own positing act so that the opposed can be excluded absolutely from each other. This complex, yet self-contained, intellectual activity, called *excluding reflection,* is what constituted the independence of *positive* and *negative.* They now refer not to static entities, but are instead signs representing the two moments of this process of thought—a POSITING that DISSOLVES itself. To isolate clearly its own distinctive character as *excluding reflection,* then, intelligence must distinguish itself as agent from that which it posits. It dissolves or excludes its negative. Yet, as excluding reflection, it had posited the independence of that other. Therefore it is its own act that is dissolved; and the effort to posit its own pure identity by suppressing its relation to the other simply dissolves itself. *Excluding reflection* is this dynamic that both posits and dissolves its own identity. As such it is a single intellectual activity, positively constituted by the double process of dissolving and positing.[10]

3. Speculative reason looks at this final remnant of external reflection that dialectic has discerned. The activity of *excluding reflection* both creates a contradiction and dissolves it. From this perspective the *contradiction* does not simply go aground or collapse. Rather its background begins to become evident, and thought returns to the *ground* of its own logical operations.

The excluding reflection that constitutes *contradiction* reflects on itself. To do so it must exclude self-contained opposition from itself as its external negative—as something only posited. But this means that the latter's components, the self-contained opposites *positive* and *negative,* now lose their independence and become simply determinations of the opposition inherent in reflection. For the simple unity of the one reflective activity shows itself to be the essence of the whole movement of opposition and contradiction—its essence as its *ground.* By excluding from itself its own act (namely, the act of excluding opposites from each other), it shows itself to be a simple unity that is negatively determined, and yet identical with itself. When *excluding reflection* excludes this mutual exclusion, it is maintaining its own distinctive activity.[11]

The relation between self-contained opposition (i.e. *contradiction),* and its *ground* needs to be made more explicit. Thought starts with the opposition as immediately given, and only reaches *ground* by dissolving this posited structure. From this perspective, *ground* is posited by the dissolving act of reflecting—it comes to be. But a *ground* is not the simple result of opposition. It has shown itself as well to be the essential origin of some explicit difference and therefore presupposed by it. *Ground* refers to an act that posits a contradiction yet dissolves this very act of positing. It persists as *ground* because it both grounds, and dissociates itself from, whatever is grounded. Although essentially determining the result, it is independent and self-contained. *Ground* signifies this self-contained activity of thinking.[12]

Ground is resolved *contradiction.* In *opposition* the determinations of reflection move from being simply diverse to being self-contained. In *ground* self-sufficiency is completed. It both retains and dissolves *contradiciton* and *opposition,* for it integrates them into a simple activity that turns out to be presupposed. *Ground* is positive self-identity; but as grounding, it relates to its negative, establishes it as negative, and excludes from itself what is grounded. Only when all moments of this activity are included is the term *ground* appropriate.

The Pattern of Reflection

Throughout this discussion of the *determinations of reflection* the logical movement from understanding, through dialectic, to speculative reason, has become more precisely defined. The understanding does not initially focus its attention on a being. Rather it determines what is essential in its conceptual object. Then dialectic, rather than simply passing from one category over to another, self-reflexively shows that the original term only seems to be essential, and that it is infected by inessential thought. Finally, speculative reason looks at the result not as a simple transition, but as an operation of external reflection. It discovers, however, that the external operations of thought are not inessential at all, but that they are precisely what are required to determine the essence. Therefore they are essential, and become in turn the object of understanding's determination.

The logical movements in the above sections thus reproduce the moments that were distinguished in the previous chapter. But they do more. For the essential determinations are determinations of thought as well. Therefore they apply self-reflexively to their own internal dynamic. Understanding *identifies;* dialectic *differentiates,* then *diversifies,* and finally *opposes;* speculative reason *contradicts* its own conclusions as dialectic in order to determine the *ground.* It is not surprising, then, to find that these categories are the principles presupposed in any thinking whatever: everything is what it is and not another thing; negation is an incomplete predicate; no two things are completely alike; of contrary predicates only one can be applied at any one time; every proposition is either true or false; everything has its sufficient ground or reason. Each of these principles is frequently maintained as an independent rule that can be recognized intuitively, without reference to anything else. Hegel's analysis, however, situates them in the intelligence that thinks them, and shows how they arise out of an intellectual context of reflection that ultimately grounds their validity.

Ground

Ground as such: Essence and Form

Understanding turns to the concept *ground*. It is the culminating determination of reflection, for it signifies the determining activity of excluding reflection through which the other essentials were defined. Anything determinate in an immediate *being* is taken to be posited and therefore to presuppose a ground. Yet this *ground* is to be primary and not the result of reflection. Therefore this concept signifies an act of presupposing that recoils on itself, dissolving its own positing role. Through this dissolution, thought determines *ground* to be indeterminate—an *essence* that continues to be itself through all its negative determinations.

When *essence* is understood as *ground,* two moments are used to identify it. On the one hand, the understanding explicitly contrasts it to anything that is posited; it is the ground that is not posited. On the other hand thought identifies it through a process in which something immediately present is not thought to be self-contained on its own account, but is taken to be posited. If the first represents a positive identity which is simply to exclude reference to anything grounded, the second reflects a negative identity which constitutes itself as ground only by differentiating itself from what it grounds. But the positive and negative meanings are identified in one determinate concept. Since *ground* is primarily the positive moment that is to be contrasted to the negative, the two are identified in this concept only as *essence* in general, to be distinguished from the mediating differentiation that specifies the contrast between ground and grounded.

Dialectic takes the inititative, for any mediating moment needs to be rendered explicit. Here we are not dealing with a mediating act of pure *reflection;* for the determinations involved are not dissolved into nonentities, but persist. Nor is this an act of *determining reflection;* for the determinations of reflection are no longer self-contained and independent, but have run aground through self-contradiction. Rather, reflection stipulates that both determinate moments, *ground* and *grounded,* will persist; the latter are thus not independent of reflection but are posited. When contrasted with the pure *essence,* these posited, yet persisting, determinations are called its *form.* The *ground* that the understanding identifies simply as *essence* is thus differentiated dialectically from its *form.*

Essence, HAS a form together with the latter's diverse determinations. However, only as one of these determinations (as *ground*) can it be posited by thought as immediate and as substrate. On its own it is simply the activity of reflecting that identifies the two contrasting moments, leaving them undifferentiated within its movement. Since reflection is unable to distinguish such a pure *essence* as something external to its own dynamic, its task is made more difficult. For the formal relation between a *ground* and a *grounded* comes forward only after reflection dissolves its own activity. Thus, when it identifies *essence* as a relating substrate, or *ground,* it *posits* that essence as determinate, and therefore as essentially *formed.*

When, on the other hand, dialectic considers the formal determinations (*ground* and *grounded*), it finds them to be no longer simply diverse, but determinations with respect to *essence.* The latter sustains them, indifferent to their diversity, even while they reflect its underpinning. Earlier the *determinations of reflection* were to persist independently, each on its own; in this case the independence has been resolved into a self-identical *essence* that grounds their persistence.

Anything determinate belongs to the *form* insofar as it can be differentiated from that which is to be formed. As *quality,* determinateness was one with its substrate, *being,* since reflective discrimination was lacking; through the essentials—*identity, difference, diversity* and *opposition*—reflection was diversely determined. What identified this diversity as form, and is therefore distinct from form, is a single reflective dynamic: by distinguishing *ground* from *grounded,* reflection becomes fundamental to their formal persistence. While *form* reflects the simple *essence,* the simple *essence* can be essentially determined only by its formal contrast to the form.

In other words, thought cannot keep *essence* distinct from *form;* every attempt to define it slips over into the opposite. The *essence* as simple unity is posited not simply as other than *form,* but also as its *ground;* since the relation of grounding is one of the formal determinations, *essence* becomes *formed.* At the same time, *form* does not remain simply the surface determination of *essence,* but goes on to include the complete relation; for it is essentially defined by the way it differentiates. It is no longer a bare abstraction but a determinate contrast. And *essence* is reduced to a merely indeterminate and inactive base which is but one moment within that contrast.

We have already moved beyond dialectical thrust and counterthrust to speculative integration. For the relation between *essence* and *form* has shown itself to be *form* not as static structure, but as dynamic differentiation. Any single determinate *form* is simply posited. The totality of the determining relation, however, is nothing but the identity which was originally to be isolated as the pure *essence.* When *form* determines *essence,* then, the former is not an external addition, but is the determining process that both dissolves its distinct differences into an identity and maintains them as formal determinations. *Form* and *essence,* far from being contraries, are simply moments of a single activity—the determining dynamic of *forming.* We have lost any distinct sense of *ground.*

Speculative reason reflects on this activity more closely. In determining, *form* acts on something else, dissolving that which is not determinate in order to create a determination. Since that which is not determinate is simply identity, *form* presupposes its own identity as that which is not formed. This is no longer pure indeterminate *essence,* but rather a new term, explicitly contrasted to form—pure *matter.* The grounding relation, first defined as moving from *essence* to *form,* has changed its connotation. The term now refers to the transition from formless *matter* to determining *form. Matter* is to be the necessary *ground* of *form.*

Ground as Such: Form and Matter

Understanding turns its attention to the new definition of ground: *matter. Matter* is a formless, indeterminate substrate; since all determination is part of the *form,* it can be thought only by abstracting from *form*—all form. The very act of abstracting, however, is itself determinate, and therefore formed. The concept *matter* results, then, when the concept *form* excludes from itself all that is formed, including its own forming activity.

Dialectic explores further the relation between them. *Form* presupposes *matter* as whatever underlies all determination; the latter is thought as in itself indifferent to the determinate *form*. On the other hand, the concept *matter* presupposes the self-dissolving process of *form*. It is not simply *essence;* its positive independence results in thought only because its negative relation, as *not form,* has been made explicit. The two concepts presuppose each other.

But this is not the full story. For the concept *matter,* by dissolving all determinateness of *form,* also cancels any relation. It is thought as groundless, subsisting on its own. Similarly since no *formal* determinations are to be found in *matter,* they also are groundless. While the two terms presuppose each other, then, they do not ground one another. This mutual indifference is a contrary aspect of their mutual relation.

Speculative reason reflects on the diversity of this definition: *matter* and *form* presuppose each other but they do not ground each other. This double relation can be maintained only because *matter* is thought of solely as a base, as a bare identity set over against the explicit relation of forming and contrasted to *form* as passive is to active. On the one hand, then, the determining dynamic of *form* can function only by imposing an ungrounded determination on an ungrounded substrate. On the other hand *matter,* although indifferent to *form,* is nonetheless open to this relation as absolute receptivity. *Form* is to form; and *matter* is to be formed. The two are related by a single determining activity. With this, the show of indifference that diversifies the two dissolves.

The mediating structure of this one process of *forming* thought, however, needs to be determined more precisely. Initially it is the transition of thought that requires differentiation: it goes from *form* as determining to *matter* as determined, and vice versa. This restless transfer, first constituting difference and then dissolving it again, is really only the ground as such.

Within this determining dynamic the concept of *form* that incorporates both *essence* and *form* in the previous section reappears. Now, however, it has acquired a more specific, contradictory character. *Form* is self-sufficient, self-reflexively identifying the whole process; but it is also only a moment, the determining in contrast to, and requiring, the determined. This double meaning cannot be maintained in thought; it dissolves. On the one hand *form's* independence dissolves because it determines itself as posited over against another; on the other hand, the contrast to *matter* as its opposite is dissolved so that *form* may persist as a self-identical process. The result is a restless intellectual somersaulting in which *form* refers to

the distinction from *matter,* and then to the overall structure of the relation. Indeed the somersaulting is itself part of the *formal* determining
activity.

In other words, *form* is independent of *matter* as pure determination;
but as determining it dissolves its own independence, for it can continue to
be determining *form* only as long as it is materialized. Its persistent independence can be maintained only through its synthetic identification with
its contrary.

Within this complex somersaulting, reflection has defined *matter* in
contrast to *form*. It is self-contained indeterminacy, isolated from precise
determinations. When *form* is materialized, however, matter loses this
peculiar characteristic—it is no longer indeterminate subsistence. Thus the
activity of *form* in determining produces a double paradox: it determines
itself only by determining *matter;* and in determining *matter* it destroys the
latter's unique determination.

This dynamic, inherent in the meaning of *form,* has as its correlate a
change in the meaning of *matter. Matter* is absolute negativity, is what
ought to be determined. But the *ought* refers to the *forming* process;
therefore, *matter* is as contradictory as *form.* For it persists in thought as
indeterminate, and completely negative, excluding any type of determination. But it persists only because it is itself being determined by the
forming activity of reflection. These two moments have the effect of dissolving each other: the persistence dissolves the indeterminacy and the
indeterminacy dissolves the persistence. This mutual dissolution gives to
matter its character of absolute receptivity, of being completely open to
external determination by form. But unlike *form's* contradiction, which
was defined in relation to *matter,* this one is intrinsic to the concept *matter*
itself.

We can now begin to see how the contradictory relation between *form*
and *matter* is mediated by reflection. *Form* is maintained as independent
only because it is materialized through its own dynamic activity. *Matter,*
persisting as indeterminate, becomes absolutely receptive to formal determination. Each relates to itself in such a way that it must dissolve the
independence of its pure self-relation and reflect the other. *Form* persists
as *form,* only as materialized; *matter* persists as *matter* only in being
formed. This reflection is implicit in both terms. The determining activity
of *form* as well as the simple receptivity of *matter* signify but two sides of a
single, integrated movement of reflection, which in *matter* is thought of as
simple movement, but in *form* is thought of as act *vis-à-vis* another.

The relation between *finite* and *infinite,* previously defined, helps to clarify what is involved. As contrasted and opposed to each other, both *matter* and *form* are finite; they cannot persist. They become self-contained only when *matter* refers to the whole unity of *form* and *essence* (the process itself as receptive movement), and when *form,* in determining, constitutes its own material subsistence as the same unity of *essence* and *form*. Their diverse meanings collapse into a single reflective activity of thought. They are identical. But pure identity is *essence* as *ground*. Rather than being simple, abstract identity, however, *ground* has become a single determining activity that *forms* in so far as it determines, and has *matter* in so far as it is determined. This unity. indifferent to both *form* as such and *matter* as such, is formed matter, or *content*.

Ground as Such: Form and Content

The understanding identifies *content* as the UNITY of form and matter. This differentiates it from the two determinations that are united so that they become simply its inessential *form*.

Thus *form* has changed its sense once again. At first it was differentiated from the simple identity of *essence,* so that its specific determinations were *ground* and *grounded*. Then, contrasted to *matter,* it became *determining reflection,* constituting the persistence of the essentials. Now that it is to be distinguished from *content,* its determinate moments are matter and itself as *form*. The self-identity of *essence,* of persistence in general and of *matter* is no longer its contrary but has been included as one of its moments.

Dialectic explores this identification of the two concepts. *Content* has been differentiated from the moments of its *form* as simply their unity. To maintain this differentiation, the unity must be reflectively determined or posited in such a way that the *form* is relatively inessential. The *content* as unity is indifferent to whatever form or matter it has, even though it is their underpinning.

But that is not all. For *content* signifies what was identical in *form* and *matter* so that only their differences are indifferent, external determinations. Even though they are posited as distinct, in *content* they are to be reflectively integrated into a unity. The self-identical, which underlies diverse determinations, is, as we have seen, the *ground*. What was supposed to have been incorporated into an indifferent *form* when *matter* became one of its determinations has turned out to be a defining characteristic of *content*.

This leads to further dialectical considerations. *Content's* identity is on the one hand indifferent to the *form,* yet on the other it is the *ground* that incorporates both form and matter into the *form.* Such a differentiation reintroduces the distinction between *ground* and *grounded. Content's* indifference to the *form* is grounded on the *formal* identity that it has reflectively incorporated into itself. The reflective movement back and forth from one sense of *content's* identity to the other is itself a transition from *ground* to what is *grounded* and vice versa. Therefore it self-reflexively embodies the *formal* relation between form and matter that was to be the content of this concept. In this context, however, the formal unity is a grounding *relation.* Dialectic has shown that a grounding relation is the *essential* form of *content;* and it has equally given to the concept *ground,* previously indeterminate, a determinate *content.*

Speculative reason reflects on the two movements within this grounding relation. First, there is the reflection of an indifferent identity into the identity as *ground.* Here an indeterminate ground that had disappeared into the *form* is given a content: it is the process of integrating form and matter into *form,* generating a formed identity. The same move transforms *form.* Since it takes the opposed moments of *content*—its form and its matter—and negates their independence, *form* becomes a grounding relation. Second, there is the reflection of the identity as *ground* into the identity as indifferent. In this process *content* is determined as a formed matter in which the various distinctions of the *form* persist materially, and thereby become indifferent to it.

These two moments together make up the *content* of ground. On the one hand it is a grounding relation—an essential identity that incorporates all the various moments into an integrated totality. On the other hand it is an identity that posits its determinate moments so that they persist independently of the grounding relation. When brought together these two moments make explicit that *ground* is determining and determinate. On the one hand its *content* is a determining relation; on the other its *form,* external to this inherent content, persists as determinate. Thought thus moves to the concept *determinate ground.*[1]

Determinate Ground: Formal Ground

Ground has a determinate content. This content provides the underpinning for its form; as immediate, however, it is to be differentiated from form's mediation. The identity that *ground* originally signified has thus introduced something negative into its connotation in that it posits its own form as distinct while yet remaining self-identical. This self-identical negativity of the concept *ground* is precisely what is to be signified by the category *content* (as that which rendered it determinate). The latter, then, is not simply immediate, but is also mediating.

Even though content is thus considered a mediating process, it is, as immediate, to surrender any determinate difference between *ground* and *grounded*. Nevertheless, since mediating introduces a negatively differentiated unity, a negativity characterizes what was to be an undifferentiated underpinning. That is to say, the way it negatively differentiates its various formal moments is precisely what renders the content determinate. Dialectic here discovers a double reflection: the posited differences dissolve themselves into the mediating process; the mediating process posits the differentiated moments of the form. But this means that the differences are the *ground* of the process that constitutes the content; and the process is the ground of the differences by which it is determined. It is thus impossible to determine which of the two moments is the ground of the content's determination and which is grounded. When the formal categories are used self-reflexively to determine what is essential, they are shown to be a matter of indifference. The concept of determinate ground appears to be self-contradictory.

To resolve this paradox, speculative reason reflects on the two transitions in the double reflection of the dialectic as they apply to this particular dilemma. First, as formed mediation, a determinate content is considered from two sides: as *ground* and as *grounded*. Because it is a matter of indifference which formal determination is to be applied to which side, it is in fact only a single activity of determining in both. It is therefore an undifferentiated mediating process. Second, in so far as it is a mediating process, a distinction must be introduced between what is original and what is derived. Because there is no inherent contrast present, it is a matter of indifference how this formal determination is applied. It does not matter which of these transitions one looks at first; for in each, one of the terms reflects the other and either can be considered as much the *ground* of its other as what is posited by it. This means that in the one determinate content the formal differentiation is a matter of indifference. It is the same content in both ground and grounded. Their difference is a matter of indifference to the content and is purely formal. Such a grounding relation can be signified by the expression: *formal ground.*

It is the complete identity in content of *ground* and *grounded* that establishes a *ground* as sufficient. For the *ground* contains nothing that is not in the grounded; and the *grounded* has nothing that is not in the *ground*. External reflection looks at the same content in two different ways, drawing a formal distinction between the ground and what is grounded. As an external distinction, the form is a matter of indifference to the content; the two are simply diverse.

Determinate Ground: Real Ground

By isolating the concept *formal ground,* the understanding can now identify what makes a *ground* determinate. On the one hand it is the determinate underpinning of the content, on the other, it is the differentiation introduced by the grounding relation. Which of these two is the *ground* of the determination and which is *grounded* is an indifferent matter, external to the content of the concept.

However, more careful reflection shows that the two characterizations are not simply external. The self-identical content is to be, on the one hand, the identity of *ground* with itself (even in what is grounded) and, on the other, the identity of the *grounded* with itself (even in the ground). This distinction is essential if the content is to render the concept *ground* determinate. The differentiation between the two is thus really contained within the content, even though each on its own is the identity of the whole. The two are to have a diverse content. In other words, to be a grounding relation the *content* must introduce the distinctions of form and differentiate itself as ground from itself as grounded.

If *ground* and *grounded* are to be differentiated, the grounding relation ceases to be merely a formal tautology. When reflection goes back to the ground and then moves from it to what it posits, there is a qualitative change in which the ground is realized. There is to be a different determination of content in the ground than in what is grounded. Dialectic explores this relation.

In the first place, to the extent that they are simply different, the ground and the grounded are to be indifferent to each other; each is immediate and self-identical. As far as their relation is concerned, a *ground* is reflected in what it posits, since its content is to be retained, while the *grounded* persists as self-identical only because it has been posited by that ground. Since that which makes the *ground* into a ground is also in the *grounded,* any difference in content in the latter is an addition. The *grounded,* then, is a unity of two distinct contents—one which it derives from, and one which is indifferent to, the *ground.* To consider it as something single, the two qualifying contents are simply externally conjoined.

When one talks about a *real ground* in contrast to a *formal ground* or tautology, then, one has a double structure. On the one hand there is a continuity of *ground* and *grounded;* the latter receives its essential content from that relation. On the other hand something inessential, external to the grounding relation, gets added. The *ground* as such is neither the ground of this inessential addition, nor the ground of the conjunction of the essential with the inessential. It is the positive basis of nothing more than the self-identical content it shares with the *grounded*. This, however, raises a dialectical question: what is the relation between this essential basis of the *grounded* and the inessential addition? It is not the relation of *ground;* for the two are external to each other, simply tied together by an external bond, a bond based on something else.

The concept *real ground,* therefore, results in two determinations, external to each other. On the one hand, the *ground* is the underpinning for the *grounded;* on the other hand something else underpins the conjunction of the latter's essential with its inessential content. The simple identity of *ground* and *grounded* falls apart. The identity of the *grounding* relation is one thing; the identity of the *grounded* result is another. Two diverse grounding structures are involved.

This difference means that it is external reflection that determines which content in the result is to be grounded and which not. *Real ground* is thus defined with reference to something else: with reference either to some content not present in the ground, or to something immediate not posited by the grounding relation.[2]

Determinate Ground: Complete Ground

1. Speculative reason has shown that *real ground* has two under-pinnings. The first is posited as essential, the *real* ground. The second is a relation in whatever results that conjoins this ground with a secondary content. It is the indeterminate substrate underlying a diversity. This secondary relation does not reflect the ground, but is introduced by external reflection. When this act of external reflection is self-reflexively identified by the understanding to be the grounding relation that underlies the concept *real ground,* it shows that what was to be the *ground* has surrendered its foundational character. It is simply posited by reflection, and is thereby *grounded*.

Understanding proceeds to render determinate this new, distinct sense of *ground*. First, this sense includes the content that is identical in both the *real ground* and what it grounds; for this concept is to ground the essential primacy of that content; but it also includes both the primary and secondary content in what results, as well as their conjunction. Second, the externality that relativized this conjunction has been dissolved; in this new ground the two moments are to be absolutely related, without reference to anything else. Because all of this is included in its significance, this new concept, *ground,* reconstitutes the identity of itself as *ground* with what it grounds; it is thus like *formal ground.* Including both moments of *formal* and *real ground* as well as grounding what is left unresolved in the latter, this grounding relation is *complete.*

2. Dialectic reflects on this grounding relation and applies its categories self-reflexively. Which moment, *formal ground* or *real,* is the primary content and which is secondary? The consideration of this involves two fairly detailed transitions.

First, we take *real* ground to be the essential moment in the content. If something is grounded, there are two determinations that apply to its content. One is the identity that it shares with its ground; the other is its posited secondary features. Since these are indifferent to each other, there is nothing inherent that specifies one determination to be the *ground* and the other not. When the content is taken immediately on its own, any relation to the ground is dissolved, and the differentiation between the two is introduced by something external. Because the *complete ground* is to introduce the formal distinction between primary and secondary content, it shares with its result the same content—that is, its two determinate moments—but presents them immediately as conjoined. But this means that in this immediacy the two are simply diverse, indifferent to each other, and reflecting no essential or absolute relation. If we compare a thing that grounds to that which it grounds, there is nothing in the content of the former that differentiates the two moments by specifying which will be the *real ground* and which will be secondary. It thus ceases to be a *complete ground,* but becomes relative. Indeed, simply a formal relation remains, since both have the same content and their difference is simply a matter of the way the content is conjoined: in one the relation is immediate; in the other it is posited or grounded. In other words, when we start with the moment of real grounding in the grounding relation, it loses its completeness and becomes merely formal.

Second, the moment of *formal grounding* is taken to be essential, positing the moment of *real grounding* as its secondary content. As we have seen, when the two formal determinations are applied self-reflexively, each identifies itself as distinct over against its contrary, and thus gives itself an independent character. There is one content peculiar to the ground, and another peculiar to what is grounded. Consider: even though the content is to be the same in both the ground and its result, a distinction has been introduced by using the two different determinations of the content. One is to be the substrate and underpinning of the relation, identical in both, and not simply something introduced by external reflection. It is the essential moment that is to posit not only itself, but also its relation to the secondary moment in the thing that is grounded. In the first thing, or *ground,* this grounding relation to the secondary moment is simply present immediately; it is an inherent conjunction. But in the second thing, or the *grounded,* only the essential moment is inherent; the secondary moment has been reflectively specified both as distinct, and as related to the primary moment. The primary moment can be called the *real ground* because in the first thing it was inherently conjoined to what became distinct. The tautology is dissolved, and once again we have lost the completeness of the ground.

If the moment of *real ground* is taken to be primary, the formality of the grounding relation is posited. If the moment of *formal ground* is to be essential it entails a relation of real grounding. Each of these transitions is relative. The complete grounding relation, however, is to include both as determinations of its content. Only in this way can the grounding relation ground itself, and thus be absolute and complete. We have shown that since both (let us say A and B) were immediately conjoined in one thing (the *ground),* then when one (A) is posited as present in the result, the other (B) is explicitly distinct yet related to it. But this entails the fact that A is equally mediated. For it is the ground of the relation in the second thing only because it was originally conjoined with B in the first. It is this immediate relation, not the essential content A, that is the ultimate ground; for it posits A, B and their explicit relation. Only thus is the totality of the grounding relation grounded in the result.

3. Speculative reason reflects on this totality. The specification of a *real ground* is now shown to be the result of something external to it. An immediate, yet mediating, relation establishes the bond of identity between *ground* and *grounded.* But this new grounding relation does not produce the tautology of *formal ground.* Because it both posits its moments as distinct from it, and dissolves its own immediacy thereby, it maintains the distinction between *ground* and *grounded* that was essential to *real ground.*

This involves two related moments. First, this new *ground,* as primordial relation, relates determinations of the content that are immediately presented. Yet as a grounding relation it has a form in which the independence of its two sides is dissolved and they become simply moments. At one and the same time it is the form of immediately presented determinations, as well as the relation in which they are negated. Second, in both the original relation and the resulting one, there is an underpinning that is identical in both. This can be identified only by the relation dissolving itself as relation and presenting itself in its immediate content. This immediate content has lost the arbitrariness that it had in *real ground* because it has been posited through the process in which the primordial relation dissolved itself.

The completeness of the grounding relation, then, involves a double reflection in which each moment presupposes its contrary. The *formal* identity presupposes the immediately presented determinations; these, as *really* distinct, presuppose the relating identity. The concept, *ground,* has now become quite complex. It signifies the *form* of grounding as an immediate conjunction that repels its terms from itself and presupposes them to be immediate, so that it can relate to them as if they were quite other. This immediate determination of the content repels from itself its own immediacy so that it now relates to an other by which it is posited. This activity of self-discrimination that constitutes a complete grounding relation can be referred to as a conditioning mediation, and the differentiated terms referred to as its conditions.

Conditioning: The Relatively Unconditioned

The concept *ground* refers to an immediate that is to mediate what is *grounded.* It is itself determined, however, by an act of reflection. For when thought posits a ground as determinate it presupposes distinct moments that together make up its content. This suggests that the dual perspective of external reflection is operative: in itself, *ground* is immediate; but for thought it is mediated. The preceding analysis has shown, however, that even on its own, *ground* is not immediate. It reflects the immediate determinations of its content. They become the *conditions,* presupposed by ground in order to render itself complete and sufficient.

The understanding clarifies the meaning of this new concept, *condition.* (a) A *condition* is *an immediate being;* it is not simple and single as is *ground,* but is one among the many determinations that make up the ground's content. (b) It is a *condition,* however, because it is involved in an act of grounding. *A being* becomes a *condition* not in itself but only as it is related to something else. There is no inherent ground or reason for its being a *condition.* In other words, its character as *a being* is indifferent to its character as *condition.* The latter is simply added on as an extra determination in light of its relation to something else. (c) These two characteristics, its immediacy and its relation, are not completely indifferent one to the other. For a condition is presupposed as immediate relative to a *ground*. Since it is part of the latter's content, it has been freed from the integration of a *complete ground* and related externally both to that unity and to other conditions. As such it can no longer be called the *content* of the ground, but only *material* for the content. From this reflective perspective it loses any indifferent immediacy and becomes simply a moment within the more comprehensive connotation of *complete ground*. The concept *condition,* then, identifies an immediate that is at the same time material for a ground. As immediate, however, it is itself *un*conditioned. In other words this concept cannot be applied self-reflexively. A condition is not itself conditioned. And reflective thought, which looks for *conditions* (as the presuppositions of a determinate ground), remains external to that which it discovers.

A single *condition,* though necessary for a relation of grounding, is not sufficient. Although it is the unconditioned immediacy of the *ground,* it is not the process by which the ground dissolves itself and produces the grounded. Thus dialectic distinguishes the *condition* from the *grounding relation.* The latter, in isolation, is an empty movement of reflection; because it lacks content, it is pure form. Therefore this dynamic moment of mediation is also not grounded in any *condition* but is independent, immediate and unconditioned. Like *condition* it can be discerned by external reflection as a necessary presupposition; but in its immediacy it is inherently self-contained.[3] It is neither dependent nor conditioned.

In so far as it is unconditioned, the grounding relation has its own distinct content: it is the *ground* as such, its essential form. By contrast, the *condition* is simply material for the ground, its being includes content that is indifferent to, and irrelevant for, the ground as such.

Dialectic has shown that there are two unconditioned moments in the concept of a sufficient or complete *ground:* its *conditions* and a dynamic *relation*—each of which has an independent content. Speculative reason considers how the two are to be related. On the one hand they are indifferent to each other and neither conditions the other. The *condition* is external to the form; the *act* takes the condition as simply passive material. On the other hand, each is mediated because it is required by the other. The *conditions* are essential because they are the constituents of a *grounding relation.* An indifferent something becomes a *condition* only when it renders a *ground* determinate. Similarly the *relation of grounding* is isolated only because the conditions as conditions are to be brought together to constitute the ground. Each moment, then, reflects the other.

Indeed this mutual reflection is as essential to their independent meanings as is their immediacy. If we put these two sides together we find that both concepts, *condition* and the *grounding relation,* are contradictory. Each includes as essential to its meaning both that it is immediately unconditioned and that it is a mediated moment. This contradiction—that of being only *relatively unconditioned*—needs to be resolved.[4]

Conditioning: The Absolutely Unconditioned

Both the concept *condition* and the concept of the pure *grounding relation* refer to immediate entities that are yet defined by their relation to each other. At first the mediating act of opposing one to the other appeared as the dialectical move of external reflection. Speculative examination, however, showed the relation to be inherent in the two concepts themselves and therefore contradictory. The *condition* shows itself to be an immediate condition only when it becomes material for a grounding relation; and the *grounding relation* is immediately present only when it forms that matter into a synthetic totality.

Yet each term has an independent meaning that is characteristic of it alone. The *condition* is *an immediate being* that happens to be related to something else which it partially grounds. In this relation it is posited by the *grounding relation* as its material and is therefore essential to it. Nevertheless, since being posited and essential are introduced by something external, they are indifferent to its *being.* Thought has simply opposed one moment of its meaning to the other.

Dialectical reflection soon discovers that the contrast is not just introduced externally, but that each moment reflects the other. Recall what happened in thought when the concept *a being* was the object of understanding's attention.[5] As *determinate* and therefore *finite* it perished and became a moment in an infinite process. In the immediacy of pure thought this logical development was simply a transition from one determinate concept to another. Now, however, reflection recognizes what is the essence of this transition: the determinate finitude of *a being* posited the infinite progress and was essential to it. These characteristics of the other moment of *condition's* meaning are thus equally reflected in the meaning of *a being* as immediate.

When it takes the other moment in the meaning of *condition,* dialectic discovers the contrary entailment. A *condition* is posited by the *ground* as its material and is therefore essential to it. But what is posited is precisely that it be something immediate: *a being.* Therefore even its immediacy as *a*

The univeluy of the Conditions as 'a being' has the prohibited the urge to be Similly medial ·sure it is determid only by ··· of to the infinite. What next to be ···
in itin bein's redewit cal escape a ginely del dsif/

100 *Reflecting*

being is posited by the concept *ground* as an essential constituent of its meaning. In other words, each of the moments reflects the other in a single contradictory relationship. As both mediated and immediate, it is a *grounding relation.*

The term, *condition,* then, has the same self-contradictory form as the *relatively unconditioned.* It involves a mutually reflective process in which the act of positing is reflected in what is immediate and vice versa so that the two are identified as simply one and the same.

When we take the other term, the *grounding relation,* we have a similar result. It started out as reflectively contrasted to something else: the process of grounding that is other than its terms. But when it is taken on its own as it is identified by reflection it requires an internal differentiation. To be a grounding *relation* what it is in itself needs to be contrasted to the determinate moments that are related. Since the latter constitute its content, they are its conditions. At the same time its immediate reality as something determinate is contrasted to its dynamic as relating process. Each moment, the process in itself as well as its immediate determinateness, is reflected in its contrary. In the term *grounding relation* the totality of this double reflection is equally self-contradictory.

The concept *condition* that was supposed to be opposed to the *grounding relation* as content to form turns out to have the same formal structure; and *grounding relation* has an identical content. Because each reflects the other not only in form but also in content there is only one totality of form and one totality of content.

Speculative reason considers this contradiction in which the two opposed terms collapse into an identity. At first each of the two relatively unconditioned terms, *condition* and *grounding relation,* simply reflected the other. Now the meaning of each is a totality that incorporates its other. Indeed they make up an essential unity of both form and content—a unity that conditions itself. No longer relative to something else necessary to complete its meaning, it is the *truly,* or *absolutely unconditioned.*[6] It is the *heart of the matter*[7] in itself.

The truly *unconditioned* (or the *heart of the matter*) contains both *condition* and *grounding relation* as opposed moments within its single comprehensive meaning. They are its posited form—posited in such a way that the *heart of the matter* is *their* conditioning ground.

As their ground, it underlies the distinction between the two moments. On the one hand it isolates conditions from the grounding relation; they are an immediate multiplicity, lacking any inherent unity and external to each other. From this perspective their integration in a ground is other than and external to them. On the other hand it is an internal simple form that takes this alien multiplicity and incorporates its diversity into a single dynamic. The concept the *heart of the matter* has this complex sense: it grounds both the opposition between diverse conditions and the grounding relation, as well as their intrinsic identity. On their part, even though these diverse moments presuppose the all inclusive totality as their inherent ground, their mutual distinctness grounds its determinate character so that the totality shows itself to be conditioned by these determinate terms, as if resulting from their combination. In other words, the totality and the distinct moments both presuppose and posit each other; they mutually reflect one another.

In this complex concept the whole preceding structure of the logic of essence is integrated. *Reflection,* using its *essential* criteria, *opposes* the *heart of the matter* (or the *absolutely unconditioned*) to its *seeming* as both a multiplicity of *material conditions* and the unity of *formal ground,* and then resolves this *contradictory diversity* into a dynamic *identity.* Indeed the *heart of the matter* is this self-reflexive process, both externalizing distinct beings as conditions and integrating them into a comprehensive totality.

The *absolutely unconditioned,* or the *heart of the matter,* is thus not a static concept. It is a vigorous self-contradictory activity, identifying itself by opposing its conditions to its ground. This contradiction shows itself, in turn, to be but a mutual reflection, for each moment reflects its relation to the other. The act of contradicting itself becomes a stage on the way to reincorporating the resulting diversity into a self-identical activity. The *heart of the matter* signifies this whole dynamic.

Conditioning: The Heart of the Matter Issues in Existence

The *absolutely unconditioned,* or the *heart of the matter,* is a concept that includes in its meaning the restless process of opposing and identifying the distinct moments of its own process. All of the various concepts , discerned by reflection as constituents of the meaning of *essence* are here integrated. The precise way that integration is achieved, however, has yet to be made clear.

In the *heart of the matter* two sides are opposed: the simple immediate diversity of conditions and grounding relation, and their identification. Within an overall synthesis each is opposed to the other so that reflection restlessly moves from one to the other. But this synthesis has not been shown to follow from the inherent connotation of the constituent terms.

Only when this is done by dialectical thought will the integration into a simple unity be complete.

First, then, the *heart of the matter* is nothing but a collection of simple immediates. It is the totality of all its determinations, not as they are identified reflectively, but as they simply are in themselves, in their positive being. Cut off, by our hypothesis, from all relation to the overarching concept, they are no longer conditions, related to something else, but are a bare multiplicity, lacking any unity. Indeed they include aspects and circumstances that have no relation to the *heart of the matter* at all. They are simply all that is.

Since any determination that might relate these beings to the *heart of the matter* has been dissolved, they are considered by thought as essentially indifferent to any reflective distinction—even that between *essential* and *inessential*. If they are to be distinguished at all from the simple objects of thought in the logic of being, it is only by the perspective of totality or completeness. A single reflection includes *all* of the multiplicity.

The structure of *being* as such does not contain explicitly this overarching totality. Rather the latter is present only implicitly as the transitions of *becoming:* the movement through which *a being* passes over to its *essence*. Reflection, however, has brought this context to thought's attention. When *a being* becomes a *condition,* then, it is not because some external reflection has posited it arbitrarily within a *grounding relation*. Rather its own *determination* or *quality* has generated a transition to something else. Thus it has become simply a moment in a process. This *becoming* does not now merely leave behind what has perished but instead retains it as a nonentity. From the present reflective perspective of totality, we recognize that the simple movement of going from one concept over to another is nothing but the way the reflective activity of thought appears when it is not self-reflexively conscious of itself. Once this has been achieved the inherent dynamic of the simpler logic shows that immediate concepts in themselves cannot avoid becoming conditions for other concepts, and thereby for the intellectual process as a whole. The *essence* of *a being* is to be a condition.

Second, dialectic isolates the opposite side of the *heart of the matter,* the identity of the *grounding relation*. It is the pure form—the dynamic act—of the *absolutely unconditioned*. If, as posited by reflection, it required determinate conditions or terms, as identified in a single form, it dissolves any such diversity into a simple process of relating that does not arise or pass away. It persists as an immediate dynamic. The self-identical persistence of this grounding process is not to be found in any *deter-*

mination of reflection posited in the presupposed condition. Nor indeed is it the paradoxical identity of self-cancelling thought that persists because it continues to relate itself as inessential to the essential that is distinct from it. Anything independent which could base the persistence through change has been dissolved into the relating process itself. This means, however, that it is no longer the self-reflexive activity of *reflection* but is the simple transition of *becoming*. The only remnant of reflective determination is that it is not itself subject to the moments of generation or perishing; it *persists* as becoming.

The constituent moments of the concept the *heart of the matter* have now been more precisely defined. Its conditions are simply the multitude of *beings* as totality; its grounding relation is the process of *becoming* as persisting. The *heart of the matter* signifies the totality of *beings* that continue to *become*.

In achieving this precision, however, dialectic has dissolved the dynamic of *reflection*—the process which, by negating nonentities, results in that which is not its starting point. Since negation, as *difference,* always involves a relation to something else, pure reflection does not collapse into a simple immediacy. Within the concept the *heart of the matter,* however, reflection has completed a process of referring its own annulling activity to itself. Because it has self-reflexively negated every negative element within its own dynamic, there is left only persistence and totality—its implicit positive content. And this content is referred, not to itself, but to *becoming* on one side and *beings* on the other.

With the recognition of this implication, the concept *heart of the matter* ceases to be a product of reflection, posited as presupposed. As its negative determinations perish, its positive immediacy is generated. It emerges into existence.

This dialectical conclusion needs to be considered speculatively. What happens in the process of transforming a negatively defined essence into a positive existence?

The concept *heart of the matter* is present to thought prior to its emergence as simple existence. It first appears as *essence,* as the presupposition (or ground) inherent in the conditioning process. It is posited as the way that relation is to be viewed—not relatively, but absolutely. It is not, however, a simple concept. It includes as its determinate moments a multiplicity of conditions as immediate beings, and a grounding or mediating relationship. It cannot be thought as immediate existence if the two constituent moments are simply brought together into a synthesis by an act of external reflection. Only when the immediate beings themselves embody the dynamic of becoming, and when the mediating relation shows itself to be nothing but that very process of becoming, does this synthesis become, not an addition of thought, but inherent. At the same time a multiplicity of beings and a simple process of becoming remain diverse until they are integrated into a persistent totality by means of this single concept. The three moments, *multiplicity, process* and their synthesis are not only (as combined) sufficient conditions for the emergence into existence, but are also (as distinct) its necessary conditions as well. It is this network of conditioning relationships that grounds the integrity of the concept.[8]

Each of the three necessary constituents, synthesis, multiple conditions and grounding process, can apply to the dynamic of the integration itself.

First, the three are a multiplcity of conditions. When brought together, however, they cease to be independent and collapse into a unity. They are therefore no longer present *as conditions*.

Second, the process of bringing them together is the act of grounding. But when the unity has come about, the process itself ceases to be; it perishes. For there are no distinct conditions left that have to be related.

In other words the conditions cease to be conditions, and the grounding relation ceases to be either a ground or a relation. The resulting unity, then, is neither conditioned nor grounded. What remains is persistence and totality, no longer as distinct but as immediate qualifications of *being* per se. Third, therefore, the synthesis ceases to be a reflective addition, distinct from its moments, but becomes equivalent to itself in its pure being; it is an integrated unity.

The concept *heart of the matter* that starts as something complex is transformed into something simple. At first it generates the distinct moments of multiple conditions and grounding relation; these moments in turn generate the synthesis of a dynamic persisting totality. In that double reflection the moments perish as distinct so that a single concept is constituted. This total dynamic from the original concept to itself as result, however, has shown itself to be but one single tautological process, immediate and self-contained. Since the intellectual activity referred to is no longer complex, but rather a simple immediacy, the term *heart of the matter* is no longer relevant. It needs to be replaced by *existence*. For *existence* signifies that immediate *being* whose *essence*, although distinguishable, is yet at one with its being.[9]

The process of logical thought that started with the single concept *essence* has finally completed an integrated unit. With *existence* intelligence returns to an immediate concept which can be considered simply on its own. We can therefore break off our commentary on the doctrine of *essence* at this point and pass on to the third book: the doctrine of *concept*.

Conclusion

When preparing the second edition of the *Encyclopaedia* Hegel noted an analogy between the becoming of *a being* and the grounding of *existence*. He therefore structured this section to suggest that *identity* is parallel to pure *being*, *difference* parallel to *nothing*, *ground* to *becoming*, and *existence* to *a being*.[10] This meant that the reflective process itself fell outside of the discussion of the categories and was treated in the introduction.

In the larger logic, the analogy is more subtle. As we have seen, the *essentials* correspond not to the immediacy of *being* and *nothing*, but to the transitions involved in *a being* and its *determination*. *Reflection* corresponds to *becoming* (the simple transition of the earlier stage), and *essence* and *seeming* are related as *being* to *nothing*.[11] Since Hegel died before revising the second book of the larger logic we can never know whether he would have restructured it to match the schema in the *Encyclopaedia* of 1827 and 1831.

The integration of *essence* into the immediate self-contained category *existence*, however, is much more complex than the earlier transition to *a being* or to *being for its own sake*. There the movement of thought, whether expressed by the terms *becoming* or *change*, *determining* or *going beyond*, is simple and direct. When a new concept enters the spotlight of attention, the former one is left behind; intelligence simply passes from one over to the other. When the concepts are such that the transition is not one way, but rather an alternating cycle, the resulting self-contained dynamic can be collapsed into a single and immediate object of thought.

With the advance to *reflection* thought becomes aware of its own active role. In the effort to ensure an adequate comprehension of its object, however, it draws a distinction between the content thought and its own activity so that it can discount the latter and isolate the former.[12] This means that the fundamental characteristic of *reflection* is negative. Since reflection as such is intelligence's own activity it is thought as a nonentity in order to get at the essential object. Intelligence then cancels its own process of "getting at," and considers the essential to be totally external to itself. Finally it annuls the positive result of its conclusion in so far as it is the result of intellectual process.

As the analysis of *difference* has shown, any negative intellectual act is not absolute but rather relative. Therefore any content of reflection (whether starting point, result, or process itself) cannot be absolutely isolated as self-contained. It always refers implicitly to something. The determinate transitions of *a being* show themselves here to be a negative relation: either *difference* or *diversity, opposition* or *contradiction.*

Reflection, however, is not simply the act of distinguishing. The latter results because thought has become aware of itself as an intellectual process. The self-awareness, which triggers the conscious effort to draw distinctions, is its implicit positive content—its subjectivity as persisting totality. And it entails that the terms distinguished, as well as the distinguishing activity itself, can be used self-reflexively. To discount its own role it must use the very concepts that have appeared as the result of its own negative activity. This is not as vicious as it might at first appear, for thinking involves the move of understanding—the act of isolating a term or concept to render a specific meaning precise. Isolated from its content the latter can be taken independently of the mediating process by which it first appeared in thought. In this way intelligence can use it to refer to its own subsequent activity without begging the question.[13]

This self-reflexive moment, however, has an important consequence. Aware of itself as vacuous and inessential, reflection can apply its own distinctive type of operation—dissolving and cancelling—to annul its own negative character. It can discern a negative determination and invalidate it. If and when this happens, the positive that is inherent becomes evident. In other words, when used self-reflexively, reflection can negate its own negations. Since these negations are always relative, such a double negation does not produce an empty cipher. Rather the positive process of reflection becomes manifest.

This process of negating the negation is already present implicitly when *external reflection* cancels the vacuous character of its posited premise. But it cannot become complete until the activity of negating is explicitly applied to itself as reflection's own essential determination. Indeed it is this very process, culminating in *contradiction* which shows that the negativity of reflection cannot be maintained absolutely, but collapses into a simple positive *becoming* which is its ground.

In the preceding discussion, each one of the determinations of reflection is used to establish what is essential to *ground,* only to find that it must also be applied self-reflexively to itself in such a way that its self-contained independence is dissolved. Pure *identity,* essentially determining *ground as such,* cannot be differentiated as *essence* or as *matter* from its *form;* rather, the two are identified in *content.* The *difference* of *content* and *form,* essential to *determinate ground,* becomes an indifferent diversity, only to be then identified as *conditions* and opposed to the contrary identity of the *grounding relation.* When the inherent contradiction that determines the structure of *conditioning* is applied to itself in all its various moments, it dissolves them into the ground of *ground*—that which is both posited and presupposed by ground, or *existence.* In each move an essential *determination of reflection* is not simply thrown out of court as invalid. Rather, when used self-reflexively, it sets itself within the context of a persisting totality that transforms it from an absolute into a relative.

This reflexive negation of the negative determinations of reflection does not return thought to its immediate origin. The first negation remains, but as dissolved into a more comprehensive perspective. The immediacy of *existence,* therefore, is also a mediated result. It retains within its self-contained meaning inherent distinctions that will become explicit in new forms as the logic proceeds. The essence of *existence,* its immediate identity, will be distinguished from the way it *appears;* and the negativity which, as reflection, was thought to be the activity of external thought, will now be inherent in the object thought. *Appearance* and *existence* will be integrated in the concept *absolute*—that which transcends all partiality. The distinctions internal to both the activity and the content of thought must then be made manifest as negative relations within a comprehensive context. When thought has worked through the processes of *appearing* and *manifesting* as well as that of *reflecting,*[14] it will be completely aware of itself. Positive *becoming* and negative *reflection* will be recognized as two complementary moments within a single, persisting comprehensive activity that both positively relates and negatively distinguishes—namely *conceiving,* or *comprehending.* While this activity has been implicit in the preceding analysis (as *reflection, comparing,* the *positive-and-negative, excluding reflection, content, grounding relation,* and the *heart of the matter*)[15], it needs to become the explicit focus of attention if thought is to become fully master of its own operations.

The preceding commentary, however, is sufficient to suggest how Hegel maintains the necessity of the logical development throughout the doctrine of *essence.* Understanding does not simply identify a transition of thought; by holding it together with its two terms, it isolates its negativity. Dialectic, in turn, by questioning this differentiation, shows how it is relative to something else and opens the door for speculative reason. The relation shows itself to be a doubling in which each term reflects the other. This mutual reflection then becomes the focus for understanding's attention.

The transitions of pure thought, therefore, not only distinguish, but also mutually reflect their two terms. When both of these operations are explicitly integrated in the activity of conceiving or comprehending, the comprehensive necessity of the logical development will be established.

Part Four

Comprehending

9

Conceiving

As the logic proceeds, the attention of pure thought broadens in scope. At first it is simply directed towards categories that result from immediate transitions. Then as it becomes aware of the negative, dissolving character of its own intellectual activity, it distinguishes its own reflective processes from the content of thought. This self-reflexive act does not remain simply a negative discounting, but now becomes a positive comprehension of itself as a persisting totality. The focus is enlarged to include the whole dynamic within which concepts are considered by intelligence. Specific terms are no longer isolated categories; nor are they simply differentiated from reflection. Now they are constituent moments of a comprehensive dynamic activity.[1]

Since this commentary has used Hegel's psychological analysis of intelligence to unravel the dense skein of logical terminology, we have already incorporated into our discussion something of this more comprehensive perspective. New concepts signify the intellectual processes that result from rendering earlier concepts precise. For us, then, the transition to *conceiving* is not as abrupt as for the reader who approaches the *Logic* for the first time.[2] We are now simply integrating interpretative form with substantial content to form a complete self-referential totality. Thought has reached the point where it explicitly thinks itself.

In the doctrine of comprehending, then, the comprehensive dynamic of thought becomes explicit; it includes the activity of conceiving, the legitimate types of judgement, and the valid forms of inference. We have here what corresponds to a philosophy of logic. The various categories of concepts, judgements, and syllogisms are not just listed; rather, comprehending thought makes explicit the conditions that need to be fulfilled for them to be used appropriately.

Since Hegel's time, symbolic logic has made considerable progress in rendering precise the processes of judgement and inference. By placing these more recent developments in dialogue with the Hegelian analysis we can take up Hegel's own suggestion that the method followed in the system of logic is "capable of greater completeness, of much elaboration in detail."[3] We can thus progress beyond the specific limitations of both, to comprehend more broadly the role of logical operations. To prevent confusion, however, these extensions of the Hegelian discussion are indented and added as appendices to the relevant commentary.

The Universal Concept

To conceive is an unconditioned, free act. It is intelligence aware of itself as a comprehending dynamic, truly infinite in that any finite distinctions are but constituent moments. The complex interplay of *the heart of the matter* has been integrated, not into the objective category of *existence* but rather into the subjectivity of pure energy.[4] Implicit in *being* as *becoming,* and in *essence* as *reflection,* the intellectual process now becomes wholly transparent to thought, and may be signified by the single term *concept.*

As first isolated by the understanding, *concept* does not have a complex connotation. It is simply the immediate identity of the comprehending activity; and distinctions have been dissolved into its unity. It is, then, the pure process of intellectual relating as it brings together anything which could be discerned as moments or terms. Since the relation is common to all it relates, to conceive is simply to universalize.

Having defined *concept* as *universal,* the understanding is unable to render it more precise, for any precision would introduce determinations and distinguish it from something else. In that case it would not be universal; for *universality* as pure relation incorporates distinctions into a unity. Any determinations that might distinguish it have already been included within its own relating structure as pure intelligence; and any others are excluded by the isolating focus of the understanding. The *universal,* then, is simply related to itself, not as the mediated result of a distinct intellectual process, but as the mediating activity itself.

(Ordinary unreflective thought thinks of the *universal* as abstracted from all determinations, opposed to what is particular or singular. But this involves a much more complex intellectual process than the one considered here. For it takes specific determinations that have been thought and cancels them as invalid. The two distinct moments, namely of thinking determinations and of cancelling them, are isolated from each other. Because the determining activity of conceptual thought has not yet been made explicit, however, such a complexity is not yet involved in the *universality* of conceptual thought.)

If the understanding cannot define the *universal concept* more precisely in itself, it can provide a comparison with the earlier categories of *being* and of *essence*. *A being, something* and *being-for-its-own-sake* were implicitly the identity of all their qualitative determinations. But since each distinct moment was thought independently, it was left behind when intelligence moved on to another category. The *universal,* however, continues through all its various moments, remaining explicitly present in each, unaltered and complete.

The *determinations of reflection* are relative. They cannot be thought simply in themselves but only as they are related to something else. Indeed they only show themselves in this relation—as the *identity* of *different* things, or as the *ground* of a *contradiction*. The relating, however, appeared as an external and independent reflection. By contrast, the *universal* which is distinct from its determinations as their essence, nonetheless defines their inherent positive character. It is a substance that allows its modes and attributes to develop, not contingently, but as the necessary result of its own mediating dynamic. Thus the negative differences are not simply excluded as other, but are incorporated as constituent moments of the relating identity. The *universal* is thus free power. While remaining self-identical it overreaches that which is other, not by force, but by quietly being present in it.

Dialectic takes this final definition of understanding and examines its implications. The *universal* is not absolutely indeterminate, like *pure being;* it is defined as the relation between terms, a relation rendered determinate by their particularities. The preceding contrast, with the categories of *being* and of *essence,* showed that these determinations are not introduced externally, but are inherent. Insofar as it has distinct moments, then, the *universal* itself acts negatively, and this introduces *particularity*. Insofar as it absorbs these moments into its unity it negates this negation, so that these determinations are relative not to something else but only to the universal itself. Acquiring concreteness by this double activity it *indivi-*

dualizes itself. The *universal,* then, is equally *particular* and *individual.*[5]

To escape this paradoxical conclusion of dialectical thought, the understanding attempts to distinguish the *universal* from any *particularity* and any *individuality* whatsoever. What remains, however, is no longer the original comprehensive concept with which it began, but only a bare abstraction. The dialectical result is that the concept *universal* cannot be isolated with impunity. Either it includes *particular* and *individual* or it is a bare abstraction, neither of which is intended.[6]

This contradiction triggers speculative reason's effort to explore its ground. What is the nature of this relation between the *universal* and its determinations?

The *universal* is the comprehensive totality. As such it includes its terms as determinate moments. These can be discerned within the totality, not as self-contained and independent, but rather as essentially permeated by the relating universality. Therefore that which determines a *universal* is not different from it, but is reflectively included within it. In due course this determination will be isolated as the *particular per se.* At this point, however, speculative reason is interested in the way it renders the *universal* determinate while yet not being distinguished from it. How does the *universal* in its totality exhibit its determinate character?

Its determination may become evident as it differentiates the one universal from another, external to it. Since these two now become particulars within a more encompassing universal relation, the first is transformed into a relative universal, no longer complete in itself. Yet the relativising determination is not to be thought as distinct from the original *universal,* the result of an external reflection. It is intrinsic, permeated by the universal just as the universal is permeated by it; it is the immanent character of, and is indistinguishable from, the universal as genus. The determination thus both particularizes the universal and articulates its inherent generic character.

This synthetic response of speculative reason to the paradox of dialectic needs to be rendered more explicit. For it leaves unresolved the dual perspective of external reflection. How in fact is the external determination as particular related to the internal determination as character? It appears as if the universal simply becomes a sub-genus for a more general universal, in which case the perspective of totality is lost and the synthetic conjunction of the two moments disappears into a progression of ever more abstract genera that are related simply by external reflection. The move to a synthesis will break down unless the process of external reflection is itself included within the totality. The genuinely *universal* act of relating, then, must reflect on itself; the moment of reflecting is not something distinct and independent but a constituent moment of the universally relating dynamic of conceptual thought. By considering what it *would* be like if it *were* to show itself, the *universal* gives itself a determinate character. There is no longer need for a reflection that is external; the difference is proposed only to be immediately cancelled.[7] Through this intrinsic, active process the *universal* escapes the dialectical paradox. Any relative universal would fail to signify the comprehensive dynamic of conceiving—that totality whose self-determining activity would make it a particular only if it were related to something else. By particularizing itself, the genuine *universal* constitutes its own individuality. Speculative reason then comprehends the intellectual process signified by *universal concept*—namely as that which relates its terms not simply positively but also negatively by distinguishing hypothetically whatever is not originally distinct. In this way the process of *conceiving* remains self-identical and self-contained. This non-relative, and hence absolute, negativity is its creative power. Now made explicit, it can itself become the object of the understanding's precision.

The Particular Concept

That which renders a concept determinate is its *particularity*. This determination is neither the simple *limit* of *something* by which it is distinguished from something else, nor an isolated *determination of reflection* distinct from that about which thought reflects. Rather it is inherent in the *universal* as its own character, requiring no external reference to become defined.

Understanding isolates the concept *particular* to render it precise. A *particular* contains the *universal*. It is *particular,* however, because it can be distinguished from other diverse *particulars,* which contain the same *universal*. The genus, for example, does not change its character from one species to another; nor are the species distinguished from the genus but only from one another.

The *universal* permeates all particulars and is their inherent identity; they in turn incorporate the totality of the *universal's* diverse determination. When the moment of difference (or sheer diversity) is comprehended, however, it provides an exhaustive specification of the universal's character. Both of these references—to the totality and to the exhaustive completeness of the universal—are contained in the connotation of the concept *particular,* because it is not referred to something external, but is the inherent determination of the *universal* itself—is its essential principle. When considered within the comprehensive context of conceptual thought, then, *particularity* has three specific features: totality, exhaustiveness, and determining principle.[8]

In the realm of pure thought all that we have is conceptual activity itself, which has shown itself to be *universal.* Therefore, when we isolate the concept *particular* with all of its connotations, there is no alien particular to which it can be related as diverse. The only difference left that is relevant to such a relation is the self-reflexive one between *particular* and *universal* itself. If conceiving universally has species, then, these species are: a) the universal as such, and b) its particularity. Indeed, it is determinate (i.e. *particular*) only because its own dynamic introduces the distinction between these two. The principle of its diversity is its own self-determining activity; and it is the ground of its own inherent distinctions.

With this, dialectical thought has begun to show the implications inherent in the isolated concept *particular.* But there is more to be said. For the two particulars that have been distinguished have a paradoxical structure that needs to be rendered explicit. The species *universal* is immediate and indeterminate in contrast to the determinate *particular.* Its indeterminate immediacy constitutes its determination and makes it one particular co-ordinated with another. As determinate, however, each species is simply a particular of the more general *universal* and is subordinated to it. The term *universal,* then, means two things at the same time: the general contrasted with specific particularity and one of the particulars. However, since it is the contrast that makes it into a particular the first meaning appears to be no different from the second.

The meaning of *universal* as immediate, however, does not include the sense of contrast or opposition. The latter is the determining characteristic of *particularity. Particularity,* then, is not the same as simple *diversity,* where several particulars are held together by external reflection, but rather is an explicit *opposition* or contrast. It is nothing but pure negativity now inherent in the dynamic activity of conceiving. In this context *difference* is no longer relative to an independent *identity;* on the contrary, as it differentiates, it identifies. Although this comprehensive structure of universal thought—identifying by differentiating—was implicit in the earlier logical development (in the concept *limit,* for example, or in the relations *positive-and-negative* and *excluding reflection*) it is now posited as the explicit result of the logic itself. With the concept *particular,* this dynamic process has acquired a category appropriate to its own activity.[9] For when its determining negativity is made into its very principle, the *universal* is exhaustively *particularized.*

Universal conceptual thought has as its single principle this process of determination—of introducing a distinction into itself. This act is nonetheless relative; it is directed against the simple unity of the process of conceiving. When speculative reason applies it to its own operation, however, the activity of particularizing is no longer considered to be simply a relative moment, but is itself particularized as what is both determined and determining. Isolated from the immediate universal, it is given the form of a determinate being. Because it is now explicitly posited as the single principle of conceptual thought, it is no longer a transitory moment that passes over to something else, but is explicitly thought of as itself enduring and *universal*.

In other words, when dialectic first thinks of the determinate character of the *universal*, it considers this particularity to be a dissolving moment that disappears into the comprehensive identity. The speculative result of referring its determinate activity to itself, however, shows that the process of particularizing persists; it is a universal constituent of the *universal*, and essential to its dynamic comprehension. At the same time, as explicitly distinguished from the *universal*, it is not complete and concrete; indeed it is quite abstract. When thus particularized by self-reflective thought, the differentiating moment of particularity is given the abstracted form of a distinct being. The simple determination that is its content is no longer thought within the comprehensive process of universalizing thought (which originally posited it), but as independent and self-contained.

When thought particularizes the determination from its context, it equally particularizes the context from its determination. The universal itself, therefore, is no longer thought under the form of conceptual activity, but also as something abstract and distinct. The process of conceiving, then, falls apart into discrete categories or objects of thought: the *universal,* the *particular,* and their external conjunction. Even though intelligence remains the implicit process by which these various moments have been differentiated, it has disappeared from view; what is explicitly thought is not the process but only its particularized elements. Because the dynamic context even though presupposed cannot be explicitly posited by particularizing thought, the abstractions are taken to be immediate—as simply present in intelligence—and each is thought to be indifferent to the other, as well as to the conceiving process of intelligence itself.[10] While the abstract universal is a concept, then, it is a concept isolated from the activity of conceiving; it is a thoughtless thought.

What we have thus made explicit is how the intellectual activity of understanding operates. It is not the original act of intelligence from which all else follows. Rather, it distinguishes a determinate moment within the comprehensive dynamic of conceiving and, by particularizing this distinction, gives it the form of being other than thought, and makes it into an enduring (and hence universal) term. What at first appears as simply a moment in an ongoing process is isolated and persists because the particularizing activity of conceptual thought continues to posit this isolation. When we use the term *understanding* in our commentary, then, it is to this process that we are referring.

An abstraction of the understanding is not empty; it is the abstraction of a determinate concept that is itself the result of conceptual activity. But insofar as it does not signify the totality of the conceptual process, but only a one-sided determination, it could be called empty. For it does not contain any reference to the principle that has defined its specific connotation. Since the context through which it develops and is realized in the mind is left aside, it is simply a bare form of thought.

Because the understanding fixes the determinations and finite formulations of thought so that they become invariable, it is sometimes dismissed as a fruitless playing with inconsequential symbols. In reaction some people turn instead to non-logical intellectual processes—intuition, simple association, and the stream of consciousness that reflects subconscious influence. Understanding, however, is not to be despised.[11] For it provides the motive force by which intelligence can become fully conscious of itself. It takes the "booming, buzzing confusion" of intuition and by particularizing distinct determinate characters gives them an independent existence in thought. Even though the constant change of sensation or the transience of immediate intuitive feeling points in the direction of the dynamic activity of conceptual thought, it contains no inherent principle by which its integrity can be defined. Only the infinite power of understanding introduces into this wide-ranging multiplicity fundamental distinctions that persist through the simple transitions of time, or space, or indeed of subconscious intelligence itself. The formal determinations introduced by the abstracting universality of intelligence provide the means for transforming an immediate totality of intuition into the objective totality of self-conscious deliberate thought.

Understanding by itself does not lead to this result. However, by particularizing its concepts to the limit of their fixed simplicity, it initiates its own demise. In the process of *particularizing* the moment of difference and distinction has its place too. In *universalizing* it was only implicit; now it is posited explicitly, namely as that which is itself particularized from its universal context. Speculative reason has shown that the *determinate concept* has thereby been transformed into a simple object of thought. As simple, it is not related to anything else but only to itself. It is then no longer a *particular* concept, inherently related to a *universal,* but rather something *individual,* which cannot be understood, but to which thought can only refer. When the relation between *universalizing* and *particularizing* is dissolved, and all that remains is something particularized and immediate, understanding ceases. All that is left is pure reference, or *the individual.*

We have here not a peculiar, Hegelian, sense of the term *concept,* but rather the justification of the process that leads logic to the use of abstract categories and of pure reference. This abstractness makes possible the introduction of formal symbolism as well as of a denotative criterion of meaning.

This means that the whole discussion that continues from this point to the end of the section on inference is characterized by the formalism of understanding, even though the dialectical and speculative moments inevitably introduce what is now called a meta-theoretical reflection. Since this meta-theory is as much a component of comprehensive thought as the abstractions, the two are included in a single, self-referential discussion.[12]

The Individual

Individuality is explicitly posited by thought when the act of particularizing is absolutely particularized. It is pure determination that is related solely to itself.

1. The category *individuality* is first generated by conceptual thought when the latter reflects on its own process, and then differentiates its determinate content from itself. In making its mediating dynamic explicit, it segregates the universal comprehension from its terms. But there now remains no further comprehensive perspective under which activity and terms can become particulars of the same universal. Since any relation between the two has been dissolved by the clear discrimination of understanding, each is related only to itself. When thought thus thinks each as absolutely independent of all relation the negative fact that one is not the other no longer reflects a positive context but is absolute. Rejecting any conceptualization, since such would involve a relation, the terms are purely individual. They can be REFERRED to by thought but neither COMPREHENDED nor CONCEIVED. We have now the thought of *the individual*—not, be it noted, of an individual *concept,* but rather the act of thought by which it refers to what is completely other than thought. *The individual* signifies that act of reference.

In contrast to the negative essentials, which are always reflected either in external reflection or in their dialectical counterparts, what is here involved is absolute negativity, negation purely and immediately in itself. The negative distinguishing process of thought has been negated by thought, leaving nothing. Because it cannot think, it can only point.

This move can be rendered more determinate if we recall the two ways in which the negative characteristic of the *particular* showed itself. Considered as inherent in the conceptual process, it was its character and remained universal. Viewed externally as related to something else, it was simply determinate. By isolating this latter moment from the universal relating dynamic two things have occurred. On the one hand the universal character became simply an abstraction that can be ordered in a pyramid of genus and species; on the other hand the determination, having nothing else to determine, became pure individuality. When conceptual thought explicitly cancels its own activity, then, two consequences follow for its content: on the one hand, its categories become pure abstractions, isolated from any dynamic process in which they may have their validity or ground; on the other, what is not abstract is the *individual,* either despised as not worthy of consideration or simply indicated by an act of reference. This double result is the culminating achievement of conceptual thought when it explicitly comprehends itself.

From the standpoint of ordinary logical thinking, the term *individual* simply follows the thought of *universal* and *particular* in a process of transition or becoming—what novelists call the stream of consciousness. We have already recognized, however, that the immediate *universal* is a comprehensive dynamic of conceiving, and that it renders itself determinate (or particular) and concrete (or individual). It is the ground that underlies this apparently simple transition. The distinguishing act that explicates this implicit dynamic of conceptual thought, however, is nothing other than its inherent principle and determining character. Therefore it simply refers to itself. Since it has thus been identified by understanding, the comprehensive dynamic has been dissolved. Any universal is insubstantial and indeterminate. What is concrete is pure individuality. This process, then, ends with nominalism: the claim that thoughts, as abstract, have no reality, and that individuals, as concrete, cannot be thought.

Dialectical considerations push further to show that this absolute contrast cannot be maintained. For the implicit unity of conceptual thought will continue to manifest itself even in its dissolution. Those products of abstraction that were to leave all individuality aside, for example, are themselves individual. When a thought is abstracted from something concrete, it does not encompass the whole determinate character of that concrete, but refers to only one of its determinations. Each abstraction is thus but an *individual* property. The abstract category no less than the comprehensive conceptual dynamic is both *universal* and *individual*. In the abstraction, however, these two moments are not integrated but set side by side as content and form: the content is individual; the form is universal. Even though the two are thus simply diverse, in the abstract universal they are yet inextricably conjoined, making it determinate after all.

For the same reasons, the *particular* is also referred to as an *individual* determination. On the other hand the *individual,* because it is THOUGHT as individual, is determined conceptually; it is *particularized.* For, even though thought cannot comprehend individuals, it yet *thinks* of them as *individuals.* This latter term, then, does not simply refer to something not thought. It is itself a conceptual category, one of the particular determinations of the self-dissolving process of conceiving. Since this category is universal and does not refer in any particular way, it is abstract. There are, then, three ways something can be thought: as an abstract *universal* concept, as a *particularized* concept, and under the category *individual.* Since the latter is not itself explicitly a concept, these three are not species of the same genus, but are rather indifferently diverse ways in which thought refers to its abstracted content.

When it lists these three ways of *thinking* a concept or category, intelligence finds that it has difficulty distinguishing the *particular* from the *individual.* Each refers to the moment of determination. The concept *particularity,* however, refers to the comprehensive totality of determinations—all of the distinct moments of the universal—and does not isolate one. This itself leads to a paradoxical conclusion, for as the totality of determinations, it is itself a concrete act of reference, and therefore *individual.* On the other hand, as comprehensive, it represents the *universal.* These two aspects of its determinate character, however, are not explicitly differentiated, but remain simply conjoined in thought in an immediate synthesis. The importance of this point will only become evident as we proceed to the doctrine of inference, when the *particular* will serve as the middle term of a syllogism relating an *individual* and a *universal.*

Dialectic has shown that even when abstracted from the dynamic context of intellectual thought, each of the three determinations—*individual, particular* and *universal*—cannot be isolated from the others as self-contained. Since understanding can identify one only by using the others, their differences become confounded. Only when the effort to think is left behind and they are simply represented by means of discrete spatial symbols can one hold them to be unalterably distinct and count them as independent units.

In other words, the unity of the three determinations of the concept (which we saw in the discussion of *universality*) is now made explicit. They are not integrated simply because the *universal* concept envelopes the others into its encompassing embrace. Rather each one in isolation inevitably requires the others for its definition. With the category *individuality* this becomes explicit, because pure reference not only involves the act of distinguishing, but also dissolves this act so that each moment is left independent of the fact that it is thought. In such isolation each shows itself to be at the same time an abstract universal, a particular differentiated from the others, and an individual. Inherently it is *universal;* as posited it is *particular*; as self-contained and taken simply for its own sake, it is *individual*. In other words, the clear isolation of the concept *individual* does not simply produce a third term alongside of the other two. It also makes clear that each is *inherently posited* as *self-contained*.

2. The dialectical paradox of the category *individuality* is that each of the three terms contains both of the others; they thus appear to be identical. To avoid this contradiction speculative reason refers to the process through which the comprehensive integrity of thinking dissolved itself. For it was this development that was to distinguish *individuality* from its correlates. To be sure, the abstracted *particular* and the abstracted *universal* are also individuals; they are specific determinate concepts with a unique content that makes them concrete. But they are still concepts, determinations of the activity of comprehensive thought. The *individual* on the other hand is to be the pure moment of difference as difference. Fixed as that difference which persists simply in being different from thought, it is posited as that which is abstracted from all abstraction. The term *individual* refers to that which is not a moment in the conceptual process at all; as pure reference it is absolutely other than thought.

By referring to its own operations as immediate transition or external reflection, comprehensive or speculative reason can characterize the specific difference of the *individual*. It exists *for its own sake,* segregated from all intrusive concepts; it is in itself immediate, unrelated to any mediating process.[13] These definitions imply that it is thinkable; it can be characterized by earlier categories. It is thought as *one,* repelling any relation to anything like itself. However, even if thought does suggest that there are innumerable other ones, the transition to these others is not simply allowed to occur, but is self-referentially excluded. The fact that they happen to be thought at the same time is to reflect no inherent liaison. Any relating universal, then, does not follow from the individuals themselves. They are simply to subsist, indifferent to each other. The universal refers to thought's own transitions as something introduced externally: an association of common characteristics that collects them into a set. "The lowest representation that one can have of the universal insofar as it is related to the individual is this external relation of the same as bare commonality."[14] Because the act of self-reference that particularizes the universal is distinct from the act of reference to an individual object, they remain distinct even in their individuality.

When considered reflectively, the *individual* can be distinguished from its material characteristics as *this*. Thought no longer needs self-referentially to exclude other *ones* in order to have it completely self-contained. The negative moment is already included in the process of reflection, for it recognizes the externality of its own activity in generating the secondary qualities of *this,* whereby it discounts its own role. *This* is indicated as immediate in such a way that the act of positing expressly dissolves its own significance. When the category of *individuality* is added to *this,* however, it is no longer considered indifferent and immediate simply with reference to external reflection. Rather the reflective relationship of *this* to its secondary qualities is also referred to by thought as its own addition.

Thought segregates *the individual* as a pure act of reference by referring to itself as in its turn absolutely individual; it is reflected into itself in such a way that the process of comprehension is explicitly dissolved. This is why the intellectual process can posit something that is to be absolutely other than thought. Because its own processes are indicated self-referentially, its abstract categories are themselves absolutely individual, immediate in themselves, isolated, and excluded from each other. However, because the act of self-reference points in a contrary direction to that of simple reference, such categories are essentially characterized as absolutely opposed to individuals. Only when this absolute repulsion between reference and self-reference is strictly maintained are *individual* and *universal* clearly distinct.[15]

With this the dynamic of conceptual thought that overreaches all determination has completely disappeared from view. It is no longer thought as the relating unity of diverse determinations which are simply its constituent moments. The latter have become self-contained individuals, devoid of reference to anything else. And the former is but an abstract commonality, an individual transition of thought, or an individual result of external reflection. Thought contains only indicated individuals that are externally related by individual intellectual operations; these latter appear to have nothing in common with this content. Indeed, the lack of relation between abstract category and indicated content is the only thing they have in common—the only unity that speculative reason can discern. Because of this lack of anything common, the intellect itself has to arbitrate on how the two are to be brought together. An act of judging, then, must take the place of the discriminating process of conceiving.[16]

Judging

When it particularizes its content, conceptual thought ends by simply referring to diverse individuals. This act of reference can be isolated absolutely because intelligence has also referred to itself as being a particular relating agent that has brought the various individuals under an abstract universal category. Because the contrast between reference and self-reference has itself been introduced by the particularizing intelligence, however, both are in some way conjoined by its activity. This implicit conjunction, signified by the term *judgement,* now becomes the focus of attention.

In an act of judgement there are three distinct moments. There is the *subject* to which thought refers; there is the *predicate* that is applied to the subject by intelligence; and the two are coupled by a *copula*. These general characterizations of the three moments are quite distinct from any particular content that is ascribed to them. As we shall see, the point of some dialectical puzzles that follow will be to establish which of the earlier categories (*universal, particular,* and *individual*) is to be the appropriate characterization for the subject, and which for the predicate. Similarly, the technical term *copula* signifies any coupling and is not bound to the verb "to be" with its implicitly ontological reference, nor to the identity of pure equivalence.[1] Indeed Hegel includes the "if-then" of implication and the "either-or" of disjunction under the category of copula. As *subject* and *predicate* become more precisely defined by means of the three conceptual determinations, then, the *copula* will also acquire a more comprehensive connotation.

The preceding considerations have an important implication: that not every sentence is a judgement. The latter is a logical process, following from the nature of the intellectual activity itself. It can be applied to nonlogical reality, but only on the basis of those criteria and conditions that are inherent in its own structure. This integrity of form and application alone validates its use.[2] There are sentences, however, that connect two terms, not on the basis of their intrinsic logical characteristics but because of contingent factors—temporal and spatial contiguity or abitrary association. The correctness of such sentences does not depend on their logical structure. Only when a sentence is appropriate to the structural demands of conceptual determination can it be validly regarded as a judgement.

Judgements of A Being

Positive Judgement 1. When we take the function of *judging* in its most primitive simplicity, its two contrasting moments, subject and predicate, are rendered determinate by the particularizing process of conceiving alone. The latter, as we have seen, reached its culmination when an abstract *universal* was separated from the self-contained and independent *individual*. These two contrasted determinations, then, provide the concrete content for the judgement's terms.

In judging, however, the two are to be related, not by external reflection, but in light of something inherent. The universal has been abstracted by conceptual thought from its consideration of certain individuals and particulars. It has been conceived or mediated by that particular intellectual process. In contrast, the *individual* is thought of as immediate *per se,* as a pure something, external to the reflective procedures of thinking. When judgement relates these two, then, it takes the *individual* as primary—the subject—and it expresses the fact that the *universal* has been abstracted from it by a judgement in which the abstracted predicate is said to inhere in the concrete individual. The two are thus related *positively,* and the judgement form 'S is P' acquires the content: "The individual is universal."

In more recent philosophy of logic the subject of a primitive judgement refers not to a concrete individual existing in space and time, but to a logical individual—that to which thought refers but which it cannot grasp conceptually. This is symbolized by "a". The act of judging conjoins to that individual the qualifying universal that has been abstracted from it: Q. Their relation in the judgement does not require a verb but can be indicated by simple juxtaposition: Qa. Placing the individual at the end indicates that it is the ground of the relation of inherence.

2. Dialectical reason explores the implications of this definition. The pure *individual,* because it lacks all universality and is simply a point of reference, is a transitory and unstable object of thought. By relating it explicitly to the *universal,* however, thought gives it a positive conceptual subsistence. It is now thought of as that in which this abstractly conceived quality inheres. Because the *universal* quality abstracts the peculiar characteristics of intelligence, it persists in thought and is common to a number of individuals. On this basis it could be considered to be primary—the subject. The process of predication would then indicate that individual in which the quality inheres. The *positive judgement* then becomes: "the universal is individual."

Because this claim presupposes the primacy of thought, understanding rejects it. Yet it cannot escape, for dialectic pushes further and shows that this connotation does not simply reflect the dynamic of thought but also the characteristics of the original subject and predicate. The individual subject, as that from which the qualifying predicate is abstracted, includes more than this one quality. If this were not the case the two terms could not be distinguished by the act of abstracting. The subject, then, is a being with many qualities, a thing with diverse properties, a substance affected by a number of accidents. As integrating this multiplicity, it is a comprehensive relation that includes a number of terms and is therefore *universal.* The predicate, on the other hand, is simply one individual quality, property, or accident. Paradoxically, the original *positive judgement* could just as well be expressed by the formula: "The universal is individual."

A double shift has taken place. 1. The subject is first thought as an immediate individual; it is simply there. Because the act of judging expresses the inherence of the predicate in the subject, however, the latter must be that which incorporates this quality into a more comprehensive structure and is thus universal. 2. The predicate that started as an abstract universal is to inhere in this subject. It is not, therefore, an indeterminate quality but one of the individual determinations that pertain to this thing.

This reciprocal process by which the content that establishes the criteria for applying the form flickers back and forth results from the way that the two terms have been related in *positive judgement*. They are simply conjoined as if there were nothing preventing their identification. But the two sides ought to be contrasted, for this is how conceptual thought rendered precise their determinations. Indeed if that contrast were not maintained, the resultant sentences "The individual is individual" and The universal is universal" would simply collapse into a simple identity where no act of judging would be involved at all. Where there is no difference between subject and predicate there is nothing to be related. Therefore the two contrary characteristics of *positive judgement* alternate: when the subject is considered as individual the predicate is universal, but when it is universal the predicate must be singular.

The two ways of expressing *positive judgement*, then, are to be distinguished one from the other and not simply identified. The second, "The universal is individual," considers the content of the two terms: the content of the subject must be a concrete universal, and the content of the predicate must be an individual quality. By contrast, the initial one, "the individual is universal," refers to the form. The subject is that to which thought simply refers; the predicate is the abstracted conceivable category. In the simple positive judgement these two distinct relations are synthetically conjoined. Two distinct sentences are not required because the subject and the predicate are indifferent to their particular interpretation. The copula, however, does not adequately express the relation. It simply conjoins by juxtaposition and fails to articulate the contrast that is essential to the content. There is, then, a contradiction between the form of the *positive judgement* "S is P" and the conditions that must be fulfilled for its valid use.[3]

3. Speculative reason reflects on this dialectical operation. *Positive judgement* conjoins two relations: "The individual is universal" and "The universal is individual." This means that both subject and predicate are at once determinate individuals and relating universals. As determinate universals they would be *particulars*. Such a synthesis would not do justice to their specific character in *positive judgement*, however. On the one hand, a judgement that said "The particular is particular" would collapse into a bare meaningless tautology. On the other hand, the characterization of each as particular follows simply because the two perspectives, the content and form, are synthesized by an act of thought external to both. Since the pure *individual* and the abstract *universal* are given immediately in *positive judgement* neither defines specifically how it is particular.

The relation between subject and predicate in this type of judgement, then, cannot be captured in a simple conjunction. The subject and predicate must be distinguished not only in interpretation but also in form. Since the latter relation can be expressed only by modifying the copula which asserts their relation, a *positive judgement* is no longer sufficient.

What is required is already implicit in the two interpretations of the judgement. Consider the first: "The individual is universal." The individual as immediate and self-contained is opposed to all abstracted universality. As opposites they are not identical but different. In the second, "The universal is individual," the subject is something concrete, having an indefinite number of qualities. Within its totality thought can discern an infinite range of properties and accidents. It is, therefore, contrasted to the one individual quality that is predicated.

Neither statement can be taken as expressing a simple identification. Such a positive conjunction is to be denied. Speculative reason discovers, then, that it is referring to a new category of judgement in which the predicate is to be differentiated from the subject: *a negative judgement.*

Negative Judgement 1. What made the *positive judgement* inadequate was its failure to express the stark contrast between a pure *individual* and an abstract *universal*—the sharp distinction between subject and predicate. Since the universal predicate, in contrast to the immediate subject, is mediated by the abstracting process of thought, it is not a comprehensive universal, but one that is particularly determined. Thought has differentiated it from the subject. A concept that is thus distinguished from something else is a *particular*. Therefore the new form of judgement could be expressed "The individual is particular."

The same result follows if we take the other way of expressing the *positive judgement:* "The universal is individual." The predicate is not simply an individual quality. It results from a discriminating process of thought, and is therefore *particular*. On the other hand the subject is universal as concrete—as other than the abstract particularity of the predicate—and is therefore individual.

When speculative reason previously attempted to synthesize the two forms of the positive judgement in "The particular is particular," this conclusion was rejected as externally imposed. Now, however, the necessary distinction between subject and predicate has resulted in transforming the predicate at least into a particular. Because the subject explicitly resists all conceptual characterization it is not to be affected by the change in the activity of judging.

This change in the content of the judgement requires a change in its form. The relation between subject and predicate is no longer a simple conjunction. Rather, one is immediate while the other is mediated. This contrast implies a negative contrast: the copula "is" becomes "is not" and the appropriate form is a *negative judgement* "S is not P." This form expresses the content: the individual is particular.

This result can be symbolized by using a bar over the symbol for a universal quality to indicate that it is determined or particular: $\bar{Q}a$.

The nature of this negation needs to be made explicit. It is not to mean that there is no relation at all—that the subject simply disappears when the predicate is thought and vice-versa. Nor is it to deny the copula; for a conjunction is to be expressed. The individual subject remains the solid foundation from which the predicate is abstracted, and the relation is still one of inherence. Rather in the *negative judgement* the inhering relation reflects not simply the abstract process of generalizing but something more determinate. And this negative determination affects all aspects of the judgement: subject, predicate and conjunction. It matters not, then, whether the "not" is independent or is referred to the predicate. If the individual is not universal, then it is equally non-universal or particular.[4]

Even when understanding tries to isolate the moment of pure negativity in the *negative judgement* it cannot avoid this result. In this case the negation would not determine the universal predicate and make it particular but would express the fact that the subject, since it is not the universal, is left completely undetermined and indeterminate by the judgement. It could be anything, other than the indicated quality. The fact that a judgement is made, however, indicates that something is to be predicated of the individual subject. Therefore the abstract isolation is not maintained: to give content to the indeterminate predicate, thought either refers to some intuitive content that is not thought (and is therefore not a universal), or it finds itself passing over from the indicated predicate that is to be negated to some other.

The most general terms for that which lacks all determination are pure *being* and pure *nothing*. The latter alone includes the sense of being *not* universal. But we have already seen that thought cannot isolate it as a pure concept. It passes over to *being* in a process of *becoming*. In other words, a thought "not" inevitably introduces a transition to something positive: a *negative judgement* is expressed. Because a relating, and therefore universalizing, transition is united with a moment of determinate differentiation, the act itself is *particular*—a determinate universal.

2. Dialectic makes explicit what is implicit in understanding's precision. *Negative judgement* expresses a relation of inherence. Even though it contrasts the predicate (as concept) to the subject (as individual), it maintains the inhering relation because the predicate has been abstracted from the subject.

Were the determining negation to deny absolutely the validity of the predicate, there would be nothing left to inhere. What is negated is the predicate's specific content—this particular determination abstracted by thought. Quite apart from the negative limitation of the "not," then, the predicate can no longer be thought as a pure universal. It has a specific content contrasted with other content; it is related as one particular to others, as species of the same genus. In a *negative judgement,* even though the specified predicate does not inhere in the subject it appears as if another one that belongs to the same genus does.

The result of this dialectic is, as always, paradoxical. For now there is introduced a second negation. The overall relation is negative, to be sure, but in addition the predicate is independently determinate and thus thought negatively. Understanding left us with two forms for *negative judgement* "The individual is not universal" and "The individual is particular." Now, however, these are combined into one: "The individual is not particular."

3. Speculative reason now reflects on the dialectical relation that has developed. A double determination has been introduced: the predicate is a determinate particular, and this particular predicate does not inhere in the subject. The form, however, has only one negation.

Considered more closely, the double negation implies that what is predicated of the individual subject is neither an abstract universal, nor the particular universal mentioned in the predicate, but instead the individuality that inherently qualifies the subject. This implied reference of the predicate would produce the tautology: "The individual is individual." Hence, the *negative judgement* "The individual is not particular," is not a primary negation (the simple particularization of the predicate), but rather a self-referential negation, isolating the positive individual.

A similar tautology results if we take the alternative interpretation of the relation of inherence: "The concrete individual, as an integrating universal, is not the particular abstracted determination." By denying the abstractness of the particular term, the predicate implicitly refers to the integration of the subject: "Integrating universality is universality as integrated."

Positive judgement appeared to result in a tautology for external reflection, but this was rejected because it did not correspond to the determinate character of the terms involved. In *negative judgement,* however, the only positive content is the same tautology, now recognized to be intrinsic.

In the sentence "the individual is not particular," however, the copula need not refer to the particularizing determination of conceptual thought as it did in *negative judgement.* Rather than having the "not" determine the predicate to transform it into an individual, it can indicate an independent negative that completely denies the inhering relation. What is then negated is not simply the particular predicate as one species among many, but its positive universal genus as well. Once this operation has been self-referentially individuated by speculative reason, we have a new category: *infinite judgement.*[5]

The difference between the two negations is represented symbolically by $\sim \bar{Q}a$: $\bar{Q}$ implies that the generic universality implicit in the particular Q remains; $\sim$ denies all relating universality.

Infinite judgement: Because the simple coupling of subject and predicate in the *positive judgement* does not do justice to their difference its form is inadequate to its content—the implicit criteria. Therefore it is not inherently true.[6] On the other hand, because the negation of *negative judgement* cannot maintain the difference in content between subject and predicate it is equally untrue. While the *negative judgement* was proposed to counteract the inadequacy of the positive, the *infinite judgement* is to express the valid perspective of the negative. In fact, however, the act of judging itself falls apart.

In the first place, the infinite judgement can be taken as a negative: "The individual is not particular" or "The individual is not non-universal." Since the two negations are explicitly distinguished so that the "not" does not simply determine the "non", the infinite judgement expresses the fact that there is no relation at all between subject and predicate.[7] But if there is no relation at all, the act of judging itself is absurd since it is supposed to couple the two on the basis of something inherent to the abstraction process. To couple them so as to indicate a lack of relation may produce a correct expression, but one that is so insipid that it abandons the rationale for judging altogether.

If, in the second place, the positive intent of the infinite judgement is considered, the result is no better. To obtain a positive, the second negation must negate the negative determination of the particular predicate, and this produces a tautology: either "the individual is individual" or "the universal is universal." While both express a relation between subject and predicate, they contain no differentiation. Therefore once again the act of judging collapses, and the statement is an insipid combination of words.

This dialectic shows that *infinite judgement,* which was designed to get at the truth of the act of judging in such a way that it includes both the distinction and the relation, fails to do so. Either it distinguishes and cannot relate; or it relates and cannot distinguish. In either case the act of judging becomes totally irrelevant.

Speculative reason reflects on this paradox.[8] While the dialectic appeared to destroy the act of judging, it did so in two contrary ways. On the one hand judgement collapsed into an absolute identity; on the other it broke apart into an absolute difference. But both moves were performed by the same reasoning dialectic and can therefore be combined in a synthesis. This synthesis requires that what establishes the identity be distinguished from what establishes the difference. They are diverse acts of the same intellectual process. In judgement, however, the two are not of equal value. Because it starts from the original partition in conceptual thought between the pure individual and the abstract universal, its task is to introduce a relation between them. What is essential to a *judgement* is this act of relating, or identity.

This self-referential consideration changes the way in which the terms of the judgement are to be considered. They are no longer simply present immediately in intelligence. They are more precisely defined.

We take the predicate first. It is no longer a simple concept, abstracted from all individuality. In that form it was thought as a pure quality, a determination that could be considered simply in itself. Now, however, it is thought as that which is inherently reflected in the subject, even though it can be distinguished from it. In this way the positive moment of the dialectical paradox acquires its pre-eminence over the negative. The predicate, therefore, is *essential* to the subject.[9]

In the previous part we saw that what is *essential* is not transitory and changing like *a being* or a *qualifying determination* but persists through the reflective process. Because it can be common to a number of individual moments, it brings them together into an essential relation. As a *determination of reflection* rather than a simple *quality* the predicate defines how a number of individual properties can be identified under a single term.

What is essential in the predicate, then, is common to a number of different changing qualities. Using the ampersand to symbolize any positive conjunction, we can represent this by $Q \& \bar{Q}$ which we can use to define the symbol C (for category).[10]

If the predicate is the essential characteristic, the subject is no longer thought as simply an abstract individual, isolated from all conceptual reference—a being distinguished from any predicated quality that might inhere in it. Reflection has now made clear that it is both identical with, and different from, its predicate. Since for the purposes of judgement its identity with the predicate is what is essential, any difference is inessential. The individual subject, then, is the concrete integration of the essential and the inessential. Because this consideration of speculative reason is external, and does not follow from the logical development so far, it will become explicit only as we proceed. All that can be expressed at this point is that the subject, as individual, is not a being, independent of its quality, but a *this,* referred to as an instance by the same reflective act that determines the essence, and indicated by a simple act of pointing.[11]

These refinements in the nature of subject and predicate require a change in the copula. For the coupling is no longer founded on the process of abstracting from the individuality of the subject, independent of all thought, but on the persisting essential characteristic expressed in the predicate. In this coupling, then, the subject is not thought as primary, with the qualifying predicate inhering in it. Rather the reflectively determined predicate grounds the relation, and the subject is indicated only because it is essentially qualified by the predicate. In other words the subject is subsumed under the predicate.

With this change in the expressed relation speculative reason indicates a category of judgement that includes the specific results of the preceding dialectic. As no longer grounded by the simple transition of the abstraction process, but by the reflective determination of what is essential, this type of judgement can be called a *judgement of reflecting.*

Judgements of Reflecting

Singular judgement. Since the predicate as essential is common (and hence universal), while the subject remains an individual, this judgement resurrects the structure "The individual is universal"—this time more precisely defined as "This is an essential universal."

The change in relation requires a change in symbolism for the copula. Simple juxtaposition will not suffice. By introducing an " ε " between subject symbol and predicate symbol to indicate essential relation, and by moving the predicate to the end of the expression (since it is the ground of the assertion), the judgement can be represented by aε C.[12].

Dialectic points out that the subject, insofar as it is only an indicated "this," is quite distinct from the universal predicate. Even though its individuality stands out against this essential characteristic, the difference is not expressed by the straightforward positive copula. Speculative reason reflects on this dialectical relation between the implicit difference and the judgement form. Since what is different is inessential to the judgement, it can refer neither to the predicate nor to the copula, but only to the subject. This can be expressed by "Not this is essentially universal," (and symbolized by ā̄ε C).

Such a negation does not dissolve the subject completely, else no judgement would remain. It only cancels that in the subject which distinguishes it from the universal—its pure individuality: "This, insofar as it is not purely individual, is essentially universal." The subject of the reflective judgement is now no longer simply indicated by a referential act; because its radical individuality has been conceptually cancelled, the subject is determined by reflection to be indeterminate.

This new operation needs to be indicated by a new abstract category. A deliberate indeterminacy, which is differentiated from the essentially determined universal, is particular. By taking *singular judgement* together with its implications, then, speculative reason has produced a *particular judgement:* "A particular is the essential universal."

Particular judgement: Because in a particular judgement what is essential to the subject is not its individuality, the act of reference is no longer restricted to this singular entity; it could apply to others as well. This extension in the range of the subject, however, does not have any determinate limits. On the basis of the essential predicate, reflection can indicate an appropriate subject; but it is unable to specify what, if anything, would constitute an appropriate difference between subject and predicate, since any such difference is inessential. We have, then, an act of reference that is indeterminate, and expressed by the pronouns "some" and "several."[13] The only thing determinate is that there is an essential act of reference.

To express the indeterminacy of the subject, symbolic logic does not use the symbol for "not-this": ā, but rather a variable defined as indeterminate: x. If the subject were left absolutely variable, however, the judgement would dissolve into an empty form, expressing no relation at all. Therefore some indication of the limiting act of reference is necessary even though, as implicit, it cannot be included in the statement form itself. By placing the variable in parentheses prior to the form we can indicate that it is in some way determinate. Further, the fact that the act of reference is derived from the essential concept, but is not specifically limited by it can be symbolized by reversing the letter E prior to the variable in parentheses. We thus derive the form: $(\exists x)\, x\ \varepsilon$ C. "Some are the essential universal."

We can now interpret the symbols more precisely. C does not signify a quality inhering in the subject, else the act of judgement could not move away from *this* individual. On the other hand, it does not signify a relation between the various individuals indicated in the subject, since that relation is essentially indeterminate. It signifies simply a universal under which these individuals are subsumed, and the relation is constituted simply by the act of reference or denotation. This has two implications: The predicate is thought as a *class;* and the essential relation symbolized by " ε " is *membership.* "$x\ \varepsilon$ C" means x is a member of class C.

Dialectical thought makes clear that *particular judgement* combines both forms of the *judgement of a being:* the *positive* and the *negative.* The positive is explicit in the judgement form; the negative is implicit in the "some", for it denies the subsumption of the individuality of any indicated individual under the predicate. The individuals indicated, then, are *not* to be considered insofar as they have any characteristics other than the essential one. But because the act of reference is indeterminate, it cannot discriminate between what characteristics are to be included and what not. Even though the *positive statement* "some are essentially universal" implicitly presupposes the *negative judgement* "some (*as individuals*) are not essentially universal," this limitation is not expressed in the subject "some." There is a contradiction between what is intended and what is explicitly stated.

If instead of this ambiguity in the act of reference we consider it insofar as it determinately particularizes, we have the same result. The limitation in its range implies the possibility of going beyond to something else—to some other individuals for whom the predicate is not the essential characteristic. Once again the result is "Some are not the essentially universal," (or($\exists x$)$x \, \varepsilon \, \bar{C}$).[14] This dialectical conclusion raises a problem, for the *particular judgement* does not in fact refer to individuals that are not members of the predicate class. Simply taken as a class the predicate is a universal, not a particular range of individuals related negatively to another range of individuals.

Speculative reason must bring together the two statements: the explicit form: "Some particulars are the essential universal"; and the implicit: "Some particulars are not the essential universal." The two, however, cannot be simply synthesized into a single particular sentence. To say that "Some particulars are and are not the essential universal" would be self-contradictory. The second "some" needs to be distinguished from the first: "Some other particulars are not the essential universal." This involves two negatives, one cancelling the subject, the other cancelling the predicate. The synthesis would then be: "Some and some others are and are not the predicate." Two things happen in this synthesis. In the first place the original predicate is no longer a simple universal, but a particular contrasted with its opposite. As such it refers to another universal that includes both. The original class simply becomes incorporated into one more comprehensive. In the second place the subject is no longer indicated by an indefinite act of reference. It is not simply *some* that are referred to but *others* as well. Thought moves beyond the indefinite particularity of the original subject to include its contrary. It thereby determines the whole range of reference. It is no longer simply *some*, but *not some*, or *all*.

The universality of this *all* is not a conceptual universality—a genus. Rather it indicates the fact that the act of reference is completely specified. "All those individuals referred to are the essential universal." With this we move beyond a *particular judgement* to a *universal judgement*.

This change in the meaning of the subject and predicate requires changes in the interpretation of the symbols. The predicate becomes a universal class that can specify its membership, not simply a category that incorporates several qualities. In the subject the act of referring becomes determinate; it specifies what individuals are to be included in the subject, not only those actually indicated but also those that would be. To signify the latter we could use ($\exists x$) and combine it with ($\bar{\exists} x$) to indicate the universality intended: ($\exists x \, \& \, \bar{\exists} x$). To simplify we will use (ϕx) for this complex. Alternatively all the individuals that make up a class could be named: [a, b, c, . . . n]. Either of the resulting statements, (ϕx) $x \ \varepsilon$ C, or [a, b, c, . . . n) $x \ \varepsilon$ C can define C as a denoted set.

Universal judgement: The diversity inherent in the judgement of reflection becomes fully explicit in the *universal judgement.* The universal predicate takes its members insofar as they are similar. Their dissimilarity is expressed by the multiple individuals collected in the subject. The comparing relation is expressed in the act of judging.

To clarify the change, understanding focusses its attention on the subject. The "all" does not refer to the same conceptual universality as the predicate, for that would simply collapse the sentence into a bare tautology. It is explicitly diverse, representing a number of different individual acts of reference that have been related by an external act of comparing reflection. Because there is nothing in this act that would suggest comprehensive totality, "all" simply refers to *not some* as a complete set of individuals. And that set is determined by a rule established by external reflection.

Dialectical reflection, however, shows that such a definition of "all" does not do justice to the universality intended. "Not some" does not refer to a distinct group, but to everything that is indicated by the predicate class—a bare tautology. Yet a number actually pointed out, no matter how many, never includes all that is intended by the class term. Hence the "all" in this judgement is simply what ought to be indicated by the external rule; but an *ought* is essentially limited and leads only to an infinite regress, never completed. Thus the method of indicating never exhausts all the individuals subsumed under the predicate class, but is to be repeated ad infinitum. It "rests on the tacit agreement that if only no contrary instance can be addressed, the plurality of cases shall count as allness."[16] Something is taken as all when it is not in fact all.

There remains a discrepancy between what is intended in the *universal judgement* and what is actually expressed by it. What is expressed is the specific reference to the indicated individuals. What is intended or presupposed is a complete universal, the exhaustive enumeration of all members of the class. The presupposition, however, is precisely that definition of the class as a denotative universal which is to be the function of the judgement as a whole. In other words when the presupposition in the subject is made explicit, the distinction between subject and predicate collapses. Since *universal judgement* is supposed to maintain this distinction even in the relation, speculative reason must reflect on what specifically has changed in the subject and in the predicate. Only then can it make explicit what characterizes the dialectical discrepancies.

In the whole discussion of the judgement of reflection it is the subject that has been progressively modified in its definition. Originally one individual it has become an exhaustively specified set of individuals. This expansion took place because of what was already implicit in the *singular judgement*. There the subject was not taken as a pure individual, absolutely isolated from all thought, in which a quality inhered. That is the perspective of *judgements of a being*. Rather the subject is indicated in light of its essential predicate. It is constituted as subject not in itself but by the act of judging. This became explicit when *particular judgement* abstracted the subject from all determinate individuality, and when *universal judgement* determined its subject by means of the implicit "ought" of the act of reference, i.e., the rule followed by external reflection.

This determination of the subject, however, is an operation of comprehensive thought. Such an act contains within itself the criteria by which those characteristics that are appropriate can be distinguished from those that are not. On this basis it can specify what individuals are in fact members of the predicated class. In other words the rule by which the subject is denoted is an operation of particularizing. This type of particular is not a quality simply abstracted from the individuals, but a species that characterizes itself in the process of differentiating its terms. It is not something multiple, but single. "Instead of *all men,* it is to be expressed by the simple substantive *man.*"[17]

This change in the subject affects the status of the predicate. The latter no longer simply inheres qualitatively in an indicated individual as something abstracted from it, as in the *judgements of a being*; rather the subject specifies the individuals that are to be included within its comprehensive universality. Nor is the subject simply subsumed under a denotative class as in the *judgements of reflection.* For the self-specification of the subject justifies the predication of the general term. If the subject is a species, then the predicate becomes its universal genus.

Having rendered determinate the change in character of the two terms, speculative reason can make explicit the transformation in the relation or copula. Insofar as both subject and predicate signify conceptual operations, they have surrendered the absolute difference between pure reference and abstract concept. Yet they operate in opposite ways. With regard to the subject, thought specifies how its particulars may be determined; the procedure earlier called denotation has been self-reflexively recognized as a particular operation of thought distinct from the universalizing process of abstraction. These two processes are opposed to each other: one is determinate, the other is comprehensive; one is differentiating, the other is identifying. They are, however, brought together in one judging act because the particularizing activity of the subject specifies what is to be comprehended in the predicate. Because this generic predicate follows from the criteria specified in the subject, the act of judging is not an external addition, but renders explicit what is implicit in its own terms. It is to this extent necessary.[18] The next set of judgements to be considered, then, can be called *judgements of necessary relation*.

Judgements of Relating Necessarily

Categorical judgement: The subject of this new type of judgement is no longer qualified by an indication of quantity. *This, some* and *all* are adequate when referring individuals to an essential characteristic or class, but not for a particular operation that specifies the criteria for determining its individual terms. In ordinary language the new subject is frequently expressed by a singular noun with a definite article: "The cow is an animal." "The number three is odd."

The relation signified by such a judgement is one in which the self-specifying subject, which contains the criteria for its own operation, determines what is to be coupled with the predicated genus: "The particular is universal."

In the move to categorical judgement there has simply been a change in what is coupled in the universal judgement. There an indefinite variable, determined by ϕ, is coupled with an abstract class by the symbol $\varepsilon{:}x\varepsilon C$. Now, however, speculative reason has shown that the coupling in fact is between the ϕ and the C. Since the denotative reference has not disappeared, these two terms continue to include an inherent act of reference, signified by x.

The two are not simply to be identified but are equally to be differentiated. This type of coupling can be symbolized by a dot "." that is placed between them. Thus the judgement form would be: $\phi x.x\varepsilon C$. To the extent that both subject and predicate now signify intellectual operations there is no need to use qualitatively contrasting symbols. The pair p and q serves to identify them as of the same order, yet to differentiate them in content. The simplest form of the categorical judgement, then is p.q. (An alternative symbolism would retain ϕ and C and indicate that they intersect by $X{:}\phi X C$.)

Dialectic shows that the form of this judgement is ambiguous and does not adequately express the nature of the relationship. The contingent judgement "The rose is red" has the same form as the necessary judgement "The rose is a plant." This common structure fails to indicate the difference in the act of judging. In the former the term "rose" refers to an individual in which a quality inheres. In the latter it signifies a species that is particularized in individuals. The necessary relation that couples this particularizing species to the predicated genus is only implicit, however, because the form is ambiguous.

The same contingency follows from the introduced symbol ".". It indicates simply a conjunction of two distinct terms. Although it rules out both inherence and subsumption because of its distinct form it does not indicate any positive base of relation. Nor does it make clear that the x indicated in the subject ϕx has the same range as the x indicated in the predicate $x \varepsilon C$.[19]

Speculative reason recognizes that the form of the judgement is to indicate the necessary relation implicit in the content. In that relation the two terms, subject and predicate, are not simply conjoined to each other, but are explicitly opposed as particular to universal. The specifying differentiation of the species does not simply intersect with the comprehensive genus. As self-specifying it is complete in itself. But on the other hand, as comprehensive, the genus is also complete in itself. The subject and predicate, then, are no longer incomplete terms or moments requiring the coupling in a judgement to be self-sufficient. They are opposed to each other in such a way that each is in some measure complete in itself; they are clauses.[20]

That change, however, does not capture all that was lacking, for the one as self-specifying is to be contrasted to the other as comprehensive. Indeed it is this contrast in the operations signified that is to establish their relation. The subject specifies itself as that which would be comprehended in the predicate; it is the condition that grounds their being coupled in a single judgement. The conditioning relation thus individuated by speculative reason can be signified by the category of *hypothetical judgement:* If p then q.

Although the simple categorical judgement in symbolic logic expresses the conjunction of p and q, or of ϕx and $x \varepsilon C$, it cannot express any necessary relation between them. The copula "." is ambiguous.

Because it relates differentiated conceptual terms it simply states that variable x in ϕx *may* be the same as the x in $x \varepsilon C$. But the judgement was to express the necessary relation between differentiating denotation and identifying class. In other words, the two were not simply to intersect, but the former was to be included in the latter such that if the former is specified, then the latter cannot fail to be specified.

If a class is not exhaustively specified denotatively, then there is no conceptual relation to be expressed between any individuals actually indicated and the class term. Thus we can introduce here the symbol "$\sim$" defined earlier under *infinite judgement*. Speculative reason has indicated an operation not yet signified: the relation in which the conjunction of the presence of the subject p with the absence of q is ruled out. The absence of q is $\sim$q; the conjunction to be excluded is p.$\sim$q and the total judgement is $\sim$(p.$\sim$q). This can be indicated by a single coupla: a U placed on its side to signify the way in which the subject specifies the comprehensive universality of the predicate: p⊃q. In the alternate symbolism of the algebra of classes this could be indicated as ϕ<C: ϕ is a sub-class of C.

In this move to a hypothetical judgement a change has been introduced into the symbolic reference of p and q. The unspecified x in each is no longer a significant component of the judgement. What is important is the coupling relation; it is a matter of indifference whether both are specified in the same way or not.[21]

Hypothetical judgement: Understanding individuates what is specifically stated in this judgement: that the relation is necessary and not contingent. In this regard the terms related are inessential. What is explicitly expressed is not what they are in themselves but how they are coupled. Therefore the act of judging does not pay attention to the immediate character or content of the two clauses. Any content at all will do as long as the relation holds. Since the relation is explicitly universal, the *hypothetical judgement* expresses nothing about the determinate terms: whether they are actual or merely possible, whether they are individuals, particulars or universals, whether they are particularizing species or comprehensive genera.

Because it focuses on the act of relating, the *hypothetical judgement* is able to articulate the necessity inherent in the earlier logical discussions. It can express a transition in which something finite changes into something else, and it can show what reflection determines to be essential. In the discussion of *ground* we have already seen its antecedents: *ground* and *conse-*

quent, condition and *conditioned.* In later logical development it was presented objectively as *cause* and *effect.*

But, as Hume showed dialectically, the fact that a *hypothetical judgement* individuates only the relation has as consequence its failure to specify what it is in the antecedent that generates the consequent. It does not specify which other will follow necessarily; it introduces instead a general term: "something else" or "a phenomenon." Because it thus expresses only the relation and says nothing at all about the determinate content, it is an indeterminate form. Although a necessary relation is expressed, the conditions of this necessity are ignored.

The judgement form that was to express a necessary relation between the two parts of a judgement, then, turns out to be opposed to a content that is indifferent to any such necessity. What was intended in the judging act was that the necessity of the relation be expressed. What in fact occurs is that the expression abstracts from any conditioning characteristic of the terms. Thus their character as self-specifying particular and comprehensive genus has disappeared. Because *hypothetical judgement* cannot express this inherently self-specifying content it fails to articulate what was intended.

Speculative reason, realizing that the form needs to express the intention, brings the two together and reflects on what would be necessary for a judgement to integrate the two. A necessary relation is not simply between *ground* and *consequent.* Rather it is a *grounding relation* in which a genus specifies itself. In the act of specifying it drives a wedge between its various determinate species so that they become disjoined one from another. At the same time, however, the fact that they are intrinsically comprehended within the universal cannot be ignored. Both the differentiation implicit in categorical judgements and the identification implicit in hypothetical need to be conjoined in a single expression. In one operation the two moments need to be opposed to each other and yet identified. This operation is signified by the category of *disjunctive judgement.*

A wedge not only symbolizes the fact that the two terms are divided. Its very form "v" has two lines that are united at one end and divided at the other. Therefore it can be used to symbolize disjunction: p v q. Its traditional interpretation in symbolic logic as "and/or" has recognized its double sense, both distinguishing and relating. In the alternate algebra of classes this can be signified by $\phi + C$.

We do not come directly to this judgement form, however. The *hypothetical judgement* is inadequate because it is possible that neither antecedent nor consequent be actual. Because that possibility is now to be excluded, $\sim(\sim p.\sim q)$ is conjoined to $\sim(p.\sim q)$. To symbolize the new relation we use the wedge: $pvq = df.\sim(\sim p.\sim q)$. We have the following series of transformations:

1. $\sim(p.\sim q).\sim(\sim p.\sim q)$ Hypothesis
2. $(\bar{p}vq).(pvq)$ Definition "v"

(The symbol $\bar{p}$ uses the symbol of neaqtion that appeared under *negative judgement*. It indicates that any negative characteristic inherent in p is cancelled, although its positive content is maintained. It must be used since no rule for double negation has yet been defined.)

3. $q(\bar{p}vp)$ Distribution.

(Under the judgement of reflection we have already recognized that what is common to several individual particulars can be distinguished from them as the class of which they are members. Since q represents the specifying relation between a class and its members, the complex form $(x\varepsilon C)$ is unnecessary and the parenthesis simply serves to indicate the range of members of the class).

Judgement form 3 thus becomes the basis for subsequent discussion.[22]

Disjunctive judgements. In *disjunctive judgement,* the form articulates explicitly the relation between the self-specifying universal and its specified particulars: "The universal is either one particular or the other."[23] On the one hand this expression is not like the *hypothetical,* ignoring the actuality of its terms. On the other hand, it is not like the *categorical* because the subject specifies itself not in relation to an abstract genus, but in relation to the either/or of the predicate.

Since the either/or does not refer only to one particular, but to the totality of particulars that are included in the self-specifying universal, subject and predicate have the same range, content and universality. They are distinguished simply by the fact that one is the universal as genus and the other is the sum of its particulars. These conceptual differences are introduced into the substantive identity that is expressed in the coupling of subject and predicate through a simple conjunction; the diversity of form simply makes explicit the implicit content. From this perspective, the more comprehensive term is the predicate as the totality of the particulars, in contrast to the simple universality of the subject.

This definition becomes the object of dialectical consideration. The primary change from the categorical judgement is found in the predicate, because it refers not to a single concept, but rather to the relation among several. On the one hand this relation positively includes all of them in one genus: "The universal subject is *as much* one particular *as* the other." This "as well as" expresses the fact that the particulars are not arbitrarily associated but have a common essential structure.[24] On the other hand, the particulars are not included in each other. Therefore the relation equally involves a negative exclusion: "The universal subject is *either* one particular *or* the other." This differentiation is the determining characteristic of the relation, specifying the particulars as particulars and not as qualities or classes.[25]

This double structure of the disjunctive "or" defines the criteria for its valid use. On the one hand it implies an integrating identification of its terms, on the other a determining differentiation of one from the other. The pure form of the *disjunctive judgement,* however, can be applied to things that include one of these relations without the other—empirical species, for example, or abstracted synonymous concepts. Because the formal structure does not articulate its inherent criteria, it does not adequately represent the necessary combination of both moments.

If we turn to the subject of the disjunctive judgement, we find that it can also change in its reference. It is not simply to be a self-determining universal concept, containing the criteria for its specification, but it is also to distinguish and relate the predicated particulars. It is therefore to be the next proximate genus. Just as the form of the predicate allows an application to particulars not specifically intended by the relation of disjunction, however, so the form of the subject allows a use abstracted from this proximate relation; it need only be more universal than the predicated particulars. This means that the relation between subject and predicate may be determined not necessarily but contingently. It is a matter of chance whether the universal subject proposed is in fact that genus that specifies these particulars. Equally it is a matter of chance whether the particulars named completely exhaust the disjunctive relation. This is the same contingency that bedevils *categorical judgement,* for *disjunction,* retains the categorical form in asserting the relation between subject and predicate.

Dialectic shows, then, that *disjunctive judgement,* no less than the others, fails to render explicit in its form the criteria that specify its application. The simple "or" of the predicate does not articulate the essential integration of *as well as* and *either-or*. The categorical form "S is P" fails to show how the disjunction in the predicate is essentially integrated with the subject. This discrepancy initiates the move to speculative reason.

Subject and predicate are essentially the same. That identity is the basis of the necessary relation to be expressed in the judgement but not found in the categorical form. To this extent the hypothetical form would be more adequate, even though it says nothing explicit about its terms.

The identity intended in the *disjunctive judgement,* however, is not independent of its terms. The act of judging specifies its constituents—opposing the subject as simple self-determining universal to the predicate as the totality of its determinations. It is thereby a dynamic relation, both integrating into a common structure and distinguishing contrasting moments. This dynamic structure we met earlier when considering the process of conceiving: the universal of conceptual thought is self-determining and hence particularized. There, however, the distinction between universal and particular was internal to a single intellectual operation, at one and the same time universal and particular. In the context of judgement, however, the particulars have been distinguished as other than, and independent of, the universal. Nevertheless the dynamic of comprehensive intelligence remains the ground that underlies the *disjunctive judgement* and that mediates the coupling of subject and predicate. In the earlier stage it considered only its own immediate process; now it brings together the sharply distinguished categories of universal and particular.

In judging disjunctively, a valid generic universal specifies its own particulars, and these particulars are considered only insofar as they are determinately distinguished by the universal. Any other contingent characteristics would be irrelevant.[26]

These speculative considerations transform the relation expressed in the judgement. It is no longer a simple categorical conjunction in which the identity of the subject is opposed to the difference of the predicate. Rather the identity generates the difference; and the difference articulates the identity. It is a self-determining process—one that identifies by differentiating and distinguishes by identifying. The opposition does not result from an independent intellectual operation that applies external criteria, but is intrinsic to the act of judging itself.

We have already encountered this dynamic integration of *as well as* and *either-or* in disjunction. There, however, it was simply a component of the predicate; now it has become the copula—the relation between subject and predicate. The two terms are both integrated into a comprehensive universality and determinately opposed to each other. This coupling is also a universal; but unlike the earlier categories distinguished by conceptual thought (even those that specify their own criteria), it does not require an independent operation of intelligence to be applied. It is a self-determining process. The previous universals, as abstracted individual concepts, were purely subjective; this dynamic relation is objective, for it is explicitly an activity that individuates itself. As functionally operative in both subject and predicate as well as in their coupling it integrates what was previously distinguished.

This total dynamic is what is to be expressed in the copula of judgement. Now no longer simply expressed, however, it is explicitly asserted. When one says: "Either the universal or its particular determinations," one does not simply say that the relation would hold if the terms were actual. Nor does one say that the terms and the relation are both actual but not necessarily related to each other. Rather one says that the relation holds in such a way that it determines the status of the terms, and they constitute the relation. The expression comprehends the operation by which it is expressed. When speculative reason makes this reference explicit it no longer expresses simply a *judgement of necessary relation,* but rather a *judgement of comprehensive conceptual thought.*[27]

In the speculative synthesis the two implicit criteria of a *disjunctive judgement* are explicitly expressed. The first states that the disjunction in the predicate is not simply between diverse predicates $(p \& \bar{p})$ in which the essential relation is what is common. Rather what is essential is their explicit difference—that one excludes the other as the exhaustive specification of their proximate genus. This is expressed in the symbol $(p \vee \sim p)$. The second presupposition is that the subject is not simply conjoined with the predicate, but entails or determines it: $q \supset (p \vee \sim p)$. This expression leads to the following transformation.

1. $q \supset (p \vee \sim p)$ Hypothesis
2. $q \supset \sim (\sim p . \sim \sim p)$ Definition "v"
3. $\sim (\sim q . \sim (\sim p . \sim \sim p))$ Definition " $\supset$ "
4. $q \vee (\sim p . \sim \sim p)$ Definition "v"

Since "$\sim$" symbolizes absolute exclusion the predicate would state not only that p is excluded but also that the exclusion of p is also excluded. This mutual exclusion destroys their conjunction. As a contradiction it cannot be thought. This does not, however, destroy the total disjunctive judgement for "v" says that simply one or the other holds. Since the predicate is impossible, then q must be actual in itself. For the first time thought isolates a universal from a judgement form. The judged relation, then, simply expresses the fact that q is self-contained; it is the act of assertion. That is to say, a self-contained universal is coupled with its inherent reality.[28] This can be symbolized by $\vdash q$.

Judgements of Conceiving

When the *disjunctive judgement* is explicitly integrated with its implicit presuppositions it produces a comprehensive structure of internal relation. Therefore an external act of judging is not necessary to relate one term to the other. The relating structure of universality expresses itself. But as an individual judgement it is limited by the specific relation expressed. It contains no reference to a wider context.

Dialectic, however, does not discover the single judgement to be isolated. For it passes over to considering the context to see whether in its specific form the judgement conforms to that context. There remains, then, one further set of judgements to be considered. In this, the self-contained structure of internal relation is the subject; and the predicate indicates how it is integrated with its comprehensive setting. Such a judgement is essentially evaluative; it says that the complex of relations is "good, bad, true, beautiful, correct, etc."[29]

These predicates indicate how the relations expressed in the subject are themselves related to that which is external to the subject. In other words, the subject provides the criterion for its own assessment. If the relations expressed contradict the relations in fact operative in the comprehensive context, it is evaluated negatively. If on the other hand the two are compatible, it is evaluated positively.

We have moved beyond isolated acts of judging. From this new perspective, the earlier judgements are shown to be subjective; they are forms used to express a relation but assert nothing. The context alone gives to these forms objective validity.

To be sure, we have seen that the forms contain implicitly the criteria for their objective use. But these define only schematic possibilities, not specific actualities. Any reference to the latter has been explicitly excluded, leaving only a formal logic.

Formal logic itself, however, does not rest content with pure forms. It refers to something external in saying that an asserted proposition is true; or to the distinction between an assertion ($\vdash p$) and that which is simply a form (p). Both references follow from the preceding discussion. With the recognition that $\sim$p and $\sim\sim$p are incompatible, speculative reason discovered that positing p would exclude its opposite. This is what would be expressed in asserting that p is true.[30] Similarly the operation of assertion resulted when the implications of the *disjunctive judgement* were made explicit. For what remained was a q that was self-contained. No longer is a relation expressed between a p and a q. q stands on its own; it simply is. This is pure assertion.

Assertoric judgement: The judgement of conceptual thought simply is. The act of judging, having comprehended the concrete network of relations expressed in the subject, immediately applies an evaluative predicate. The latter asserts whether the subject corresponds to the actuality to which it refers (true/false, correct/incorrect); whether its determinate characteristics are consistent with its comprehensive design (beautiful/ugly, good/bad); or the way in which its specific interaction with its environment constitutes what is particularly intended (good/evil, right/wrong). It can be expressed in the statement: "This self-specifying individual is thus."[31]

Dialectic looks more closely at this definition. On the one hand, the move to this type of judgement indicates that the subject is not absolutely independent and self-contained. Although expressing a comprehensive network of relations, and therefore universal, it is yet incomplete, for it *ought* to be something it may not in fact be; it refers to an independent state of affairs. A new type of judgement is required because the subject does not self-referentially evaluate its relation to the individual content to which it refers. On the other hand this limitation also distinguishes it as something individual. A subject is individual not simply because it is only immediately present in thought and no mediating justification is provided, but also because the self-specifying act of its assertion can be distinguished from the comprehensive universality that it expresses. In other words, the integrating dynamic of the subject that specifies its constituent terms is to be considered not as a comprehensive universal but as a concrete individual. It is this individuality that is evaluated in the predicate. In the *judgement of conceptual thought,* then, the expressed universality of the subject contradicts the specific individuality of the evaluative assertion. These two characteristics, although referred to the same subject, are simply coupled and not yet integrated into a comprehensive unity.

This leads, however, to a paradox. The judgement asserts a relation between an individual evaluation and its universal expression. But because the two are contradictory, they fall apart into a predicate and a subject.[32] Their coupling, however, is simply a subjective declaration, lacking justification.

But the intention of judgement is not to assert that the subject is good or false, ugly or right simply because of some arbitrary act of intelligence. The relation is supposed to be objective and universal.[33] What is intended in asserting is not expressed by an assertion.

This paradox becomes the object of speculative reflection. In making an *assertion,* the act of judging affirms a positive objective relation between the subject and its evaluation. But since this positive relation is not justified in the judgement itself, it is contingent on the agent that judges. This means that the evaluation could be the exact opposite. What one says is beautiful, another could call ugly; good from one standpoint appears evil from another; the simple assertion of a proposition does not guarantee its truth. This contradiction between the subjectivity of the act of asserting and the objectivity intended can be resolved only by changing the judgement form. To reflect the inherent ambiguity, its *assertoric* quality needs to be modified and made *problematic:* "It is possibly thus."

> The problematic judgement recognizes that the propositional form "p" can be as much true as false. This disjunctive relation suggests that truth and falsity are not mutually exhaustive, but that there is an evaluative context in which neither holds in isolation. This requires a. third value, distinct from p and $\sim$p: $\Diamond$ p. In this move the abstractness of judgement forms and expressions becomes explicit.

Problematic judgement: "In saying "p is problematic" the possibility is expressly entertained that the subject p can be evaluated negatively as well as positively. To this extent it compares with *particular* and *hypothetical judgements.*[34] In all three, the previous statement (the *assertoric,* the *singular* or the *categorical*) is recognized to be in some way purely subjective, the result of the contingent judging act. The implied content does not justify what is expressed. But the ambiguity of subjectivity becomes evident only in *problematic judgements* because the evaluative predicate explicitly asserts a relation between the individual subjective operation and its conceptual content. Therefore the discontinuity between the immediacy of the assertion and the expressed mediating relation cannot be ignored.

In evaluating this judgement form, dialectical thought first applies the problematic determination to the copula: "This concrete universal possibly is thus." Its ambiguity expresses the contradictory relation that holds between the subject and its predicate. The evaluative predicate comprehends in a single term the total relation between the individual state of affairs and its constituent moments. As embodying the evaluative norm it is universal and thus independent of any problematic considerations. The question, therefore, concerns whether it has been correctly coupled with this subject.

What in the subject could contradict the predicate? It cannot be its universal expression, for that is the pure concept, comprehensively incorporated in the predicate. Nor can it be its pure individuality (that to which it refers), for that is beyond doubt—as something immediately present and contrasted to thought. What is in question is the relation between its individuality and what is conceptually expressed in universal terms. The two are not integrated in the way the predicate says they are. They are simply conjoined in an arbitrary synthesis.

In the subject, its individuality is immediately coupled with its universal expression. This is what makes it concrete and allows the conjunction of the definite article (or demonstrative adjective) with conceptual adjectives and nouns in a definite description. What the problematic consideration makes explicit is the need for a third term that would justify conjoining the two. This third term would not be simply an object of reference, nor would it be what the subject specifically expresses. In neither case would the problem be raised. Rather it reflects the relation between the two: whether the individual is *constituted* in such a way that it embodies what is expressed.[35]

What is contingent about the subject is its particular constitution. A distinction has been introduced: on the one hand the use of the universal expression has to be justified with reference to this constitution; on the other hand, the individual is to be particularly identified by means of it. In contrast to pure reference, both operations are conceptual. One, however, expresses a comprehensive *universal* relation, the other may be arbitrary and *particular,* relevant only to this determinate situation.

Because reflection on the subject of this judgement has shown that the heart of the matter[36] is its internal discrimination into these diverse moments, it has been entertained only subjectively, even though it intended to be objective. If it were objective, the integration expressed would have maintained itself in the face of the negative dissolving pressure of dialectical reason.

Within a problematic judgement, then, the individual subject is thought in a double way: first as constituting a universal and objective integration; then as it actually is determined in its particularity. This separation of the *grounding relation* from its concrete *conditions* reproduces the structure of the *heart of the matter* and grounds the ambiguity of the evaluative predicate. An operation explicitly contradictory to the coupling dynamic of judging has appeared. The act of entertaining a possibility implies a fundamental partition—not between subject and predicate, but within the subject itself. Although essentially an *individual,* its *particularity* may contradict what it expresses *universally.* The three determinations of conceptual thought thus fall apart into radically distinct moments; the contradiction basic to the form of the *judgements of conceiving* has become central to its content. It is not simply that the objectivity implied by the assertion is contradicted by the subjectivity of the asserting act. Rather the subject may contradict itself.

Speculative reason considers this contradiction that has appeared in the subject of the judgement. The radical contrast between the universal constitution and the particular determination has made it subjective not only in the logical sense but also in the psychological. When the grounding relation that is to be the heart of the matter is opposed to the particular way it is conditioned, we have something subjective in the sense that it is present only in the subject thinking. The contingent way it is determined is subjective in the sense that it may pertain only to this individual subject and not to what is expressed in the comprehensive universal.[37] As we have already seen, it is characteristic of the *heart of the matter* that it refer to both moments—the *grounding relation* and the constituting *conditions.* If this distinction is not maintained, it will collapse once again into the simple *existence* of assertion. Yet it is precisely this distinction that makes the subject something subjective, only problematically related to its evaluative predicate.

Speculative reason has found that it must reverse the process of simple reflection as it developed in the doctrine of essence. It has moved from the assertoric assumption that the subject exists, and has broken it apart into the complex structure of the *heart of the matter,* which is only subjective and contingent.[38] The subject thus loses the immediate conjunction of immediate object of reference and universal expression that characterized it in the simple *assertion,* and which distinguished it from the more comprehensive perspective of the evaluative predicate. And it breaks apart into its conditions and a grounding relation. By individuating the conditioning determination, speculative reason has expressed it in a distinct term that contrasts both with the individuality referred to and with the universality expressed. With this the subject of the judgement becomes a complex thought, *constituted* out of distinct and determinate moments. The predicate in turn evaluates this specific *constitution*.[39]

Thus the problematic relation between subject and predicate itself becomes problematic. The subject makes explicit the determinate moments that are included in the comprehensive universal concept; the predicate simply expresses the essence of the relation. In other words, the justification of the predication is clearly established by the constitution of the subject, and the judgement is no longer in question. It is *apodictic*.

That p is possible means that p could be true as well as false. This is symbolized as $\Diamond p = p \& \sim p$. To say that the same thing could be true as well as false seems to call in question the definition of *assertion* that became explicit at the end of our discussion of *disjunctive judgement*. Therefore thought turns back to the complex of symbols that the symbol p was to simplify. The simple *positive judgement* ϕa will not suffice because its negation $\sim \phi a$ has been ruled out in the discussion of *infinite judgement*. The only alternative is to use a εC; that is $\Diamond a\varepsilon C = (a\varepsilon C) \& \sim(a\varepsilon C)$. What is in doubt, then, is whether a is essentially categorized under C or not. This can be resolved only by discerning how a is specified (that is ϕa) to see if it is such that ϕ is a subclass of C; that is, whether $\phi < C$. $\sim(\phi < C)$, then, would state that ϕ is not a subclass of C. We can now state that if ϕa and $(\phi < C)$ then $a\varepsilon C$; if ϕa and $\sim(\phi < C)$ then $\sim(a\varepsilon C)$. p, then, is to be elaborated into the form: $a(\phi a \& [\phi < C])\varepsilon C$.[40] In this form the problematic moment in the judgement $a\varepsilon C$ is isolated: it is not whether ϕa but whether $\phi < C$. In $\Diamond p$, then, p can be conjoined with $\sim p$ because the immediate operation ϕa is common to both, while the reflective operations $\phi < C$ and $\sim(\phi < C)$ are contrasted as true and false. The subjectivity of the problematic judgement lies in the fact that although ϕa is immediately known and $a\varepsilon C$ is asserted in the act of judgement, each is isolated from the other. They lack the mediating relation of "$<$". In this fully explicit form of p, however, it is no longer problematic that $a\varepsilon C$. It is absolutely necessary.

Apodictic judgement: In a *judgement clearly justified,* the subject is not left as a simple, immediate term. It includes both its immediate *conditions* and the *grounding relation* that connects it to its expressed essence. This combination provides the ground or justification for applying the essential predicate.[41]

At this point the judgement form fully expresses its intention. Subject and predicate correspond, since each expresses the heart of the matter. The comprehensive integration of the predicate is made into a concrete universal by means of the network of logically distinct relations that have been differentiated in the subject. In other words the psychological subjectivity of arbitrary *assertion* is transcended, for the justification of the assertion is expressed in what is asserted; and the contingency of this particular subject is overcome because its particularity has been expressly isolated as a distinct term and then related to the universal expression. In other words this judgement is objective.

Dialectic examines the three parts of the apodictic judgement: predicate, subject and copula. The evaluative predicate contains the heart of the matter as pure essence, integrated into a single term. It renders explicit an abstracted *ought* that is contrasted to its limited constitution. In the subject, however, the limiting conditions are distinguished from their grounding relation. This not only articulates the nature of the constitution, but it differentiates this constitution from the essence that it constitutes. Any judgement about actuals involves this absolute differentiation. The fact that this is explicitly expressed in the subject, however, prevents the act of judging from adding anything when the predicate is coupled to the subject. The pure essence—the integration of the various conditions—is already the animating soul that constitutes the subject as such.

When the judgement couples the subject to the predicate, then, it reflects nothing but the passing from a complexity over to the simplicity of the predicate's comprehensive totality; conditions and grounding relation are brought together into an integrated whole. In other words, the distinction between the subject as object of reference and the predicate as its conceptual expression, which is the necessary condition for all judging, dissolves. The copula simply disappears.

This leads to the final paradox of the activity of judging. For the judgement that finally expresses the objective truth to which it refers results in its dissolution. There is nothing distinct left to relate. In the first place, subject and predicate have inherently the same content. In the second place, the self-determining character of the subject justifies coupling it to the predicate. Thirdly, the distinct content of the predicate expresses nothing but this determinate character. The form of judgement has been reintegrated with the self-referential operations of conceptual thought. Because there is no immediate differentiation between subject and predicate, reference to an independent act of *judging* is simply irrelevant.

Speculative reason, as always, takes this paradoxical conclusion of negative dialectic and shows its positive implications: the dissolution of the act of judging is grounded in nothing other than a process of inference. In the act of conceiving, thought particularized the pure individual from the abstract concept. Because it identified itself only with the latter, it had to arbitrate the way in which what is independent of thought can yet be coupled with a thought. This introduced the process of judgement, in which the subjective act of judging always remained differentiated from its expressed content. It was this difference that generated the dialectical transitions and reflections; and it was the effort to individuate and then express what had been unexpressed that marked the task of speculative reason. Until this distinction was resolved, the act of judging remained somewhat arbitrary and simply subjective.

The dissolution of the act of judging, however, came about because the coupling of subject and predicate was already expressed by the individuated terms that had been particularized within the subject. Although a single object of reference, the subject had been articulated into determinate moments that were explicitly contrasted to each other. It is thus not merely referred to, but is also thought of as composed of abstractly distinct moments. At the same time, what was originally simply a coupling indicated by the copula has become a term, abstractly isolated within the subject.[42]

The copula, then, has not simply disappeared along with the act of judging. Because self-referential thought has individuated its determining role as a distinct moment within the comprehensive subject, it has been given a specific and determinate character of its own. It is nothing more than the particular conditions that on the one hand determine the individual object of reference, and on the other justify applying the universal predicate.

Because it relates the two terms, however, it is not simply referred to as an independent third. Rather it is immediately conjoined to both subject and predicate, to the one as determining, to the other as grounding. This means that it cannot simply be set beside them as one immediate among others. It is mediated by the immediate relation it has to each of the terms, and it in turn mediates their relation. This double character has been expressed in its definition as determinate constitution.

Dialectical reflection has shown that the content of subject and predicate is identical. Therefore the reference to the mediating relation as a distinct term is simply a matter of form. Insofar as articulate form and self-identical content can thus be distinguished, independent unexpressed intellectual operations have not disappeared absolutely. Within the single intellectual content, speculative reason has abstractly individuated a formal structure of mediation. Its concrete character needs to be clearly understood.

As mediating, the new middle term signifies an operation of thought; it is conceptual. This operation is one not of comprehensive integration, however, but of conditioning determination. No longer an immediate coupling, it has a determinate character. As a determinate concept, or *particular,* this new term is distinct from both the individuality of the subject and the universality of the predicate. The process of conceptual discrimination has dissolved the act of judging with its contrast between reference and thought, and incorporated its diversity into a single self-identical content; but at the same time it has transformed the judgement form: what couples subject and predicate has been individuated as an independent term. The self-identical intellectual operation that moves from one distinct concept to another by means of a third is called *inferring;* its formally differentiated structure is a *syllogism.*[43]

In the *apodictic judgement,* the relation between the subject a and the predicate C is mediated by the fact that a was determined by ϕ and that ϕ was categorized by C. We have, then, three judgements: the result: aϵC; and its conditions: ϕa and the relation ϕ<C. ϕ here plays two roles: on the one hand it determines a, on the other it is, or is not, a determinate constituent of C. It thereby mediates between the two, replacing the simple copula ϵ. When ϕ<C and ϕa become the conditions for asserting aϵC in one intellectual operation the transition has already been made to *syllogistic inference.*

The Dynamic of Conceiving

In the logic of comprehensive thought the immediate transitions of intelligence, and the mutual implications of reflection are not simply allowed to happen. When some such process takes place, intelligence turns on itself to discriminate clearly what the process involves so that it can individuate that operation and signify it by means of a determinate name or symbol.

Understanding starts by trying to comprehend a concept or category. This implicitly universalizing procedure inevitably leads to the dialectical process of particularizing, which seeks to distinguish what is expressed in the category or form from what is implicit and not expressed. The task of speculative reason, then, is to individuate both what is explicitly referred to and what is self-referentially implicit so that both can be explicitly comprehended in a new category.

If the three sections of the chapter on conceiving throw some light on the logical process, the combination of that chapter with its successors adds a further perspective. As we have seen, the initial process of comprehending involved in understanding leads to a precise individuation that opposes the object of thought to a subjective addition. When this process of individuating is self-referentially comprehended by intelligence, however, it discovers an act of transition that couples what is subjective with what is objective. This copula becomes expressed in judgement forms, but because the copula represents a transition or passing over from one term to another, it is not itself individuated as an independent term. Speculative reflection identifies the mediating process and differentiates it as an independent third from its two terms. By *referring* into itself, it articulates the *inferential* process of intelligence for comprehensive thought.[44]

For Hegel, then, the abstract forms of logic are not simply to be relegated to a subordinate level of understanding, to be transcended within the comprehensive totality of reason. Rather these traditional forms that have been rediscovered and re-expressed in modern symbolism in fact represent the results when intelligence self-referentially identifies the pattern of its own processes. The failure of logical discussions is not their formalism. That indeed represents the high-point of their achivement. It is rather that the effort to avoid self-reference leads to a theory of types, which ignores the necessary transitions from symbolism to meta-theory, and from meta-theory back to a revised symbolism. The service that Hegel provides is to make explicit this dialectical moment so that speculative reflection, holding up a mirror (in Latin, *speculum)* to its own operations can articulate what would be essential for an adequate meta-theory. Far from being arbitrary, this procedure attempts to avoid the contingencies inherent in much contemporary logical discussion.

11

Inferring

Syllogisms of A Being

In the comprehensive perspective of conceptual thought, that which is the object of thought (or category) is its own integrating activity (or concept). At first thought simply acts, and in acting becomes particularized; an abstract universal is distinguished from a pure individual. Once these, its products, have been completely alienated from its activity, however, the nature of the dynamic changes. For the only way thought can determine these categories further is by arbitrating how it is justified in relating them. Because the act of coupling remains external to the terms coupled, the dialectical effort to achieve a judgement form appropriate to the operation performed ultimately leads to a contradictory conclusion. On the one hand the terms of the judgement are not really independent but are rather two different ways intelligence regards the same content. On the other hand, as formal terms, they are isolated and detached. Indeed because the act of coupling has itself been individuated, a third, middle term has been distinguished. The one content is inference—a movement in which only the perspective of intelligence alters; its determinate form is called syllogism.[1] This contrast between the identity of inference and the differentiation in the syllogism transforms once again the nature of thought's activity. Because the two refer to the same operation, they need to be brought together. This simple synthesis should prepare the way for a final integration where content and form are completely compatible.

In other words, what remains is to render explicit the operations of speculative reason. The syllogistic form should articulate all aspects of the process of inference; and alternatively the determinate moments of its inferring activity need to be explicitly represented.

First Figure: 1. At first the forms of inference are subjective in the double sense we have already noted: on the one hand the three terms of the syllogism are abstract and therefore contingent—not inherent in the nature of things; on the other, the subjective integrating inference is other than what is expressed objectively. Because of this the syllogistic structures remain formal, simply the product of abstracting understanding.

What conceptual thought distinguished in *apodictic judgement* are the subject, the predicate, and that which justifies their relation. The subject is isolated as an individual—that which is referred to as independent of thought; the predicate is the universal genus, abstracted from all particularity; the middle term is both a specific category within the universal genus and also a determination that inheres in the individual. As a determinate category, it is a particular concept.

Since the comprehensive context of conceptual thought is set aside as irrelevant when the understanding focuses its attention on the syllogistic form, each of the three terms is taken as immediately presented to intelligence—as a self-contained individual to which any relation is added externally. The process of reference is represented simply by the determinate character of the middle term, or particular. Thus, though the latter is self-contained in itself, it is nevertheless to be the ground of the relation between the subject (or individual) and the predicate (or universal).

The schema of this type of inference can be represented by I - P - U. The *individual* is thought as not *universal* in itself, but only as determined in a *particular* way; the abstract *universal* is thought of not as having an *individual* instantiation but as a category that has determinate species. Each of the extremes is related to a *particular* determination that leaves open the possibility of inference even though, as extremes, they are clearly distinguished from that *particular*.

The formal structure of this inference allows several interpretations, all of which conform to its basic intention. In the first place, the *individual* can be thought as absolutely self-contained, as a simple object of reference. Through its particular differentiation, however, it can be thought as *a being* and brought into a conceptual relation with others similarly differentiated under a generic *universal*. Alternatively, the *individual* can be any representation that has been absolutely isolated. The particularizing, or isolating, operation, however, is itself a species of conceptual thought. In this latter case the subject is not only a logical individual simply referred to, but also a category negatively determined by reflection on what is essential.

In both perspectives the movement from *individual* to *universal* is introduced by a subjective intervention of thought. It posits the distinct moments of *individuality, particularity,* and *universality,* and thereby imposes this form on the intellectual content so that the inference can be represented. To be sure the three particular determinations are essential moments of the inference. The fault is not that these are used, but rather that there is no intrinsic relation between these forms and the content to which they are applied. The categories do not require any specific reference; the material is indifferent to the particular determinations used.

Two interpretations of this form, then, are possible. If the subject is taken as the ultimate basis of inference, a *particular* quality is thought as inhering in it, and a *universal* is the general category that inheres in this *particular.*[2] Alternatively, if the *universal* genus is taken as normative, then it subsumes a *particular* species, and the latter subsumes an *individual.*[3] In both cases, however, it is because the inference symbolized is a simple transition from one inherence or subsumption to another that the *universal* can be predicated of the *individual* subject in the conclusion. Thought passes over from an *individual* subject to a *particular* predicate in a simple transition. It then passes from the *particular* to the *universal.* When inference moves to the "therefore" of the conclusion (the sentence which asserts the relation between *individual* and *universal*), it simply collapses the two transitive relations into one.[4] As we shall see, the various figures of the *syllogisms of a being* are valid only insofar as the underlying inferential process is this simple transition.

In the syllogistic form conceptual thought does not start with simply the three terms: I, P and U. Rather its premises are two immediate transitions: I to P, and P to U. Each transition is a judged relation, either of inherence or of subsumption. And the transition expressed in the conclusion is equally a judgement. Unlike the others, however, it is preceded by a "therefore" indicating that it is mediated by the previous judgements. This "therefore" is not a convenient addition of the referring subject; it is rather an essential constituent of the conclusion, distinguishing it as a mediated transition from the immediate transition of its premises.

Thus three distinct judgements constitute the form of the syllogism. This form makes it appear as if each is independent and taken in itself. The heart of the matter, however, is that the various elements of the syllogism are not thought in absolute isolation, totally indifferent to each other. Rather one is specifically thought as *individual,* another as *universal,* and a third, common to both, as *particular* so that inference can pass from one immediate transition to the other. In this first figure the formal distinctions of the syllogisms stand in contrast to the essentially identical transition that grounds the inference.

2. Dialectic evaluates this definition of the syllogism. As we have seen the inference is based on the formal relation of *individual, particular,* and *universal.* But these forms are referred to an indifferent content; they introduce their qualifications into something independent.

The *individual* subject to which the syllogism refers can be any immediate and concrete object of reference; the *particular* can be any one of its qualities, properties or accidents; the *universal* can be any one of the more abstract genera under which the *particular* can be subsumed. This indefinite reference allows the syllogistic form to apply to an indeterminate range of intellectual transitions, from contingent association to essential identity.

But this unlimited range of application introduces difficulties. For a concrete individual has any number of qualities or properties. It is a matter of arbitrary contingency which one is selected as the middle term of an inference. If one of the other determinations were selected, a quite different argument would result. Similarly, the particular quality can be subsumed under widely diverse universal genera, each one of which follows from its determinate character. Once again it is a matter of chance which one is in fact used as the conclusion's predicate term.

In other words, for any one subject, an indefinite number of syllogisms are possible. This diversity, however, is not simply a matter of relative indifference; by selecting appropriate qualities and appropriate generic categories, explicitly opposing conclusions could be reached. When thought abstracts a quality or a character from an individual, it ignores the other qualities or characteristics that are in dynamic tension with it and that help constitute this unique individual entity. A turquoise object could be called blue or green; a man could be called both an animal and a rational being; the force involved in the solar system is centrifugal and centripetal. By taking one of these qualifying determinations in isolation, thought can infer to a universal genus that would be the explicit contradictory of the one it would derive from the other. It is this arbitrary and contingent character inherent in the formal syllogism that has led all reasoning to be called sophistical. In formal argument anything can be proven, as long as the appropriate middle term and appropriate predicate are selected.

This conclusion does not result simply from the fact that the content is independent of the form. It follows from the essential requirements of the form itself. For in specifying that the terms *individual, particular,* and *universal* are simply applied subjectively to an indifferent content, and in maintaining that they are forms abstracted from all other determinations, conceptual thought leaves aside any reference to concrete relations between these terms. It does not specify that the particular quality *essentially* characterize the individual, or that the genus be the *next proximate* generality. It is this formal lack of specification, not simply the recalcitrance of the content, that produces the contradictions.[5]

3. Speculative reason considers this dialectical paradox. Inference is to establish a necessary relation between subject and predicate. But the syllogism represents a contingent and arbitrary sophism. What is required is a syllogistic form that will justify the relations expressed in its own premises so that the conclusion is in fact necessary. The immediate transitions in both premises need to be grounded.

In the first figure the conclusion is justified by a transitive relation. Both premises, however, are immediate: the particular determination immediately passes over to its generic category; the individual is immediately determined. Neither transition is itself justified. It is this lack of a mediating ground that produces the bedeviling contingency.

Each premise, then, must itself be proven and become the result of a mediating inference. This can happen in two ways. In the first place, because the *particular* can be considered as an *individual* when coupled with the *universal* and as a *universal* when predicated of the *individual,* thought can look for new particular middle terms to mediate each of the premises. Instead of resolving the problem, however, this proposal aggravates it, for it produces four immediate premises instead of two. If one were to proceed, the number of unjustified assumptions would increase in geometrical progression. This infinite regress fails dismally to avoid the radical contingency that produced the dialectical paradox. For it presupposes the arbitrariness used in assigning the three formal determinations to the content. Each new *finite* judgement *ought* to be justified, but it is not. The recurring dialectic between *finite* and *ought* simply leads to a bad infinite.

The other alternative consists not in arbitrarily altering the formal characterization of an indifferent content, but in specifying that each term essentially determine that to which it refers. To justify the coupling of *particular* and *universal,* then, an *individual* would have to serve. Similarly a *universal* would have to mediate between *individual* and *particular.*

This general requirement, recognized by independent reflection, follows from the content of the inference. For the immediate transitions from one term to another in the premises are a matter of arbitrary contingency. As such there is no general principle inherent in those expressions—neither a principle of universal relation, nor one of particular differentiation. The movement is purely immediate. As such it is radically *individual.* It can be pointed to, but not conceptually expressed. It is this radical *individuality* that mediates between *particular* and *universal,* as well as between *individual* and *particular.* Both premises are grounded on an *individual* act.

The implication follows equally from the form of the syllogism. The conclusion asserts that the relation between *individual* and *universal* is grounded by the inference. The minor premise states that the *individual* subject is immediately determined—a judgement needing no further justification because it follows from the conceptual process of particularization. The *individual* is thereby coupled to both quality and universal category, and can mediate between them. Even though in itself it is a pure *individual,* in the syllogism it has been thought with some justification as related to both *particular* and *universal.* It can therefore be used to mediate the conjunction expressed in the major premise.

Second Figure:[6] 1. The truth of the *first figure* is that its inference is based on arbitrary contingency. Such contingency is purely *individual;* it simply happens as a singular event. The real mediating agent is not a *particular* quality, but is this immediate transition. The process of inferring dissolves this immediacy and establishes a relation that is grounded. The conclusion will then express a mediated conjunction, which can be contrasted to the premises as necessary over against contingent and as conceptual over against *individual.* Through this negative contrast the concluding judgement is rendered determinate.

In this type of inference the two premises relate the contingent *individuality* to a *particular* quality on the one hand, and to a *universal* category on the other. Since the latter relation has already been mediated in the first type of inference, the two figures presuppose each other. The inference of the first presupposes the form of the second; the form of the second presupposes the inference of the first.

In the conclusion the *universal* remains the predicate, but the *particular* becomes the subject. It is posited *as* an *individual,* even though it retains the characteristic of a *particular* concept. Similarly the individual is posited *as* a determining middle term, or as a *particular,* even though in itself it remains a pure *individual,* simply referred to by thought. This "positing as" is an operation only of external reflection; it does not touch the characteristics of the terms in themselves.

This syllogism has as its determinate and objective interpretation that a *universal* genus in itself is not specified immediately in any *particular* way, but as simply a generality, common to a wide range of *individuals*. Its species can be *particularized* only when there are *individuals* thus differentiated.[7] Similarly the specific characteristics of a *particular* are not sufficient to categorize it as a *universal*. Rather, only because an *individual* embodies both specific and *universal* features can the *particular* be identified with the genus.[8] But a pure *individual* can serve as a predicate for a *particular* concept neither by inhering in it nor by subsuming it into a more comprehensive class. In both premises, therefore, it remains subject.

2. The objective sense of the second figure, outlined in the previous paragraph, is the result of interpreting reflection. It is not contained in the new syllogistic figure. What has happened is that two of the terms, still externally related to each other as in the first figure, have changed places. Instead of an *individual* being related to a generic category by means of a *quality*, a *particular* quality is related to a generic category by means of a contingent *individual*: P - I - U.

This change, however, initiates a number of dialectical steps. The *individual* which is to serve as the mediating term is to exclude all reflective characteristics; unlike the *particular* of the first figure, it has nothing in common with the two conceptual extremes. Indeed it is this exclusive character that generates the mediating dynamic. Since both specific quality and generic category as abstract concepts are external to its essential *individuality,* they can legitimately be related by thought quite apart from the contingent reference.

The alteration in the form of the syllogism, however, changes the relation between the form and the inferential content. As we have seen inference involves a double transition of thought. In this *second figure,* however, the transitive relation from the first to the second premise does not hold, for the middle term has been subsumed under the *subject* of the conclusion as well as under its *predicate*. Although the *second figure* was supposed to be simply a species under the genus of immediate inference, it does not reflect the simplicity of its transition. For thought is unable to pass directly from the premises to the conclusion.

This discrepancy between form and content exposes the radical contingency of the immediate, individual transitions symbolized in the middle term. The syllogistic inference would be valid only if these subjective and arbitrary connections reflected an actual state of affairs. In other words, the conclusion of the second figure—that a particular quality is subsumed under a universal genus—would have to be true independent of the inferring process. The *individual* transition is simply a contingent way in which this relation comes to be thought.

If understanding nevertheless wishes to maintain the second figure as a species of immediate inference, it must ignore this reference to an independent conjunction and consider the form alone. The transitive relation of the premises can be restored if the *individual* that is the middle term ceases to be the common subject of two different predicates and becomes the predicate of the term that will be the subject of the conclusion. The transition of thought in the minor premise will then be from *particular* to *individual*.

This poses a problem, however. An *individual* is a being immediately present, to which one only refers. As subject it is a *this,* as predicate it must remain one: "A *particular* is coupled to this; this is subsumed under a category; therefore a *particular* is coupled with a category." The copula in the first, or minor, premise can be neither inherence nor subsumption. Inherence involves an immediate transition from an *individual* to its qualification, but is irrelevant to a transition from a qualification to an *individual*. And subsumption involves an *individual* being a member of a class, but a determination cannot be an instance of an *individual*. The transition from a *quality* to *an individual being,* which was identified in the doctrine of being, was simply an association that presupposed a previous logical transition. This association produced the term *something,* which later was adapted to serve as the subject of a *particular judgement.* Therefore the minor premise must be expressed as "Something *particular* is associated with this." Since this relation passes over to be subsumed under the category, the conclusion would be: "Something *particular* is associated with a category." Only in this way can the transitive relation be maintained.

But the necessity of the inference is affected. A *particular judgement* implies both a positive and a negative: "Some are; others are not." Therefore the association of subject and predicate is not immediate and inevitable. Whereas the judgement "I is P" (or "Individual is particular"), the minor premise of the *first figure,* could be accepted as unquestioned, its inversion "P is I" is not obvious. Such a coupling would now need to be justified if the inference were to establish necessity.

The conclusion is equally indeterminate. The coupling of a *particular* determination and a *universal* category reflects the contingent fact that both have been associated with a single *individual.* As thus conceptually indifferent to each other, *particular* determination and *universal* category could change their places in the syllogism; it matters not which term is subject and which predicate; which premise is the major and which the minor. A relation that was supposed to be well-grounded by the inference turns out to be arbitrary.

3. Since the determinate characteristics of *particular* quality and *universal* category are indifferent to each other, the conclusion simply afffirms that they are associated at some point. What associates two terms in a common perspective, however, is a *universal*. In other words, what mediates their conjunction is not a purely contingent *individual* that can only be indicated. Intelligence is operative, because it holds both of them in the mind at the same time. This universalizing, comprehensive activity underlies both of the premises as their inferential content.

It remains contingent, however. For when a *particular* quality is associated with a *universal* category in the conclusion of the *second figure,* all conceptual necessity has been surrendered. The two have simply been brought together by an intellectual process of association that has dissolved any reference to an objective *individuality.*

Whenever thought refers to an *individual* to justify coupling a quality with a category, the resulting conceptual relation has no reference to anything objective. Since the middle term was to be that which is independent of all conceptual determinations, the other terms are conjoined not because they share some common conceptual content, but only because both happen to have been associated with the same *individual.* With no independent justification for coupling these concepts, the conclusion reflects a purely intellectual transition—a universal concept.

The lack of justification for this conjunction is quite different from the problem posed by the immediacy of transition in the *first figure.* There, when thought simply passed from one term to another, the movement was thought to be grounded in an inherent relation between a being and its quality, between a quality and its category. Now however, the judgement expressed in the conclusion is mediately *posited* as subjective and arbitrary. All reference to *being* has been explicitly left behind by the process of inference.

The conjunction of determination and category in the conclusion, then, does not follow from any independent individuality of the inferential content. Through the comprehensive universality of simple association, intelligence passes beyond any reference to individuals; and the arbitrary subjectivity, which we already recognized as present in the form of the *first figure,* has been introduced into the inferring process.

But if it is the subjectivity of intellectual association that mediates between the terms, then we have identified a type of inference that is neither a determination, nor something individual and unique, but is common to all intellectual operations. This mediating process is *universal,* both in the sense that it is present in all thinking, and because association relates terms within a general perspective. We need, then, a different syllogistic figure in which the *universal* serves as the middle term.[9]

Third Figure: 1. Each premise of this third figure I - U - P has been the conclusion of one of the others. *Individual* and *universal* were mediately coupled in the first; quality and category in the second. In its formal structure, then, it presupposes them. But equally, as dialectical and speculative reason have shown, they presuppose the intellectual operation that it represents. For it asserts that the associations involved in immediate intellectual transitions are the universal products of all thinking.

In other words, this figure expresses the truth of the formal syllogism: all immediate inference is simply the product of associations that may be represented in universal concepts. Its validity is subjective in both senses: the inference requires no reference to what is other than thought; the formal structure of the syllogism reflects nothing inherent in its content. The third figure, which asserts that inferential mediation is the product of universalizing intelligence, makes explicit this purely formal character of symbolic logic.

2. Through dialectical evaluation, the middle term is shown to be effective because it abstracts from any determinate character of its extremes, whether *particular* concept or *individual* entity. It simply isolates something that is common to both. This poses problems for the simple identity of the inferring process: thought can associate an *individual,* or something *particular,* with a *universal* class, but this does not entail a transitive relation from one association to another. If there is to be a single inferential move, some way must be found for passing from the mediating *universal* to the *particular* as predicate of the conclusion. Since a *universal* is more comprehensive than anything *particular,* however, it cannot be subsumed thereby, nor can the latter be said to inhere in the generality of the former. The transition from *universal* to *particular* is simply a passing over from *something* to *something else,* a process of *becoming other* which can be expressed only by a *negative judgement.* "The *universal* is coupled with the *particular"* becomes "The *universal* is not the *particular."* Any difference will serve to justify the negative judgement. But by formalizing the relation, the terms are isolated; each one is abstracted from its context.

Since the transition of inference would move from *individual* through *universal* to this abstracted predicate, the conclusion of the syllogism would also have to be negative: "The *individual* is not the *particular.*" But this means that its subject and predicate are simply differentiated from each other. In such a relation of pure abstraction, either could be the subject for the other's predicate.

This indifference makes it possible to alter the order of the premises. It matters not which term in the conclusion is predicate and which subject. For there is no conceptual determination that would require one to be predicate for the other. As purely abstract they can be associated in any order. Thought simply stipulates one pattern rather than another. All necessity has been lost.

3. What the third figure shows positively is that the essential mediating content of the inferential process is purely intellectual—it is a function of conceptual thought that is clearly differentiated from both indicated individuals and distinguishing determinations. Inference has become a purely formal operation; it abstracts from all specifying content. Any distinguishing features of the extremes are irrelevant to the differentiation of *something* from *something else.* They are brought together in the inference, then, only by ignoring particular determinations. But as thus abstracted from any conceptual differences, there is no basis on which the extremes can be distinguished as *individuals* and *particulars.* Because they are considered only to the extent that they have been abstracted by intelligence, they are all abstract *universals.* The self-identical content of the figure of universal mediation is a process of association in which all the terms are equally abstract and *universal:* "The abstractly *universal* is associated with the abstractly *universal* by means of the abstractly *universal.*" In this *fourth figure,* the indifference of the formal terms to each other and to the self-identical content becomes fully explicit.

Fourth Figure: 1. When all determinateness has been put aside, we are left with the abstract inferential process of mathematics: when two things are both abstractly (or quantitatively) equal to the same thing, they are equal to each other: U - U - U. With the reference to pure equality any need to introduce a transitive relation as the identity of the inference has disappeared. At the same time, there is nothing inherent in the character of the three terms by which one is to be specified as the mediating relation and the others simply as extremes. Any pair of relations could be taken to ground the third. It is a matter of external circumstances and accidental conditions which of them happen to be primary and which derived.

2. Mathematics claims that this form of inference is self-evident—an axiom that requires no proof. Dialectical reflection soon shows, however,

that it is not as unmediated as mathematics claims. For it involves abstracting from a network of concrete relations those universal features which can be equated. Because these features have been isolated from all determinate relations, they are brought together in the syllogistic form simply because they are identical. And since there are no differences left, their comparison involves no ADDITIONAL activity of conceptual thought. This axiom is 'intuitive' and requires no inferential movement from one term to another—not because there is something objective and independent of thought that is acknowledged, but rather because subjective intelligence has so constituted it that no mediation is required.[10]

3. This dialectical conclusion makes evident by contrast the fact that an immediate *inference of a being* presupposes more than is expressed in the abstract mathematical syllogism. The formal structure of proof is simply one side of a process that, when reversed, exposes the self-specifying activity of conceptual thought. Not as abstracted do the figures represent the essentials of the inferential process, but only when they, as form, are grounded in a determinate content.

This determinate content cannot be provided conceptually, for the *third figure* has shown conceptual thought to be abstract. To become concrete it must refer to *individuals,* not as absolutely other than thought, but as reflected in their contrary. This grounding of formal thought by referring it to an individualized content is the intellectual act of denotation. It brings together into one reflective perspective the three inferential moves. For each one has been shown to reflect the others. When the mediating moment of inference was formalized as a determinate *particular,* reflection showed that an *individual* transition was presupposed; when reference to an *individual* was used to bring together the two extremes, thought discovered that in both premises it had been externalizing and abstracting itself from individuals; when, finally, a self-identical and hence abstract *universal* was identified as the middle term, the collapse into the formal identity of the mathematical syllogism exposed the importance of the differentiating process by which *particular* distinctions were introduced into a comprehensive content.

Reflection identifies these three as the self-identical content that is represented in syllogistic form. They are synthesized in the act of denotation because it brings together a differentiating act, an indicated individual, and an abstract identity. This conceptual totality grounds inference. Because the figures of the formal syllogism were each isolated in turn, they were shown to be empty, divorced from the dynamic process of intelligence.[11] It is their synthesis alone that grounds inference.

To determine what is essential about the content of the inferential process so that it can be given a determinate form, then, reflection must represent formally the three operations of differentiating, identifying and referring, but also conjoin them in an explicit synthesis.

First Figure:[12] Apodictic judgement resulted in three different propositions: on the basis of $\phi<C$ and ϕa, $a\varepsilon C$ was asserted. This then provides the formal structure of immediate inference.

Dialectic evaluates this structure and discovers that, while ϕa is immediately evident, the other premise $\phi<C$ is the result of reflective thought. For the definition of C as $\phi\&\bar{\phi}$[13] presupposes a type of negation that implicitly retains a positive relation to what is negated. An individual determination is subsumed under its universal context. This means that ϕ and $\bar{\phi}$ are related to C through an intellectual transition that is not justified by anything independent of thought. Therefore objective necessity has not been established. Indeed, through the immediate reference of the category C to the individual a the conclusion can be more readily established than can this particular premise.

A new type of inference is required — one that establishes the conceptual relation between the two universals ϕ and C, thus making it objective. A reference is needed to that which is clearly independent of thought — an objective individual simply indicated. This produces a new syllogistic figure: one which has as its premises the immediate relation ϕa and the essential relation $a\varepsilon C$ and concludes that the relation between ϕ and C is grounded.

Second Figure: When we take the two premises along with the desired conclusion and attempt to determine the nature of the inference we are faced with a difficulty. For the simple fact that both ϕ and C can be predicated of the same a does not necessarily imply conceptual relation between them. On the other hand, the common reference to a shows that it is impossible for ϕ to be categorized as absolutely unrelated to C. If we symbolize the negation of a category (as distinct from the negation of a quality) by $\tilde{C}$, we can symbolize the conclusion as $\sim(\phi<\tilde{C})$. Since this means that the two terms have something in common, we can use the symbol X and replace $\sim(\phi<\tilde{C})$ with $\phi X C$. Understanding has defined the valid inference of the second figure: on the basis of $a\varepsilon C$ and ϕa, one can infer $\phi X C$.

Dialectic evaluates this definition. The conclusion conjoins two universals, abstracted from reference to any individuality. Since each is taken simply in itself, there is no inherent difference between a determination and a category that would ground the relation of subsumption.[14] Since the determination is equally isolated from any inherence in the individual, both ϕ and C are simply categories (or classes) distinguished from individuals because they are thought to be essential.[15] This raises a problem, however, for in both previous inferences, the one premise that was unquestioned was ϕa — the fact that ϕ determines a. But ϕ is now recognized as abstracted. from a. How can an abstraction determine the reference to an individual object?

This dialectical doubt can only be resolved if we find some form of inference that grounds the relation between an individual and a determinate abstraction. It can take as one premise the fact that a has been denoted as one member of the class C, ($a\epsilon$C); as the other, ϕXC, justified on the basis of some other individual. We have, then, the structure of the third figure.

Third Figure: The fact that ϕ and C overlap in one case implies nothing at all for another, since both have been explicitly abstracted from all inherent relation to individuals. Therefore the two premises are not sufficient to determine any relation between a and ϕ. The figure needs to be reconsidered to see how a valid inference can be established. The minor premise $a\epsilon$C, being established denotatively, cannot be altered. The major premise, coupling ϕ and C, however, can allow some modification, since both terms are categories of thought. The act of abstraction has abstracted each from the other so that they have become indifferent to each other. Therefore there is no conceptual relation by which one categorizes the other. This can be symbolized by $\sim(\phi<C)$ and equally by $\sim(C<\phi)$.

This makes possible the following pair of premises: $\sim(C<\phi)$ and $a\epsilon$C. The grounded relation that is to be expressed in the conclusion needs to be specified. The major premise states that C cannot be conceptually categorized as ϕ. The minor premise states that a has been denoted as a member of C. But the only conclusion is that no relation can be asserted between a and ϕ. If there is no relation, it is left absolutely indeterminate by the syllogism. And this requires the negative *infinite judgement:* $\sim\phi$a.

Dialectical reflection exposes the implications of this definition. Through the process of inference the individual is explicitly defined as unrelated to any differentiating determination. Since this conclusion is the result of an intellectual operation of inference, it can no longer refer to the subject through an act of reference, but only by means of an abstracting operation of thought. It is nothing but an abstracted category, excluded from other categories. In other words what was supposed to be an individual has lost its determinate contrast to the other two categories. It is something abstractly thought. In the effort to establish strict objective necessity, symbolic logic ends with a purely formal pattern of abstractions, lacking reference to any determinate individuality.

The syllogistic forms relate abstract concepts that have been isolated through conceptual operations. They are absolutely indifferent to one another; and as long as thought maintains their abstracted character they can be related in any fashion whatsoever. When the subjectivity of intellectual activity (or inference) is thus isolated from any determinate form, the result is pure phantasy—symbolizing, allegorizing or poetic imagination.[16] When, in contrast, formal symbolism is abstracted from the intellectual operations of thought, only the procedure of pure mathematics remains. In the latter process, which alone is logically significant, the process of abstracting is pushed to its limit where all determinate and differentiating characteristics, even that of reference, are excluded, leaving only abstract quantitative identity and the "axiom" of equality.[17]

Speculative reason undertakes to synthesize the two. What intellectual activity is appropriate to differentiate one pure form from another? Once pure reference has been excluded, the only type of differentiation possible is reflective: denotation.[18] A formal category is a class that is reflectively identified by denotation. But this act equally differentiates the members of the class from all other individuals (who make up the complementary class $\tilde{C}$).

The abstractness of thought, then, involves a double reflective process. The abstract class is identified by the members that have been denoted. But the latter are equally differentiated from the individual members of its complementary class. These two operations, the one universally identifying, the other particularly differentiating, were symbolized earlier as $x \varepsilon C$ and ϕx. By recognizing (a) that the relation expressed in each of these forms is not a judgement since x is an open variable; (b) that even though both are operations of thought and are therefore abstract, they yet operate in contrary directions and can themselves be differentiated; and (c) that this very differentiation means that in their conjunction the ambiguity of the variable in one corrects the ambiguity of the other: speculative reason can use the combined symbol $\phi x.x\varepsilon C$ to represent the denotative act of reflectively defining a class.[19]

Syllogisms of Reflection

The collapse of the *syllogisms of a being* into the empty formalism of mathematics triggers an act of self-reference on the part of speculative reason. In the conclusion of a syllogism, the subject and the predicate are not to be coupled immediately, but their relation is to be grounded by the inferential process. This grounding relation is to reflect something essential in each of the two extremes. For the failure of the formal syllogism lay in the contingency that bedeviled the relation between the middle term and its counterparts—a contingency that could be avoided only by relying on the reference to *individuals* (in the *second figure)* and the exclusive abstraction of all conceptual *universals* (in the *third*).

This change in the inferential content will be symbolized by a change in the middle term. It is no longer referred to as a simple determination differentiated from both the more comprehensive category and an indicated *individual*. It is to be essentially related both to the subject, or minor term, and to the predicate, or major term, of the conclusion. These latter relations are not immediate transitions of thought, but are grounded in the determinations of reflection.

This modification of the middle term is reflected as well in the two extremes. The subject is not simply indicated by thought; it is differentiated by means of the middle, specifically indicated as an instance. The predicate, on the other hand, is to be an abstract class that is denotatively identified by the specific differentiation. *Reflective inference* will subsume a specified *individual* under its essential class.

Since the middle term is coupled to its two extremes through reflection, we can now define its character more precisely. It is that which differentiates the individual subject; that is, it does not simply refer to its pure *individuality,* but rather employs a determination of reflection (or *determinate ground*). On the other hand, it is that which reflectively determines the *universal* predicate by identifying a class of denoted *individuals*. The middle term synthesizes the two as that which identifies the differentiating characteristic.

Syllogism of totality: 1. In the first form of *reflective inference* the earlier forms of the syllogism acquire their complete expression. Indi-

vidual entities are still thought as *individuals,* the class as purely denotative is still thought as abstract. The only addition is that the middle term is
no longer a simple determination. It is rather a reflective determination
that specifies what is essential in the subject and in the predicate.

This change in the middle term, however, resolves the dilemma that dialectic posed to the first figure of the formal syllogism. Because it differentiates the individuals to which it refers, the middle term determines which
individual may be the subject of the conclusion. Therefore the relation is
no longer contingent. The middle term, for example, is no longer simply
"green" or "circular". It differentiates individuals by means of the quality: "All green things", or "Everything circular".[20] And the major premise can be asserted to be true not on the basis of a simple transition of
thought from a ϕ to a C, but rather because the predicated feature is in fact
identified by the denotative determination of the middle term.

The *first figure* of the *formal syllogism,* I-P-U, thus acquires a formula-
tion that does not depend on a subjective transition but is determined by
reflection using its criteria for what is essential.

2. Dialectic soon shows, however, that in this form the claim that there
is an inference is a pure illusion. For the major premise asserts that all the
identified individuals are members of the predicated class. But this "all"
includes the individual that is differentiated in the minor premise. Therefore there is no transition at all. The conclusion is already referred to in the
major premise. This form, which was to resolve the problems of the formal syllogism, turns out to represent no inference at all but a simple tautology. There is no differentiation, but only identity.

3. Whereas in formal syllogisms it is only through dialectical reflection
that the contrast between the immediacy of the premises and their need for
a mediated justification became evident, in this syllogism the required contrast is explicitly expressed. For the conclusion is one of those judgements
used to justify, and thus to mediate, the major premise. The whole simply
seems to be an inference—a formalized differentiation that does not
reflect the simple identity in thought's content. The middle term only *formally grounds* the conclusion. Thus the differentiation between form and
content is purely subjective, for the identification of this particular individual as a member of the predicate class is immediately known before it is
proven. Indeed such an immediate identification underlies the validity of
the major premise since it expresses the fact that *all* of the members of the
class have been denotatively identified. Thus speculative reason individuates a different kind of inference: one in which the immediate differentia-

tion of individuals identifies the membership of a denotative class. This inference is called *induction*.

Inductive Inference: 1. Induction involves grounding the relation between a *particular* process of denotative differentiation and an abstract identification in a class. This conjunction is to be established by differentiating the *individual* members of the class. Therefore it stands under the general structure of the second figure, in which individuals mediate between a particular and a universal, P-I-U. But unlike the second figure of the formal syllogism, the middle term is not simply one contingent *individual*. All the *individuals* in the class are to be identified by being differentiated from all other individuals.

The fact that all *individuals* are to be considered in an exclusive totality resolves the difficulty posed by the *second figure* of the *formal syllogism*. There the particular quality could not be subsumed under the individual.[21] Now, however, the two have the same extension, but are considered from differing perspectives. Particular refers to the criteria for differentiating; individual refers to the members differentiated.

Looking behind the formal structure of this syllogism we can discover its objective import. It means that a class is not simply identified denotatively. Rather, because something specific is used to differentiate its members from all other individuals, the class is recognized as being an essential determination of the individuals.[22]

2. *Induction,* however, does not escape the dilemma of subjectivity. For the mediating process of inference always differentiates only a finite number of diverse individuals; it can never determine if it has exhausted the class. Whether all its members have been specifically identified is a matter of subjective contingency. Thought ought to encompass all, but has taken only those individuals that have in fact been immediately differentiated. This *limitation* in the middle term to what have actually been identified reduces the comprehensiveness of inductive denotation to a bare *ought*. To ground the inference one ought to consider all, but that remains a task yet to be achieved.

As always, when *limitation* and *ought* confront each other in explicit opposition, an infinite regress results. Whenever one has established the conjunction of a *particular* differentiation and an identified class in one *individual,* one must move on to the next. The totality of all *individuals* is never exhausted. The conclusion, then, is never finally assured. On the basis of the actual *individuals* considered, one can entertain the possibility that differentiation and class are essentially related, but it is equally poss-ible for a future *individual* to show that the conjunction is only contingent. The process of reflective inference that is supposed to determine an essential connection produces only a problematic conclusion. There is no real identity, only difference.

3. Speculative reason considers this paradoxical result. The *ought* of in-duction reflects the fact that the total extension of the genus class is to be identified by the middle term. Its implicit assumption that any finite collec-tion is sufficient to ground the *universality* of the conclusion presupposes some inherent relation between specific differentiation and class that is not contingent on identified *individuals*. Induction, then, is grounded on an intellectual conjunction that is to be contrasted to the simple identification of two classes because they have the same members. It assumes that there is an inherent relation between a specific difference and its class such that a finite sample is sufficient to ground a necessary synthesis.[23]

If induction maintains the nominalistic premise that only *individuals* can mediate between conceptual categories, then the middle term falls apart into two: individuals actually considered, and individuals that ought to be considered. But because this internal division destroys the identity re-quired for the inferring process, no conclusion is possible. Only when an *individual* is differentiated, not as something indifferent to the abstract *universality* of the class, but as essentially identified by it, is it possible to infer from a differentiated set of individuals to a general conclusion. The *individuals* are not identified by the *universal,* but the *universal* is identified by means of the *individuals* denoted. This presupposition of an essential identification on the part of a finite set of *individuals* is implicit in the differentiating process. It identifies those differences that are significant because they manifest the essential determinations. Speculative reason has thus individuated a distinct inferential operation in which a process of identifying instances of a class serves to differentiate the essen-tial determinations of that class. For this we need a new syllogistic form: *analogy.*

Analogical inference: 1.In analogical inference the premises (a) that a dif-ferentiating characteristic identifies one member of a class, and (b) that another individual is a member of the same class provide the grounds for attributing the differentiating characteristic to that second individual. Because class membership mediates the inference, this syllogism reflects the structure of the third figure: I-U-P. In the major premise, however, the class and the specific difference are not coupled indeterminately, as in the *syllogism of totality.* Their conjunction is justified by reference to an *individual* (or a finite set of *individuals)* that is different from the one identified in the minor.[24] Since the difference is a difference in reference, the abstractness of the *third figure* of the *formal syllogism* is also avoided.

2. *Analogical inference* reflects a natural tendency of intelligence when it identifies some differentiating characteristics of a set of instances of a class, and infers that other instances will have the same characteristics. In this process, reflective thought rises above bare denotation and assumes that there is an objective ground for conjoining class and determinate characteristics. This objectivity is achieved by referring to the finite set of individuals identified in the major premise. And the fact that these individuals are distinct from the *individual* differentiated in the major premise saves the inference from collapsing into the *petitio principii* of the *syllogism of totality.*

It might appear as if there were now four terms individuated in the form: the two sets of *individuals,* the class, and the determination. But the *individual* referred to in the major is not thought as something independent of thought, but as objectively embodying what is essential in the class. Therefore some of its *particular* determinations are taken to appertain to that *universal.* It is this immediate identification of the *individual* in its characteristic particularity with the *universal* that saves the inference from breaking apart.

However, the intellectual identification of what *particular* characteristics specifically differentiate a class member may reflect either a superficial association or something essential. The syllogistic form cannot discriminate between the two. Therefore the *individuality* that justifies the coupling in the major premise is not only that of an *individual* object of reference, but also that of a contingent and subjective intellectual operation.

Just as *induction* implicitly synthesizes the set of *individuals* referred to in the middle term with an indefinite set that *ought* to be identified to establish the *universality* of the conclusion, and just as the *syllogism of totality* implicitly includes in the major premise the distinct *individual* referred to in the minor to validate its inference, so *analogy* couples the differentiating characteristics of an indicated set of *individuals* with their generic class. What was only implicit in the earlier syllogisms, however, has now become explicit as the *individuality* that is the common reference for both terms in the major premise.

The fundamental weakness of *analogy,* then, lies in the contingent synthesis between the identified class and the determinate differences. There is nothing in the form of the *analogical inference* that can ensure that specified determinations essentially identify the *individual,* and do not reflect its contingent *particularity.* The example Hegel provides illustrates this ambiguity. The facts: (a) that the moon is a satellite, and (b) that the earth which is essentially a satellite has inhabitants, would lead to the analogical conclusion that the moon has inhabitants. But the inference itself cannot establish whether the fact that the earth has inhabitants follows from its essential nature as satellite, or is simply accidental. It is this contingency that frustrates the syllogism and prevents it from symbolizing a necessary inference.

This weakness is inherent in the form of *analogy.* For various determinate features are simply identified immediately with the *individual* instance of the class. Since this identification has not been determined by reflection, but is an external and immediate addition, it contains no criteria for distinguishing what, in the *individual,* follows from the *universal* essence and what from its contingent constitution.

3. When speculative reason considers this conclusion, it discovers that the major premise, in which the middle term is conjoined with the predicated differentiation, is as much a contingent relation between an *individual* and a *particular* as it is an essential relation between a *universal* and a *particular.* Both alternatives are possible. But the relation between an *individual* and its *particular* differentiation was to be established in the conclusion of the inference. To presuppose such a relation, even problematically, is to destroy the validity of the whole inferential structure.

What is needed is a middle term that is both *universal* and objective, not in the sense that it immediately refers to an *individual,* but in the sense that it dissolves the *individuality* of its various expressions into a comprehensive unity. The *universal* will then contain the objective criteria for differentiating whatever identifying characteristics are inherent and necessary from any determinations that are contingent and *particular.* Only with this type of middle term will the contingency of *analogy* be overcome.

In each of the *formal syllogisms* the immediacy of the premises required that they be justified by the alternative syllogistic figures. In the *syllogisms of reflection* it was recognized that the middle term must reflect its two extremes in a synthesis and not simply be presented immediately. With *analogical inference,* however, we realize that the middle term reflects the other two because of the reflective act of synthesis which is itself immediate and thus contingent, an act of external reflection. Such an alien reflection combined the *particular* differentiation with all its instances in the *syllogism of totality*; it collected various *individuals* into the inductive series;

and it combined the characteristics of one *individual* with its *universal* genus. Since this synthetic combination is immediate, however, it is not itself mediately justified by the concrete character of the terms themselves.

The move to the *syllogisms of reflection* negated the formal immediacy of the middle term. But this conditioning negation (the act of synthesis) is itself now shown to be immediate in terms of its content. It in turn needs to be grounded. The middle term must constitute its own relation to its extremes. Neither immediate, nor simply posited as mediating, it must unconditionally mediate its own distinctions if an inference is to be absolutely necessary.

Throughout the *syllogisms of reflection* the middle term has specifically denoted *individuals*. Only in this way could inference escape the charge of formalism. The specific differentiation in the *syllogism of totality* is defined by the fact that it identifies all the relevant *individuals; induction* collects a series of *individuals;* and *analogy* uses an *individual* to embody the *universal* essence. The formal structure P-I-U is also reflected in the inference, for the synthesis of the terms into a reflective totality turned out to be a contingent *individual* act of external reflection. It is the *individual* immediacy of a reflective, synthesizing act that conceptually constitutes the middle term and justifies the inferential process.

With *analogical inference* the essential contingency of this individual perspective is exposed, and it is recognized that an inference, to be secure, must have for its middle term a concept. For as we have seen, the comprehensive process of conceiving individualizes the particular character of its terms. Once this operation has been individuated by speculative reason as the self-identical content of inference, a new syllogistic form is required—one that will represent such an absolutely *necessary inference*.

Totality or Instantiation: 1. By using the expressions revived by speculative reason to distinguish between thought's two reflective operations, we can resymbolize the first figure of formal inference as follows:

$\phi x.x\varepsilon C$

ϕa

Therefore aεC.

2. Because the major premise asserts that the differentiating operation ϕ exhaustively determines the range of x, the particular differentiation in the minor and its relation to the universal class in the conclusion have already been included. Nothing new has been added by the latter two judgements.

3. The inference collapses into the form: $\phi x.x\varepsilon C$. This premise, however, has not been justified.That can happen only insofar as a number of individual acts of differentiation (like the ϕa in the minor premise) are identified as denoting the membership of C. This type of inference is not *instantiation,* but *generalization* or *induction.*

Induction or Generalization: 1. The inference now individuated would be symbolized as follows:
(a,b,c,d) ϕx
(a,b,c,d)$x\varepsilon C$
Therefore $\phi x.x\varepsilon C$.

2. (a,b,c,d) is only a finite set of individuals. Since ϕx was used to symbolize $(\exists x \,\&\, \overline{\exists} x)$, however, it refers not only to some individuals actually differentiated, but others that would be, but in fact are not. As the x in the conclusion is a variable that does not include all the individuals to be indicated by ϕ, the conclusion includes more than what is contained in the premises. In fact no inference would be possible if the intellect had not on its own considered the association of ϕ and C to be not contingent on the induction, but holding independently.

3. This kind of inference starts from the synthetic conjunction of ϕ and C. Since this conjunction has not been exhaustively determined, it must refer to an individual, or to a specified set of individuals. Then when another individual is identified as a member of the class C, the inference will conclude that it is differentiated by ϕ. This is an *analogical inference.*

Analogical Inference: 1. The inference now individuated would have the form:
$a\varepsilon C. \phi a$
$b\varepsilon C$
Therefore ϕb,
although the a in the major premise could be expanded to (a^1, a^2, a^3, a^4). This indeterminacy in the form of the major premise is to indicate that the *individuality* of a is not in question.

2. We have already seen that the simple conjunction "." of a categorical judgement does not establish any necessary connection. It is a contingent relation that could be otherwise. This means that the inference is radically problematic. It could be the case that a member of the class C is not differentiated by ϕ. Once again the syllogism cannot justify the necessity of the inference.

3. In the *inference of reflection* we reach one of two results. Either there is no inference because the conclusion is included in the premise, or the inference is unjustified because the middle term is insufficient to establish what is expressed in the conclusion. In the latter case either the indicated *individuals* do not encompass the totality of the conclusion, or any *particular* way of differentiating does not follow from membership in a class.

In *analogy* the fundamental problem of this type of syllogism has become explicit. For all three presuppose an operation of thought that is independent of either identification or differentiation. This operation, essential to the act of denoting, involves their synthesis. Such a process, however, is derived neither from the operation of differentiating, nor from that of identifying, and is represented by the symbol ".". When coupling two clauses, both of which contained indeterminate variables, its contingency was not evident. When, in *analogy,* it was used to conjoin two determinate judgements, it was seen to be a distinctive operation.

Once the inference to a categorical conjunction has been individuated by speculative reason, it needs to be represented in symbolic form. This will be a *categorical syllogism.*[25]

Necessary Inference

Inference is a mediating process. That act of mediation has now become more explicitly expressed in the structure of the syllogism itself. Like the qualitative *particular* of the *formal syllogism,* it is distinguishable and determinate; but it is also a dynamic relation and therefore *universal.* Like the individual *synthesis* of the *reflective syllogism* it brings together the different characteristics of the extremes, but it has integrated them into an objective *unity.* The middle term now signifies not something abstracted nor a denoted conjunction, but an intellectual operation.

In this type of syllogism, then, the inferential process is represented not simply in symbolized terms, but in what is asserted. At first assertions remain contingent and diverse. Only as the various types of *necessary inference* develop will these assertions become both distinctly determined and integrally related with the mediating process.

Categorical inference: 1. Superficially, the categorical inference appears to have the same structure as the *formal syllogism* of inherence—a *particular* mediates between an *individual* and its category. However, the mediating term is no longer referred to as something determinate. It is rather a *universal* concept or comprehensive genus whose connotation determinately defines the range and criteria for its application.[26] This process of defining, or determining, has two thrusts. In the first, it specifies the particular determinations that characterize its inherent nature. By isolating them from the internal dynamic of its own integrity, it makes them into abstract *universals,* which then serve as the predicates, or major terms, for syllogisms. In the second, its criteria of selection identify and differentiate the *individual* or *individuals* that instantiate it. The relation between this *individual* and the substantial middle term is expressed in a categorical judgement. Equally, since the predicate is not only an abstract *universal* in relation to the concrete middle term, but also an essential determination of it, the other premise can also be categorical: "Socrates is a man; men are mortal; therefore Socrates is mortal."

2. This syllogism avoids the problems exposed in the *first figures* of the two previous species of syllogism. On the one hand, because the middle term expresses the generic nature of the individual subject, and the predicate categorizes an essential determination, the contingency of the two premises is dissolved. There is no need to justify them further—the requirement that led either to an infinite regress or to alternative figures. On the other hand, the premises do not presuppose the conclusion, as in the *syllogism of totality.* For the middle term differentiates the *individual* and the *universal* category in the premises but enables them to be directly identified in the conclusion. It couples them in a judgement in which it no longer needs to be individuated. There is a genuine process of inference to a novel conclusion.

The inference, then, is no longer a subjective addition to an independent, and equally abstract, content—either in the sense that the transitions in the premises are arbitrary, or in the sense that it introduces a syllogistic structure to represent something that requires no derivation. Rather the inference both is reflected in the major and minor premises and involves a genuine transition to a judgement not previously expressed.

3. Despite this achievement, however, an element of subjectivity remains. For what integrates the inference into an objective and necessary totality is the significance of the terms. Thought must consider implicit connotations of the middle term to establish the necessity of its relation to the two extremes. These implications, however, are not formally represented. While the premises express in positive judgements that this *individual* and this *universal* category are to be coupled with this *particular* genus, they do not indicate why. An element of subjective contingency remains to the extent that both the subject and the predicate terms are to be

particularly differentiated by the middle term in a way not specified in the form.

This contingency can be shown, first of all, by external reflection. For any number of *individuals* immediately presented to thought embody the genus. The selection of this *particular* given *individual* or set of individuals is arbitrary and not itself justified by the middle term.

Such subjectivity, however, does not simply follow from external comparison, but is inherent in the structure of the syllogism itself. The middle term is the substantial genus that is to identify its individual members. The subject is coupled to that middle, however, in a categorical judgement that expresses no necessary relation. This means that the instantiating act that is one of the conditions for the inference is a subjective addition to the objective form.

If on the other hand one starts with the individual subject, it is differentiated in a number of ways that are not specified by the genus. It has an individual content peculiar to itself, which is indifferent to the middle term. Because subjective thought contrasts this independent differentiation to the one introduced by the middle term, the two become simply diverse, contingently coupled in the *categorical judgement*.

The same relation of independent externality is also found in the relation between the genus and its universal category. A number of such categories can be specified. Each one, as abstract, is more general than the concrete genus, and thus independent of it; therefore any particular predicate is not essential to determine the genus.

Speculative reason considers what is lacking in the *categorical syllogism* such that each of the extremes becomes a self-contained universal. The individual is the integration of its diverse differentiations; the category is an abstract universal common indifferently to a number of genera. Since they are not particularly specified by the middle term in the form, they are indifferent to the inferential process. The self-determining necessity of this syllogism, then, is only relatively unconditioned. The two ways in which the middle term conditions the two extremes are indifferent to each other; each condition is hypothetically entertained by thought in the premises but the two absolutely identified in the conclusion. Speculative reason thus individuates a type of inference that has not been captured in the *categorical syllogism,* one in which a hypothetical relation between contingent terms has the relativity of its necessity dissolved so that it can be asserted absolutely. This is the structure of the *hypothetical syllogism.*

Hypothetical syllogism: 1. A *hypothetical judgement* expresses a necessary relation but disregards the immediate actuality of its terms. In the *hypothetical syllogism* (or *modus ponens*) a reference to the latter is added. The grounding relation between antecedent and consequent is no longer simply an abstracted expression but becomes operative in a process of inference that actually uses one to condition the other. From this perspective the truth of the antecedent (the fact that it is the case) is not simply the minor premise but necessitates the inferential process.

2. This structure needs to be evaluated dialectically: first, the major premise, or hypothetical judgement: If A is then B is. What this expresses is an inner necessity or integrating identity that leaves as a matter of indifference whether the terms exist, or how they appear when independent and self-contained. The subject and predicate are not thought as immediate beings, but rather their content is dissolved into the relation. Since the latter is the only thing that is asserted, the terms of the judgement reflect simply the way that necessary relation becomes manifest or appears.

A necessary *grounding relation* on the one hand involves a set of differentiated *conditions,* and on the other involves the result of those conditions—an identified actuality. It is the same intellectual content in both, but considered from different perspectives. Insofar as the conditions are abstracted by thought from the simplicity of the actuality, they could be called *universals* in contrast to its *individuality.* If, on the other, they are referred to as *individuals* in a diverse multiplicity, the consequent would be their *universalizing* integration.[27]

We turn next to the minor premise: that A is the case. It mediates the inference, first, because it simply is the case—an immediate being, indifferent to anything else that might be—but, second, because it is contingent, dissolving itself to produce B. This double meaning, inherent in its meaning as *condition,* becomes explicit when A is asserted as the minor premise in a process of inference. Thought asserts it, only to pass over to something else. At the same time, thought does not simply pass over; A is to be independently asserted as self-contained and complete on its own. (In other words, the antecedent conditions that make up the minor premise A are a dispersed material, ready and waiting for the conditioning act. As individuated they are negatively defined but this negative definition is precisely the distance required if conceptual thought is to become active in moving from the two premises to a conclusion. The contingent act of assertion transforms the hypothetical relation into an actual inference.) This minor premise, then, is on the one hand the implicit necessity of the inferring process, and on the other a contingent immediate that is simply the case without regard to the necessity. It becomes the mediating term of *modus ponens* because it is asserted. As antecedent of the *hypothetical judgement* it embodies the necessity of the relation; as minor premise it is not simply a possible, but is said to be actually the case. In asserting the necessity of a relation as well as the contingent actuality of one of its terms in its premises, the *hypothetical syllogism* contrasts with the *categorical* in which the relation is contingent and the terms are not explicitly differentiated.

Dialectic turns finally to the conclusion: Therefore B is the case. This articulates a similar contradiction: although B is immediately asserted, the "therefore" indicates that it is mediated, derived from something else. As both immediate and mediate it has the same formal structure as the middle term, A; but it can be distinguished as the mediated from the mediating, as the necessary from the necessity, as a determinate individual from the determining process.

However, as we have seen when considering the grounding relation expressed in the *hypothetical judgement,* A and B are to have the same content. They are distinguished only because reflective thought differentiates them formally from the self-identical content that is expressed in the grounding relation "if-then." Thus to refer to B as what is necessary, following "therefore" from the A which is its conditioning necessity, is simply to use an alternate form to express the grounding relation. And to separate them as independent assertions is simply another way of expressing their formal differentiation; therefore the inferential process is identical with the major premise. For the fact that something is asserted does not guarantee that it is actual.

3. Speculative reason considers this paradoxical result. Just as the *categorical syllogism* articulates an inferential process by which different things are brought together into a positive coupling not previously thought, so the *hypothetical syllogism* separates off the terms of a necessary relation and makes them independent. The positive identifying of the one is balanced by the negative distinguishing of the other. But dialectical reflection showed that thought cannot maintain the distinction. The *categorical inference* presupposed a hypothetical coupling that was then explicitly asserted; the contingency of this move required the justification of a *hypothetical inference.* Now in the latter, an asserted contingency is shown to reflect nothing but a necessary relation hypothetically postulated. The apparently indifferent being by which one term is to be distinguished from the other is dissolved into the dynamic structure of their relation. This complex is simply what was asserted in the major premise. The supposed difference between the *hypothetical judgement* and the other assertions in the syllogism is simply a matter of form.

Contingency is no longer simply implicit as it was in the *categorical syllogism*. It is rendered explicit through the independence of the act of assertion. It not only asserts the necessary relation; it also asserts that one term is independently actual. It selects this term, however, with a view to establishing the independent actuality of the other. Its assertion is not a matter of independent immediacy, but reflects the total inferential structure. In this inference, the intellectual process requires terms that are to be indifferent to each other; but in fact any such indifference has no real substance. The appearance of external contingency is taken back into the comprehensive integration of conceptual thought.

The mediation underlying this syllogistic form, then, is not an immediate, *individual* act of intelligence. Its contingency has been dissolved. For the process of establishing its terms as constituent moments of its relating activity characterizes the comprehensive *universality* of thought. And this is not a *universality* of abstracted, and thus static, notions, but a *universality* of a dynamic self-determining process. The former, with its *individualized* independent terms, seemed to require something else to establish its necessity. It thus shows itself to be subjective, having no inherent validity. The latter, however, as a self-determining activity establishing the contingent independence of its terms as well as their necessary relation, does not require anything external to give itself an objective form.

The inferential process of differentiating the constituent moments of an identified unity is that of disjunction. We can represent this in a third species of *necessary inference:* a *disjunctive syllogism*.

Disjunctive syllogism:[28] 1. Even though all the *syllogisms of necessity* have made explicit the relating *universality* of conceptual thought that mediates inference, they yet represent this inference in different ways. The *categorical syllogism* sees it as a substantial genus that *particularizes* itself into an *individual* and a *universal* characteristic. Its activity is simply determin*ing,* and therefore particular (I-P-U). The *hypothetical syllogism* considers it to be the *individual* conditioning assertion that takes a *universal* relation, simply expressed, and gives it a *particularized* form (P-I-U). The syllogism to which we now turn, however, stands under the third figure. The inferring activity distinguishes its *individual* and *particular* terms from itself as intrinsically related. It is thus a comprehensive *universal*; for it not only contingently *individuates* its terms, but also couples them in *particular* determinate relations.

This activity becomes expressed in the substantial identity of a *universal* genus, which at the same time identifies its *individual* instances as differentiated species within its comprehensive totality. This can be expressed in a *disjunctive judgement:* "The *universal* is as much B as C as D" where B, C, and D are its *particular* species. But the "as much as" has a second, negative thrust. For the species are exclusively *individuated* from each other: "The *universal* is either B or C or D."

This exclusive *individuation* is not simply a mutual difference inherent within the *universal.* Rather, each *particular* relates to itself as an *individual*—as that which excludes all other *particulars.* It is this moment that makes possible the inference. For if one *particular* is asserted in the minor premise, the others can be rejected in the conclusion, or if some are excluded in the minor, the rest can be asserted in the conclusion.

2. It is the same assertion that is made in each of the three judgements that make up the inference. In the major premise, it is expressed as a *universal*—as a comprehensive totality of diverse species. In the minor it is asserted as an identified *individual,* which leads to its *particular* differentiation from others; or it is differentiated from others in the minor leading to the assertion of the *individual* in the conclusion.

The syllogistic form expresses the fact that the inferential process both *individually* identifies and *particularly* differentiates. But this double process is equally expressed by the copula in the *universal* major premise. In other words, the *disjunctive syllogism* expressly articulates both the differentiation that was only implicit in the *categorical syllogism* and the identification that was only implicit in the *hypothetical.* Because it identifies both in a comprehensive form there is no inferential process to something new. For the conclusion is simply one determinate moment in a comprehensive totality. The fully adequate formalization of inference destroys it as an inference.

3. This paradoxical conclusion needs to be examined to individuate its ground. In the *hypothetical syllogism* there is a difference between the expressed identity of the grounding relation in the major premise and the distinct assertion of its conditions in the minor. This difference reflects a contingent subjectivity, which severs the immediacy of A from that of B. In the *disjunctive syllogism,* on the other hand, the differentiating operation of inference is already represented in the comprehensive universality of the major premise: "U is either P^1, or P^2, or P^3", just as their identity is expressed by "U is P^1, as well as P^2 and P^3." It posits both essential determinations in a single judgement. The minor isolates either the negative differentiation of *either-or,* or the positive identification of *as well as.* The

conclusion corrects this isolation by asserting the contrary moment. From stating the relation in a single judgement, then, thought has elaborated it into three.

There is then no difference between the activity of inference and what is represented in the formal structure. The act is no longer a subjective process of reflection, distinct from a form that is represented; nor is the syllogism an abstract form ambiguous in its reference. The form of the syllogism refers to the complete process of inference; and the inference is completely expressed in the form. There remains neither the subjectivity of an unrepresented individual thought, nor the subjectivity of an ambigiously abstract form. The universal relating dynamic is explicitly objective; and the form exhaustively represents the process of thinking. In this way the difference, essential for inference, between the activity of inferring and what is inferred (or between the mediating and the mediated) falls away.

We can now understand some of the inner dynamic implicit in the whole discussion of the syllogism. The discrepancy between the activity of inferring and the syllogistic structure means that neither was complete. As simple transition to something else, as synthetic conjunction, and as differentiating individuation, *inference* remained in some sense an immediate and individual act of intelligence. Only when intelligence self-referentially recognized that its simple transitions identified in a synthesis, that its syntheses yet differentiated their terms, and that its individual assertions both identified by means of a transition and differentiated themselves from their contrary did it dissolve all residual elements of logical contingency into the transparent solution of its own self-comprehension.

As formal figure, as reflective operation, and as a necessary transformation rule, the *syllogism* remains external to its subject matter—the inferences of thought. The three figures of the *formal syllogism* abstracted each inferential process in turn. As abstract, however, it was limited and finite; each ought to be more, but could not because the others were explicitly excluded. In the succeeding species of syllogism the middle term became more precisely defined as overreaching this isolation. The *syllogisms of reflection* collected the various determinations—*universal, particular* and *individual*—into a synthesis that was nevertheless imposed on the extremes by external reflection. In the *syllogisms of necessity* the middle term became the act of assertion that both integrated and distinguished its various determinate moments. What cannot be represented in formal symbolism, however, is the integration of the comprehensive dynamic within which the single operation both differentiates and identifies its terms.

In comprehensive thinking, then, three distinct processes are integrated:

the differentiating act of individualizing, or *conceiving*; the particular act of identifying, or *judging*; and the comprehensive act of asserting, or *inferring*. And the whole is collapsed into a single reality because the third process self-referentially includes itself as well as the other two.

Conceptual thought is this dynamic movement in which each moment is constituted as distinct, but this very constitution mediates and determines the other moments, and thereby the total movement. Yet this dynamic of internal self-mediation is simply immediately present.[29] It is *a being*, not as pure indeterminacy, but as integrated with its mediating justification or concept. It is the *heart of the matter* that not only is implicit and hypothetical but independently exists. This is what can be called *objectivity*—a necessity that is strictly universal because it is not relative to anything else, but is absolutely self-determining.

What it determines, however, is a contingent matter that cannot be expressed in the formal structures of thought. To have content, thought must apply this absolutely necessary form to something objective. Speculative reason thus has individuated a double reference for the *objective*: on the one hand it refers to the absolute necessity of its own operations; on the other it refers to the content that will be differentiated by means of those operations. Having self-referentially identified all of its own differentiated operations it can turn to the categories that signify what is not contained within its subjectivity. To follow that path, however, would take us beyond the self-determined limits of this particular study.[30]

Categorical Syllogism: 1. At the end of its reflection on *analogical inference,* speculative reason individuated an inferential process that has not yet been symbolized: the movement to a categorical conjunction. If there is to be a movement, the terms of this conjunction must be independent in the premises. And this independence can be expressed only by their *assertion*. Thus the form:

⊢p

⊢q

Therefore p.q.

2. Dialectical reflection on this syllogism, however, serves to make explicit what is involved. For the conclusion is mediated not by q, but by the two determinate acts of assertion. The latter specifies that both p and q are self-contained universals that determine their own reference. As a result the conjunction in the conclusion must be introduced by something else, external to their assertion. This contingency in conjunc-

tion became explicit earlier in the discussion of *categorical judgement*, and leads to a contrary type of inference in which the conjunction can be the premise for asserting one or other of the terms independently:

$\vdash$ p.q

Therefore $\quad\vdash$ p.

The synthesis asserted in the original conclusion, then, is not necessitated by the premises. The only thing common is that both happen to be asserted. This lack of necessity is contrary to what inference was supposed to achieve.

3. What is missing from the *categorical syllogism* is the justification for assuming that the independent assertion of p (or q) is necessarily related to the assertion of the other. Intelligence differentiated them as particular terms that it then coupled arbitrarily. What has not been represented is the inferential process by which the independent assertion of a particular expression is related to another assertion. The ground of such a move must be made clear if the necessity of the conjunction is to be established. A necessary inference from one asserted judgement to another is represented in the *hypothetical syllogism,* or *modus ponens.*

Hypothetical Syllogism: 1. Although the *hypothetical judgement* only entertains the possibility of its constituent terms, it asserts a necessary relation between them that can become the basis for individuating one as actual. This requires that the other be independently asserted as actual. Thus the form:

$\vdash$ p $\supset$ q

$\vdash$ p

Therefore $\quad\vdash$ q.

2. Dialectic examines the structure of this inference. The following sequence results:

1. p $\supset$ q	hypothesis
2. p	hypothesis
3. p.(p $\supset$ q)	2, 1 conjunction
4. p.$\sim$(p.$\sim$q)	3 definition "$\supset$"
5. $\sim$($\sim$p v (p.$\sim$q))	4.definition "v"
6. $\sim$(($\sim$p v p).($\sim$p v$\sim$q))	5. distribution
7. $\sim$($\sim$p v p) v$\sim$($\sim$p v$\sim$q)	6. definition "v"
8. ($\sim\sim$p.$\sim$p) v (p.q)	7. definition "v"

In the discussion of *disjunctive judgement* we noted that thought cannot think the falsity of p together with the lack of its falsity, and that any such conjunction can be left aside. This leaves:

9. p.q
10. q   9. conjunction.

This train of inference, however, is not strictly necessary, for there is one step not justified by any of the inferential moves previously analyzed: the move from 8 to 9. If this inference cannot be justified, the whole syllogism collapses. For if p were false, its assertion in premise 2 would conjoin a falsity with the denial of its falsity. And this possibility is not ruled out since our reflection on *assertoric judgement* has shown that the independent truth of a simple assertion is problematic. Therefore a contingency remains in the inferential processes symbolized. What justifies the assertion of the minor premise?

This contingency becomes explicit in formal logic when it is recognized that the judgement "p⊃q" can be true whenever p is false, and that the assertion of a false proposition can justify the inference to anything. This form of the syllogism, then, is still bedevilled by an external contingency. It does not specify why the premise p should be asserted.[31] Indeed it is selected as much because it is the antecedent in the major premise as because it is independently known to be true.

3. Speculative reason considers the results of this analysis. The *hypothetical syllogism* is supposed to exhibit an inference from the assertion of p to the assertion of q. However it fails to rule out the possibility of a false assertion of p. In other words, both p and ~p could be true. It was precisely the exclusion of such a conjunction of contraries that generated the transition from 8 to 9, but was not itself justified. Since an exclusive conjunction is a disjunction, the implicit inference can be expressed only in a *disjunctive syllogism*.

Disjunctive Syllogism: 1. In *hypothetical inference* speculative reason has individuated an inferential operation that can be symbolized as:

⊢p v~p   or alternately as   ⊢p v~p
⊢p   ⊢ ~~p
Therefore ⊢ ~~p   Therefore ⊢p[32]

2. With this, thought transcends the subjectivity of assertion. For whatever the content of p, the disjunction in the major premise must be

true, and can therefore be asserted. Once that is asserted, one or other of the syllogistic forms must hold true: the assertion of one as true means that its differentiated contrary is to be excluded as false; the exclusion of one as false is to assert the other as true. While it is contingent which operation one performs in the minor premise, the conclusions must follow so that both an assertion and a denial will be justified. While the inference is no longer contingent but strictly necessary, then, the fact that there are two alternate forms retains the ambiguity between "as well as" and "either-or" expressed in the major premise.

3. Speculative reason self-referentially identifies this delimited ambiguity as the one element of contingency that thought cannot exclude from itself. There is here, then, a double reference to objectivity. The self-justification of the inference form makes it objective and necessary. But because it cannot determine which particular content is true and which false, it is a purely formal objectivity that requires reference to some objective content to discriminate which of the two alternatives is appropriate. Thus symbolic logic makes explicit the limitations of its own formalism.

Part Five

Logical Necessity and Philosophical Freedom

The Necessity of Hegel's Logic

With the disjunctive syllogism Hegel's *Logic* has articulated a logical form that is absolutely necessary. There are no subjective conditions that would render its inferential process contingent and relative.

This, however, returns us to the question posed at the beginning of our study. Commentators, friendly as well as hostile, have accused Hegel of being arbitrary and contingent in his exposition of the logical categories. We are now in a position to see how Hegel would respond to such a charge.

To begin, we need to make clear what is meant by the term *necessity*. In its simplest form, it is an *actual* whose contradictory is not *possible*. However, because of various definitions of actuality and possibility, there are three distinct senses of necessity.[1]

First, an actual is whatever is; a possible is that which is not self-contradictory; and what is necessary is anything which is in fact actual. It would be self-contradictory for anything that is to be other than what it is. Therefore, if it is, its contradictory is no longer possible. Actuality and possibility are categorically conjoined. This sense of an immediate necessity is implicit in any appeal to self-evidence.

Second, an actual is something that exists; and its possibility is articulated in a set of existing conditions that ground its existence. Any one condition by itself is only an element of its possibility, and requires the others in order to be sufficient. But when the set of conditions is complete, the actual must come to be. Relative to these conditions, the contradictory of the actual is impossible, and the actual is necessary. This sense of necessity, symbolized in the hypothetical syllogism, does not establish a strict logical necessity; for the possibility that some of the conditions do not exist cannot be excluded. In other words, the fact of their being sufficient is only contingent, and the necessity is thus relative.

Third, there is the necessity of something actual whose contradictory would be self-contradictory. Such a self-referential, negative determination specifies inherent (rather than external) conditions sufficient to rule out its own falsity. When abstracted, each determinate moment may seem to be simply a contingent possibility. But since they are all comprehended within the one actuality, they guarantee its truth. This is the absolute necessity traditionally associated with logic and rational philosophy.

If one is to avoid the accusation of being arbitrary in one's logic, one can appeal only to the third type of necessity: an actual assertion whose contradictory is self-contradictory. For even though something is self-evident to pure thought, it is a contingent matter that intelligence thinks rather than imagines or represents; therefore what from one perspective may be called necessary, from another may be called accidental. And relative necessity is contingent on the problematic character of its conditions.

Hegel's analysis of the disjunctive syllogism has shown that absolute necessity is purely formal. Despite its self-determined necessity it leaves radically open what interpretation it gives to its symbolic variables. It is a formal tautology that can justify no conclusions about the objective world, and requires a reference to this objectivity in order to acquire a content.

To meet this requirement of an objective referent, though, we are not limited to content that is external to the logical process. We can equally well refer back to the operations of pure thought. As we have seen, two alternative forms of the disjunctive syllogism are possible: in one, the immediate assertion of one disjunct entails the exclusion of its contradictory; in the other, the exclusion of its contradictory provides a sufficient condition for the necessity of a term. These two operations, however, are not present in thought as pure forms. Although they define the first two types of necessity, they also represent the intellectual processes categorized as *becoming* and *reflection*. The positive disjunctive syllogism conceptualizes the movement from the simple immediacy of a logical transition to the statement of its necessity; the negative disjunctive syllogism conceptualizes the movement in which the reflective exclusion of contrary possibilities provides the set of conditions that ground what is essential and necessary. And the whole syllogism conceptualizes the individuating act of conceiving that discriminates between pure reference (or immediate necessity) and abstracted categories (or relative necessity).

By self-referentially individuating the operations of pure thought (as the content for its own absolutely necessary form), we thus establish the fact that conceptual necessity entails *as much* the immediate necessity of pure thought *as* the relative necessity of sufficient conditions; and that it entails *either* one *or* the other. It would itself be self-contradictory if neither held.

The necessity for all three operations is implicitly recognized in contemporary logical discussions. The fact that *modus ponens* has been individuated as the most productive form of inference because it can take a number of premises and combine them to achieve a conclusion that is not expressly stated in any one is the recognition of the need for a conditioned necessity in logical argument. Otherwise we would have only tautological expressions or independent, contingent assertions.

And the appeal to intuition to justify reliance on the laws of identity, non-contradiction, and excluded middle, as well as on other more determinate logical claims, exploits the use of immediate necessity. For a logical intuition is one in which the intellect purges itself of the contingencies of imagination and representation so that what is left is self-evident, and therefore necessary.

Finally, to prove a tautology one must take the laws of thought to be self-evident, and use them as conditions for a hypothetical argument working from its contradictory. Then the self-evidence of the falsity of its self-contradictory conclusion is combined with the conditioned rejection of the hypothetical premise, in order to individuate the necessity of the original judgement.

The totality that thus incorporates all three types of necessity is the comprehensive activity of logical intelligence. As such it provides the context for each of the determinate developments within the *Science of Logic,* and enables a retrospective view to articulate the determinate necessity of each logical operation.

In "The Doctrine of Being", pure thought (as opposed to imagination and representation) found that it passed over from one concept to another: from *being* to *nothing,* from *something* to *other,* from *finite* to *infinite*. These transitions, identified by the category *becoming,* simply happened. As immediately actual, they are necessary in the first sense of the term. This operation becomes more precisely articulated throughout the first book.

It is equally present, however, in each of the detailed discussions; for dialectical reason is nothing but the transition of thought from one term to another. Even at the level of comprehensive thought in the third book of Hegel's study, there appears to be something arbitrary about the dialectical moments. They simply happen. One cannot specify any conditions that would make them relatively necessary. Yet there is something intuitively self-evident about such moves. Although they cannot be justified, they present an inherent, immediate necessity.

The first kind of necessity, one of the two that make up the exhaustive range that is comprehended in absolute necessity, is thus explicated in the first book of Hegel's *Science of Logic,* and is determinately present in each detailed discussion. Indeed, the results of the dialectic are paradoxical because they have simply happened immediately and have not been grounded in any set of conditions.

In "The Doctrine of Essence," the relative necessity that follows from a set of sufficient conditions is established by reflection when it determines what is essential in any grounding relation. This process of reflecting determines the content that is identical in the conditions and in the result, yet differentiates those conditions from each other and thereby from the result. This double determination exposes the grounding relation that is essential if the conditions are to result in something necessary. As reflection identifies the patterns of conditioning throughout the second book, it does not use single terms to signify the operations, as was possible in the doctrine of being. Instead of *becoming, change* and *alteration,* it talks about *essence* and *seeming; reflection* and *determination; identity* and *difference; ground* and *grounded.* This doubling of terms expresses the conditioning relation that holds between one and the other, making them relatively necessary.

The second type of necessity is also present throughout the logic in each unit of discussion. For it is speculative reason which reflects on the paradoxical results of dialectic in order to determine the conditions that ground them. As an independent and external reflection, it brings the original concept together with the resulting thought into a synthesis, so that it can determine more precisely the conditioning relationship that mediates between them such that each reflects the other. This grounds the necessity of the synthesis.

In "The Doctrine of Conceptual Thought," the individualizing act of reference identifies an *immediate* actual by means of a *conditioning* process that self-referentially abstracts from it the universality of thought that is its contradictory. When it then *immediately* conjoins these two in judgement, reflection shows that there is nevertheless a *conditioning* process of inference. In any conceptualizing process, this act of individualizing articulates the structure of absolute necessity.

In other words, the third operation of logical thought recognizes that the two previous operations are mutually exclusive, yet complement each other in an individual totality. The mutual reflection, which speculative reason generates, collapses into a single process that is not itself determined by anything external; thus it appears to be contingent. This conditioning relation contrasts with the apparently arbitrary transition to dialectical paradoxes which immediately give rise to speculative reflection. Since these two mutually exclusive processes complement each other, they collapse into a single comprehensive term, whose absolute contingency can be expressed only by an act of reference.

The operation of pure reference, which conditions and is conditioned by an act of self-reference, is the process of conceiving. For it individuates even its own operations in such a way that they can be represented by individual signs and symbols. The development of this single process of reference-through-self-reference is the explicit subject matter of the third book of the *Logic*.[2]

However it is equally present throughout the logic as the operation of understanding. When the mediated results of speculative reason collapse into a single unity, the result is individuated by understanding so that it will be both clearly identified and precisely differentiated from contrary terms.

The third operation that embodies absolute necessity, however, does not produce a completeness that goes no further. For it initiates in its turn an immediate dialectical transition that has its own necessity. It is this open-ended circle that gives to the *Logic* its developmental character.

We have shown, therefore, that in the total structure of the *Logic* as well as in its individual sections, all three types of necessity are operative. Closer observation shows that they structure the intermediate developments as well. Thus the immediate transitions of *becoming, reflecting* and *individualizing* lead to conditioning relationships between *a being* and its *determinations, identity* and *difference,* and *subject* and *predicate.* When their disjunction is individualized as *being for its own sake,* as *ground* or as *inference,* this initiates the process by which the complexity collapses into a single object of reference.[3]

Yet another intermediate stage is present in the *Science of Logic,* although it has not been part of the subject matter of this book. For the three sections of Hegel's work here considered are all the first parts of much longer discussions. Since they focus primarily on the operations of thought, they represent simple transitions that are to be contrasted with the reflective structure of the mutual conditioning that is present in thought's relation to a world other than thought. When thought thinks this otherness, it develops categories that apply to it, such as pure *quantity, existence* and *objectivity.* Ultimately, however, *quantity* comes to be identified with *quality* as *measure, reflection* with *existence* in *actuality,* and *subjectivity* with *objectivity* in *the idea.* When this identification becomes completely individuated, it leads over to *essence, to comprehensiveness* and, finally, to pure reference which limits itself to that which is absolutely other than thought.

In other words the comprehensive circle of the three types of necessity circulates through the logic at many levels of complexity. What might appear to be contingent and arbitrary has yet its necessary place within the totality of pure thought that has self-referentially individuated all of its own operations.

This rich complexity is not evident to the reader who endeavours to follow the text for the first time. The argument is presented as an arbitrary transition in which one category simply follows from another. Here there appears to be no other necessity than that Hegel actually thought it this way. Something completely different would have been, but is no longer, possible. Such a reaction underlies the criticisms made by both Popper and Russell.[4]

A second, more reflective, reading begins to make evident the way in which each of the transitions is conditioned by its relative context. While the arguments have no inherent, logical necessity, then, they follow from the fact that Hegel was a monist, seeing everything from the perspective of the whole, or that his "logical" inferences reflected empirical associations. Neither rules out the possibility of a wide range of alternatives, for the determinate character that Hegel attributed to the whole, or discovered empirically, arbitrarily determined which transitions were well grounded and which not. Charges such as these have been made by Findlay, Taylor and Mure.[5]

Only with a third reading is the specific, self-referential focus of the logic individuated: the absolute necessity in pure thought that specifies that a transition is either simply the case, thus ruling out its contradictory, or reflects a set of determining conditions that together are sufficient to make it necessary. Not only do these two exhaust the range of distinctly individuated logical operations, but they mutually exclude each other within the comprehensive dynamic of pure intelligence. The self-referential moment, then, integrates all of the logical moments into a single totality within which the contrasting alternative moments can be differentiated. Reflection on the three readings shows that the various interpretations and criticisms embody the three constituent moments of one comprehensive logical operation. Thus it not only establishes its own necessity but justifies the contingent necessity of its various criticisms.[6]

From the perspective of a third reading one turns back to the criticisms and discovers that the critics have themselves appealed to intuitively self-evident principles, or accepted a set of conditions not themselves justified. Since they have not reflected on the processes by which they have come to their own conclusions, and have not individuated the conceptual operation that alone can establish absolute necessity, their criticisms presuppose the very type of arbitrary contingency that they accuse Hegel of having. But their arguments tend to lack the redeeming feature that a third reading makes possible an understanding of what at first was only implicit and conditioned. In other words, if there is to be a charge of arbitrary contingency, it is to be levelled against the critics of Hegel; and it will be justified by those very principles of absolute necessity that Hegel himself has articulated.[7]

At the end of disjunctive inference a double reference appeared. As a self-determining necessity, the combination of the two disjunctive syllogisms was absolutely necessary and objective; it was the way by which pure thought determines itself. At the same time the internal ambiguity made evident its subjective formalism in that it required reference to something other than itself to provide a concrete content. This double reference raises two questions that need to be considered if the assessment of the necessity of Hegel's logic is to be complete.

In the first place, Hegel has concluded that pure thought manifests the pattern of self-determining necessity. But we have defined pure thought relative to the psychological operations of intelligence; and these are known to us only in the context of the human species. Is the absolute necessity of self-referential thought, then, simply the way in which man actually thinks when he has purged his mind of relative contingencies? If so, what is to ensure against the possibility that the way man thinks has nothing at all to do with the real world—that it is necessary (in the sense of being universal) but not true? And why is pure thinking more reliable than intuition or imagination in any case?

In the second place, if it can be established that the purely logical operations are also true, does this necessity abolish human freedom? Is their application to something other than thought, such as will or action in the future, simply a necessary reflection of the conditioning ground of its own past? Even if there be future contingency, it cannot be anticipated and is therefore irrelevant to purposeful action.

If the first question wonders about an immediate necessity in the relation between Hegel's logic and the world, so that the reflective question of truth is irrelevant, the second wonders about a conditioning necessity that rules out self-determination. To respond with the assurance that both are formally necessary is not sufficient, for it leaves open the possibility that the logic is neither true nor good.

The first of these questions is considered by Hegel in the book that was to serve as the introduction to his system: *Phenomenology of Spirit*. The second concerns the relation of the logic to the system as a whole, which is anticipated in the last chapter of the larger logic, and is sketched in the *Encyclopaedia of the Philosophical Sciences*. To round out our discussion of the necessity of Hegel's logic, we will conclude with a general consideration of this larger context.[8]

13

The
Logic
as
Metaphysics

The necessity of Hegel's logic remains a contingent necessity. Even though thought can show how its inherent dynamic differentiates various categories only to identify them again in an objective totality, the necessity of that process is not itself justified. An intelligence has become fully conscious of its own operations, and has arbitrarily decided to commit itself to the discipline of pure thought.

Intelligence, however, is but one function of man, man is but one of many species on earth, and the earth is but one planet in the vast expanse of the universe. It may be interesting to examine how man's instinctive traits come to be expressed; but does the structure of his intellectual activity bear any relation at all to the structure of the universe as a whole? Does the logic outline as much the inherent nature of reality as the necessary way intelligence thinks?

Hegel is bold enough to make such a claim:

Pure science . . .contains thought to the extent that it is the heart of the matter in itself,[1] or alternatively the heart of the matter in itself to the extent that is equally pure thought . . .Consequently, far from its being formal, far from its standing in need of a matter to constitute an actual and true cognition, it is its content alone that is absolutely true, or, if one still wanted to employ the word "matter," it is authentic matter—a matter not external to its form, since the matter is rather pure thought and hence the absolute form itself. Accordingly, logic is to be understood as the system of pure reason, as the realm of pure thought.

> *This realm is the truth as it is without veil, self-contained and complete in itself.*[2]
>
> "The objective logic," he says further on, "takes the place of the former metaphysics."[3]

The claim of an absolute necessity for the logical analysis has not been justified in the preceding commentary. Our presuppositions involved isolating the psychological functions of intelligence: leaving aside will and feeling, consciousness and self-consciousness, ignoring the social dynamic and all contacts with an alien nature. The reader was invited to refer simply to his own intellectual operations. New categories were defined in terms of the specific relating acts that speculative reason discerned; they were analyzed, using criteria derived from reflection; and the resulting integration simply completed the process. Nowhere was there any contact with an external reality. To be sure some concepts were of 'externality', 'existence', 'actuality' and objectivity'; but their definitions remained the product of thought, conscious of its own operations in thinking about what would be other than itself. The logic never makes use of sensible intuition—the sort of contact with external existence that Kant laid at the foundation of his *Critique of Pure Reason.*

Such an interpretation awakens the suspicion that the whole Hegelian enterprise is simply a house of dreams—the construct of an ivory tower far removed from the critical tensions of real life. He is, after all, called an idealist, one who has separated himself from brute material facts and principles. This suspicion can have two contrary results. On the one hand, those who are predisposed to accept Hegel's logical discussion as being more than a systematic intellectual history will dismiss the preceding commentary based on subjective intelligence as misrepresenting everything that Hegel was about. On the other hand, those who have doubts about the validity of Hegelian philosophy will use the same commentary as sufficient justification for rejecting the whole system.

The principle of interpretation we have followed, then, finds itself faced with a critical problem. How can it do justice to Hegel's claim that the logic is the truth unveiled? What kind of bridge can be constructed between the purely internal dynamic of intelligence and the external world of nature and of human history?

The first move in providing an answer is to recall several important aspects of our preliminary discussion. The act of pure thinking that concluded the analysis of intelligence did not simply make explicit a stream of consciousness in the manner of a modern novel. It involved a critical assessment of intellectual content. It discounted the contingencies that influenced its own operations: attention and recollection, imagination and memory. For understanding isolates a concept not in terms of its accidental appearance in space and time, but in terms of its internal significance; dialectical judgement explored relations in such a way that arbitrary associations were dismissed, and only those that explicitly followed from the original concept were maintained. Similarly speculative reflection refused to be satisfied with a contingent synthesis, but articulated the inherent structures that integrate a concept with its implications.

This critical activity of pure thought was applied to the intellectual processes themselves. Everything that was not fundamental to the intellectual dynamic, everything that followed from the particularity of experience whether external or internal, was rejected. Whatever might mislead thought into supposing the relative and inadequate to be true and comprehensive, and any transition that showed itself to be the contingent product of a particular space and time, or of a chance association, was abandoned. Only by such a preliminary psychological critique, submitting all categories to rigorous dialectical test, was the logic able to develop any perspective of comprehensive necessity at all.

This dynamic, internal to the individual intelligence, was articulated in language so that it could become the common reflection of various minds. In this way the contingency of an individual relativism was avoided; for the move to a common language (with its attendant need to become conscious of a shared meaning in contrast to particular connotations and associations) required that the single individual become aware of his own peculiarities and transcend their limitations. When the social dynamic of recognition expanded to the cross-cultural contact of diverse languages, those patterns of intellectual transition that characterize one or another culture were acknowledged to be only a particular way of thinking about the world and not necessarily inherent in human consciousness as such.[4]

In the earlier discussion of intelligence and language, then, a set of procedures served to recognize and thus exclude contrary possibilities. They transformed the contingent necessity of the logic into a relative one. They ensured that the logical system would not be an aethereal construction in the air, but would reflect those operations that constitute all intellectual activity, irrespective of its particular conditions. This self-critical perspective has exposed the contingencies relative to the human species. If there is a necessity that is more than purely immediate, it will be grounded in this cross-cultural self-consciousness. Because its conditions are contingent, however, the discrepancy between human certainty and absolute truth remains.

In his *Phenomenology of Spirit,* published in 1807, Hegel took as his fundamental theme this discrepancy between certainty and truth, between subjective intelligence and reality. The claim to truth of an intelligent being is not necessarily true. The experience of actual objects and of his own personal history forces him to acknowledge that some such claims made previously have been radically mistaken. The "introduction" to Hegel's system was to articulate this odyssey of spirit, showing how consciousness could eventually not only be certain of truth but also be truly certain—how the claim to truth justifies itself.

The work is an analysis of experience, both personal and cultural. Each claim of consciousness is submitted to rigorous criticism, not by an external philosophical spectator, but rather by the experience that follows from its confident affirmation. Thus experience itself leads to scepticism, and scepticism prepares the ground for a more comprehensive stage of consciousness. The *Phenomenology,* then, outlines a process of criticism similar to that contained in our introductory analysis of intelligence and language. But instead of sketching it through an atemporal analysis, it traces the temporal movement through which men and women have experienced the falsity of their relative claims, have corrected this inadequacy, and have achieved thereby a more comprehensive self-knowledge.

In this enterprise, however, Hegel makes a claim that is not at all self-evident—a most presumptuous affirmation that appears to have no truth to it at all. For he does not leave the historical development as an indeterminate progression, asymptotically approximating the integrity of certainty and truth. He ends the *Phenomenology* with a chapter on absolute knowledge—a certainty concerning truth that is alleged to dissolve all unresolved relativism. This final move, and this final move alone, can transform the logical system from the most adequate expression so far of the way intelligence comprehends the world, to being an embodiment of "the only true method," "the truth unveiled."[5]

This final chapter is intensely compact, crowding everything into sixteen pages in the German edition; it overflows with the abstract vocabulary of Hegel's philosophical writing; and it was written under the pressure of world events.[6] A full scale commentary on its content would require an independent work.[7] For our purposes, however, we can schematically derive from it the way Hegel justifies his identification of the logic with metaphysics—how an individual intelligence can have pure knowledge.

"This reconciliation of consciousness with self-consciousness. . .shows itself to be brought about in a double-sided way; in the one case in the religious spirit, in the other case, in consciousness itself as such. They are distinguished from each other by the fact that the former is this reconciliation in the form of implicit being,[8] the latter in the form of self-contained being for its own sake.[9] As we have considered them, they at first fall apart. . .The unification of the two sides has not yet been brought to light; this it is that winds up this series of embodiments of spirit, for in it spirit gets to the point where it knows itself. . .as it is inherent and self-contained, in itself and for its own sake."[10]

Specified in this passage are the three distinct moments of the final achievement: the *inherent* reconciliation, the reconciliation *for its own sake,* and the complete integration of both.

In the immediately preceding paragraph Hegel has just finished reviewing the second of these moments: the reconciliation *for its own sake,* or reconciliation self-contained. It provides, if you like, the necessary condition of absolute knowlege: that consciousness become aware of itself as containing the criteria of truth. When its capacities and its limitations become completely transparent, it no longer requires external events and experiences to test the validity of its claims. It achieves such self-knowledge through the process of developing experience, in which a claim to certainty takes an immediate determination (external or internal) as being the truth, only to discover that it in fact is limited and is not what it ought to be.[11] Each relativizing characteristic is isolated and transcended in turn. The first six chapters of the Phenomenology are devoted to showing how the totality of these individual experiences can culminate in absolute self-knowledge, i.e. in knowledge that is self-contained.

At first, the test of truth is taken to be the immediate object of sense. But changing experience teaches that the way the object is sensed, perceived and understood is a function of consciousness itself; the limitations of immediate experience are exposed. Then the individual endeavours to become certain of himself. But the variable dynamic of consciousness leads him to scepticism and beyond. He surrenders completely any claim that he, as changing individual, contains the criteria for truth, and submits himself totally to that which is other than himself.

This surrender becomes expressed in a third operation, simple observation. By refusing to be active the self simply accepts what is presented objectively. In the interim, it has changed the way the object is thought from that of pure consciousness. For it has introduced as criterion the need to avoid all change, and now searches for unalterable principles.

Because this test rises above the subjective contingency that distorts the processes of sensing, perceiving and understanding, it is taken to be independent of, and external to, subjective consciousness. At this stage of developing experience, consciousness considers its own being insofar as it is something universal, its "I" as something external.[12] When, through disappointed expectations and unexpected events, however, it becomes aware of its own role in specifying the criterion of changelessness, its perspective is transformed.

Each of the first three levels of developing consciousness are functions of personal experience, the way by which an individual consciousness, on its own, attempts to come to terms with its world.[13] But with the breakdown of rational observation a change occurs. It is no longer the individual as such that establishes the permanent criteria of truth. He has already surrendered all personal peculiarities in the transition to observation; the sense for the universal has permeated his consciousness through all the subsequent transformations of experience. Now he is aware of himself as a constituent member of a people—as part of an objective totality. The integrated concreteness of an individual culture transcends his own particular limitations.

The criterion of truth then becomes that which is affirmed by a society, self-confident in its mastery of nature, requiring no alien divinity to compensate for its limitations. The world is there only to be used. The spirit of a culture dissolves any value that may be found in things in themselves and considers them only from the perspective of its own self-conscious: "The thing is I."[14] What is found in the environment is a function of communal activity—either its presupposed matter or its created product. This process is a dynamic, not of individual experience, but of history, with each age constructing its world on the ruins of that which preceded, transforming ever more thoroughly the natural environment into one shaped and adapted for the life of man. It culminates in the French Revolution. There the demise of one culture and the creation of a new is no longer left to the contingencies of time, but is itself the explicit product of self-conscious community. At this point the human spirit becomes aware through its own action of its own awesome capacity. Not only is it positive and constructive but also negative and destructive.

The level of pure self-knowledge has not yet been achieved, however. For a culture cannot become aware of itself quite independently of all its individual members. And these members are in no way absolute masters of their fate. The onrushing torrent of the French Revolution carried its participants along in its irrepressible dynamic. Although the creation of men, it submitted tamely neither to their comprehension nor to their will. The promethean self-confidence in human capacity found itself confronted by the unbreachable barriers of human limitation in the reign of terror.

Individuals responded to this terrifying historical development by realising that culture and community were not one suprapersonal reality to which they simply submitted. They themselves as individuals bore responsibility for what in fact occurred. They became conscious of themselves as autonomous moral agents.

This initiates the final transformation of human experience. The actual life of spirit—that dynamic vitality of human community—begins to be reconciled with its own self-consciousness[15] in the person of its morally responsible members. These have been formed by the whole previous process—the traditions of their individual pasts. This comprehensive perspective has worked itself into the fabric of their lives. Therefore, when they reflect on their own moral responsibility they are integrating all those many moments into a simple intuition: the claim on conscience that this is what is right. In the concrete awareness of moral autonomy, the whole education of the human race is contained.[16] Nothing external remains that would render its self-knowledge relative.

This moral intuition of the beautiful soul, however, does not last; for the individual acts—he introduces a new and alien event into this integrated totality, thereby disrupting the simplicity of conscience. Henceforth it is affected by contingencies that contradict what was intended. The comprehensive completeness of pure self-knowledge is destroyed as the act reveals unexpected consequences—either in the motivation of the agent or in its effect on the historical environment. The simple intuition of what is right now becomes a harsh judge, condemning this act for dereliction of duty. The moral agent, aware both of his standards and of his responsibility for the deed, condemns himself; he did not perform what was required by his pure self-conscious moral intuition. This scission not only disrupts the self-confidence of the moral individual, but reproduces in miniature the disruption of history represented by the French Revolution. It is overcome when, on the one hand, the stern perspective of duty surrenders its harshness and recognizes that its own inherent necessity required the delinquent act; and when, on the other, the agonized sense of guilt perceives that it is only a moment within the comprehensive context of all actions, and contributes to this totality precisely through its perverse particularity. Because harsh judge and guilty agent are the same person, the moral individual forgives himself. The finite contingency of the individual act is no longer rejected absolutely, but is accepted as an inescapable limitation that will continue to resist the pure moral ought. Indeed it is through their conflict within one and the same consciousness, that the ought becomes actual and the limitations are transcended. Aware of himself as the individual who integrates this perpetual conflict and transition between actual limitation and conditioning obligation, the moral consciousness becomes reconciled to itself, and is thus completely self-contained for its own sake.

The moral agent, who in this way accepts that he is essentially differentiated as man by his self-constituted finitude, thereby integrates the whole range of past experience and history that constitutes his individuality. Their influence is no longer something alien, to which he simply submits. Rather he knows himself as a human agent identified with his species, who appropriates his environment by means of a limited and relative reflection, and who acts somewhat arbitrarily on this environment to achieve his ends. Because he can differentiate his own peculiar role in such interplay, he can equally identify the finitude that is not unique but pertains to all men and women. Aware of how man responds to his world, he can hypothetically contrast it to what the world would be, apart from all human intervention. The acknowledgement of the conditioned necessity of human limitation is the necessary condition for a completely comprehensive understanding of the way man deliberately interacts with his world; but it takes one no further.

This self-awareness, then, has a negative implication. Since all human activity is essentially limited, the self-aware individual has distinguished what man does not know and cannot do from what he does and can. To this extent the former is unknown—the implicit principle of the universe as such to which mankind as a whole can only refer and submit. All human achievement, including this self-knowledge, is therefore only relative, a function of one particular and finite species. The history of developing self-consciousness that achieves the first condition for absolute knowledge thus comes to an absolute barrier. It is a reconciliation of consciousness with itself that is self-contained and for its own sake. But it cannot know anything at all about the inherent character of the world as such. It knows itself as condemned to an absolute relativism.[17]

This self-knowledge of itself, then, requires reference to the second moment in absolute knowledge: the implicit reconciliation of man with his world, inherent in the being of man as such. This becomes evident in the religious spirit; for in religion, consciousness acknowledges the fundamental limitation of all mankind. Although Hegel sketches a whole history of religious consciousness (in the seventh chapter of the *Phenomenology*), for our purposes we can concentrate simply on the final stage—revealed religion. In Christianity a complex set of beliefs is presented to the individual as being the faith of the world. He has no role in formulating them. He may only accept, and then integrate, them into his life.[18]

Revealed religion reports that God is a pure essence, complete in himself, dynamically identifying himself by eternally begetting his Son, and reintegrating this differentiated other into his own life as individualized Spirit. In an act of pure freedom, the triune God created a world that was alien. This world not only lacks the inherent ability to reintegrate itself with the divine, but also contains integrated individuals, men and women, who assert their independence over against God. The stern unity of this divine will thus stands opposed to the sinful diversity of the human condition.

But the religious tradition went further and reported how man was reconciled to God. The pure will acted again, not as absolutely free and independent, but in the context of this radical alienation. He differentiated himself from the differentiated creation, not by isolating himself in an absolute other, but by particularizing himself further, relative to the particularity of the world. God became concrete, an individual point of reference in that external reality. Having submitted himself to its determinate and independent limitations, he died. Through these events, God as an abstract other passed away. The result was a new divine reality—a dynamic spiritual existence that continually submitted itself to the limitations of man, yet passed beyond them into a more comprehensive totality.

This story of creation, fall, incarnation, crucifixion and resurrection/pentecost[19] is reported to man as the *history* of God—of the absolute reality that conditions and determines the whole universe. It has as its counterpart a story of human response.

When, through positive dogma, finite man is told not simply of his finitude but also of his excluding rejection of God he becomes acutely conscious of his guilt and sin. His evil is not that of a single moral agent, but is the limiting condition of human nature as such. Man's agony reaches its culmination with the reflection that it was human nature in its most essential determination that killed God, that destroyed the pure beyond of abstract infinity to which he ever aspired. In this dark night of the soul in which all reliance on what is human is absolutely abandoned, he yet discovers in himself a living spiritual dynamic which dissolves his absolute finitude. This is the same comprehensive life that characterized the Spirit who proceeded from the death of God. At one and the same time he is the humanity that is to be absolutely rejected, and the divinity that has been transformed from pure essence through absolute limitation into vibrant life. In the knowledge of himself as dynamically related to God, he is incorporated into the company of all those who confess themselves to be both sinner and justified.[20]

Because this confession is contradictory, the congregation of the faithful believe that the present experience of the divine spirit is partial and incomplete. At present they are sinners; in the future they will be justified. A further external initiative will be required before the final and complete reconciliation of men and God will be achieved. Either it will be mediated by a church that stands as the objective agent of grace, or it will be achieved through a future divine intervention, when all human limitation, including that of a physical body, will be transcended. In the self-consciousness of Martin Luther, however, that remnant of unresolved diversity was dissolved. When Luther refused to consider that anything other than scripture and conscience—the objective history of the incarnate God and the internal conviction of the justified sinner—could justify his assertions,[21] he dismissed both the church and the future as necessary mediating conditions for absolute self-confidence of the reconciled state. It is in fact already achieved. For it is when man knows himself as simultaneously sinner and just, when fully conscious of himself as rejecting God while yet reconciled with him, that he knows himself as he is known by God.[22]

The Lutheran Christian, then, knows intuitively in his own conscience that his life embodies the inherent dynamic of the divine Spirit. But this knowledge is made consciously explicit by means of representative structures. Father, Son, and Spirit are independent names, suggesting that their referents exist external to each other. The act of creation and the process of reconciliation are retold as historical narratives, as if inevitably conditioned by the latter's contingency. The integrating unity that transcends these determinate structures remains a mystery; it is only intuited by conscience, and is never expressed in doctrine.[23]

This intuited integration, already present in the individual as believer, is reconciliation implicit, the second constituent moment of absolute knowledge. All relativism has been transcended in the profound consciousness of oneself as simultaneously sinner and just. Not only the integration of one's own cultural experience and history is to be found in conscience, but also a complete reconciliation with the moving principle of the universe as such. However, the latter remains implicit because it is only intuited as immediate, and represented in inadequate signs; it is not yet articulately comprehended.

If, then, the secular moment of moral self-acceptance brings together the total set of historical conditions that renders explicit and self-contained the reconciliation of certainty and truth, the religious experience of reconciliation points to the inherent presence of the grounding relation. For absolute knowledge, however, these two must be combined not simply in an artificial synthesis, but in an integrated unity. Already, in the conscience of one and the same individual, the history of man to and beyond the French Revolution and Lutheran certainty (in justification by faith alone) have been brought together. What is required is to integrate this synthesis—to take the diverse aspects simply conjoined by external reflection and to show how they mutually reflect each other in an objective and comprehensive totality.[24]

This requires a perspective in which an individual is transparently aware of himself as integrating all his conditions—a stage of experience already considered under the title: the beautiful soul. There the autonomy of the moral conscience marks the culmination of man's self awareness as he responds to the trauma of the French Revolution. But conscience is also the absolute conviction that triggered the Lutheran reformation. This single stage of an individual consciousness combines human secular history and the story of salvation.

The claim of the beautiful soul to truth broke down because the individual had to act, and in acting reasserted his peculiar individuality over against the universal integrating dynamic. From the present perspective this action is not simply the negative destruction of an inadequate stage but also the positive development of man's inherent nature as limited. The individual acts, distinguishing particular action from universal truth. In this way he falls into sin, or evil. But in the act of self-acceptance the two distinguished moments are reconciled. The pure universal is dissolved into a dynamic process; the single act surrenders its isolation to become incorporated into a larger context. It is the whole movement, and not the simple immediacy of conscience, that achieves pure self-knowledge. The total comprehensive process (not simply the uncontaminated purity of moral insight) is transparent to consciousness.

But this process is precisely the one represented in the dogma of revealed religion. God acts in creation like the beautiful soul that opposes concrete particular existence to its pure essence. In this his completeness falls apart; limited by an alien world he becomes finite. Through the story of reconciliation the pure essence dissolves into the actualized life of dynamic spirit, and through the experience of it particular men and women in the world are incorporated into its comprehensive vitality. This double movement reflects the moral integrity of the self-accepting individual. When the individual consciousness becomes explicitly aware of this essential identity—that, despite all difference in content, the way it becomes conscious of itself as conscientious agent has the same form as the way God comprehends all reality into his life—he has himself acquired the perspective through which he can comprehend that reality. For all reality is movement, not movement in general, but one that differentiates absolutely and identifies totally in an individual comprehensive operation. This triple process, represented by the Lutheran *simul peccator et justus,* and brought to consciousness through responsible action is the inherent principle that integrates all that is. To know this is to have absolute knowledge. All relative perspectives have been transcended.

"This knowledge—its nature, moments and movement—has thus shown itself to be the pure being-for-its-own-sake of self-consciousness; it is I, namely *this* I and no other, the I that is at the same time an immediately *mediated* or dissolved *universal.*"[25]

This stage of consciousness distills the whole range of human experience into the pure essence of its own internal dynamic. From this perspective it can look back over its experience and identify the essential structure of relations by which each stage of consciousness or self-consciousness develops and dissolves. It has the universal criterion with which to differentiate what is essential from what is inessential, even though the process itself be temporal, whether transitory or enduring.[26]

Alternatively, however, it can simply examine itself. The I can bring to consciousness the inherent dynamic of its own intelligence. This movement, internal to the I, distills into a pure intellectual process the historical accumulation of human experience as well as the cosmic dynamic of creation and reconciliation. Because the external relations of space and time have been dissolved into the dynamic of pure self-knowledge, the immediate transitions of intelligence are not arbitrary and contingent but encapsulate what is essential in all human interaction with the natural and social world as well as what is essential in the dynamic life of the cosmic order. There is thus no difference between the science of logic and that of metaphysics. Logic's "content is the exposition of God as he is in his eternal essence before the creation of nature and finite spirit."[27]

"It is not blind necessity that forces intelligence to proceed towards successive solutions, but it is necessity freely accepted, a will to reach knowledge."[28] Pure thinking comprehends a network of conditions that includes the whole human race in its self-confident independence from anything transcendent as well as the history of man's conditioned interaction with the apparently alien divinity of the cosmic order. Because both culminate in the acceptance of essential limitations, this pure self-knowledge can take account of its contraries: unconscious ignorance and deliberate partiality. "Strictly speaking, the *Logic* of Hegel proffers nothing against the rejection of truth, except the sole consolation that true knowledge can and must comprehend its contrary—excessive stupidity—while those who reject it deprive themselves forever of the meaning that truth provides."[29]

This self-defined necessity, however, still leaves open the possibility of a relation of conditioning necessity that is absolute. The internal necessity of pure thought necessarily captures all phenomenal processes in space and time. If there be any contingency, that itself is simply a function of the limitation inherent in relative necessity. Therefore one cannot rise above this necessity to achieve a genuine freedom of self-determination in which alternative futures are entertained and a choice is made between those ends that are to be achieved.[30]

Such an iron-bound necessity appears to follow from the assumption, explicit at the end of the *Phenomenology,* that the temporal processes of human experience can be collapsed into the logical processes of pure thought—that time is nothing more than "simply the concept that is there, that is presented to consciousness in pure intuition."[31] Is this simple identification of the temporal with the conceptual process justified?

The answer to this question is critical. For if time and concept are simply identified, then the necessity of Hegel's logic is simply the relative necessity of the second type. It is not at all clear how a temporal process can condition conceptual thinking in some kind of developmental process so that the history of philosophy will introduce genuine novelties into the logical assessment of reality. Nor is it clear that pure thought can condition the future to achieve an actual social order that is both more comprehensive and more diversified than what has in fact appeared.

The possibility of something new is ruled out by a relation of necessary conditioning. Even if the world is contingent, the *Phenomenology* has shown that this contingency makes the absolute knowledge of pure thought relatively necessary. Is the contrary movement from such knowledge to the world also relatively necessary? In the final chapter of the *Logic* Hegel considers the distilled essence of pure thought, which is simply its dynamic method. And he discovers that it leads conceptual thinking into a non-conceptual relation—to that which is other than thought. A final commentary is required to discern whether this transition is conditioned or immediate, whether knowledge leads to determinism or freedom.

Thought
and
Action

In the final chapter of the *Logic,* Hegel considers *the idea* that underlies the whole logical procedure. He has allowed pure thought to pass over from one concept to another in a dialectical transition; he has reflected on this process to determine what is essential in it; and he has individuated new concepts that can be abstracted as immediate categories. Because the series of moves is contingent upon the determinate transition that actually happens in the first instance, the way the logic operates at one moment is distinct from the way in which it operates at another. But once it has worked through the many levels of logical complexity, intelligence can refer back to the totality of its own operation and abstract from it the method that is common to all.[1] In this act of pure self-reference, the method identifies its own internal conditions, making no reference to anything external. As self-contained, it is not only *the idea* of the logic, but *the absolute idea*.

Method has a beginning. As beginning, it is simple, for the complex would be result; and it is universal, for there is as yet nothing from which it can be distinguished.

This characterization refers to any beginning, whether presented immediately in intuition, posited representatively, or isolated by abstract thought. What is significant is not what is taken for the starting point—its subject matter—but how it is considered. Whether independent objectivity or unsophisticated subjectivity, neither or both, it is only from something simple and universal that any process begins.

The beginning is therefore determinate; it is simple over against all complexity, and universal over against any particularity. This contrast is presented to thought as an immediate transition of thought. But it is resisted. The starting point is taken as simple and universal regardless of whatever inherent complexity and particularity it may have. To individuate itself as the beginning, these other determinations are to be distinguished from it as alien and secondary. The two sides are simply aspects of a bare diversity.

This second moment of the method, however, is not an external addition. From one perspective, to be sure, the differentiation adds something new to the beginning, creating a synthesis. But from another, it is analytic, making explicit what is already implicit in the beginning. For to identify a beginning is a complex procedure that opposes simplicity to complexity.

In the act of individuating the beginning, an immediate dialectical transition has introduced an explicit contradiction. At one and the same time the beginning is simple and complex, universal and particular. No longer is the beginning immediate, but something mediated—the result of a process in which essential distinctions have been made in order to maintain it as the beginning. Therefore this process is also not simple and immediate. In other words the immediate transition turns back on itself and reflectively recognizes its own complex character.

This leads to a third moment in the method[2]—reflection on the contradictions in order to identify their ground. Thought identifies the opposed terms to determine what is essential in their relation. Insofar as those terms have been analytically distinguished, this reflective operation is synthetic. But insofar as the immediate transition to something else was synthetic, the reflective move analyzes the process to discriminate its constituent moments.

Paradox reappears. But instead of finding that what is simple is complex and thus contradictory, reflection shows that what are contrasted as opposites are to be essentially identified. For the two moments do not simply stand in abstract confrontation; rather, they are constituents of a single relation that can be individuated only by means of their contrast. This identity is the essential ground that is genuinely immediate because it underlies the contradictions inherent in the apparently immediate beginning; the act of identifying reflects an inherent integration. Thus just as a dialectical *becoming* dissolves into *reflection,* so *reflection* dissolves into conceptual *individuation.* It refers to an immediate, simple universal that collapses its contrasting moments into its identity. This method thereby returns to where it started. But the simple universality achieved is no longer simply posited or accepted as a beginning; it is "something *deduced* and *proven.*"[3]

Between the first and the resulting immediate there are three intermediate stages—the negative thrust of immediate transition or differentiating dialectic, the identifying thrust of conditioned reflection or speculative synthesis, and the individuating thrust of conceptual comprehension or understanding. The three movements together make up the total dynamic of the method. As yet, however, they have been simply added one to another in an immediate conjunction. The structure of their mutual implication has not been articulated systematically.

Reflection considers the three moments in a synthesis. This leads to a sharp differentiation between them. The negative thrust of immediate transition diversifies its subject matter into a multitude of different finite entities that limit each other. Conditioned by this external diversity, the positive thrust of reflection incorporates into its synthesis an increasing range of identified differences. Since these two operations run counter to each other, they can be brought together in a synthesis only as essentially opposed.[4] As opposed, they fall apart into two infinite regresses: one searching for more exhaustive determinations, the other proposing more comprehensive syntheses. They are simply conjoined as alternating moments of logical thinking.

As alternating, however, there is a reciprocal relation between them. Reflection can extend its syntheses only because immediate transitions have differentiated more exhaustively; the latter provide the conditions for the former. On the other hand, when reflection establishes an essential identity, this simplicity immediately passes over into a new differentiation. The two, then, are not simply opposed, but are complementary moments in a single dynamic. In fact, it is the integration of their reciprocal relation that constitutes the complete method. The fully self-contained process of pure thinking analyzes itself into its finite components, while reconciling these components into an infinite synthesis.

The final result of the method, then, is actually identical with its own complete dynamic—the ever more comprehensive integrating of an ever more exhaustive determining. This, inherent in all the previous stages of the logic, is the comprehensive individual, related simply to itself. In this pure self-related act the method reproduces the very characteristic with which the first logical category, *pure being,* was essentially defined; it is equivalent to itself. The logic has come full circle.

The fact that the logic is developed consecutively, whether in time or in theory, means that the conclusion is not absolutely identical with the beginning. *Pure being* was originally thought simply as a bare category, accepted as the most indeterminate of all indeterminate concepts, the object of a contemplating intelligence. Now however, even when thought immediately, it includes the whole intervening development of the logic. "It is *fulfilled being,* the *concept* that *conceives* itself, *being* as the *concrete* and thoroughly *intensive* totality."[5] What was simply the content of intelligence has dissolved into the rich dynamic of its own pure form. Reference and self-reference are combined.

The pure method is the self-conscious individuality of pure personality, determining itself as it integrates itself. At the point where it becomes fully transparent to itself as this concrete double process, it realizes that this systematic network of internal relations is nothing other than its own determinate character. No reference has been made to what is external to, and in some sense independent of, its concrete integrity. The method marks the culmination of pure thought as it thinks its categories and concepts. But even though some of those concepts refer to *particularity,* contrast *externality* to *internality,* and emphasize *difference,* their connotation remains strictly intellectual. Thought remains in its own homogeneous sphere. To this extent its individuality is a simple and immediate universality, a form without content, limited by this determination of its being. As soon as this becomes explicit, intelligence recognizes on the basis of its own principles that its own simple immediacy is but a beginning to be dissolved in a further development.

A problem, however, is posed. For the move to an explicit contrast between pure thought and alien reality can be neither an immediate transition nor a reflective determination. In both operations the beginning and the result are homogeneous, and thought remains in its own sphere. The move to what is other than pure personality cannot be logical, comprehended in the self-conscious operations of pure thought.[6] And the terms that describe it will be neither concepts nor categories, but rather representations of a non-intellectual operation.

At the same time, thought contains within its range of categories terms (*other, different, external, particular, objective*) that could refer to the move, even though inadequately. For they are contrasted with, and indeed opposed to *something, identity, internal, universal,* and *subjective.* When each of the former was isolated absolutely (as a pure beginning) by the understanding, thought discovered that these moments of dialectical difference and contradiction did not remain independent, but dissolved into a more comprehensive relation. Therefore two things can be anticipated. First, any external reality opposed to its pure personality can be represented by these negative, or determining, characteristics. Since the first and third terms of each triad are defining predicates of systematic totality,[7] the second term in contrast will be the essential determination of its opposite. Second, because they can be characterized in this determinate and negative way, that which is other than thought will not remain impervious to it. For intelligence has already discovered that these limiting characteristics dissolve into a more inclusive perspective. Whatever can be characterized as other than thought will yet remain comprehensible.

The impending move, then, will not introduce a new conceptual characteristic—an intellectual transition that can be signified by a categorical term and thereby become a concept. Rather intelligence comes to its limit and surrenders the integrity of its internal relations. It lets itself fall apart.

Although this move is neither an immediate transition nor a reflective synthesis, it integrates the two. For reflection identifies what is essential in pure thinking and opposes this to an immediate activity that is in no way intellectual. And what happens immediately is to be something quite other than thought, an external event that is nonetheless differentiated by thought from itself, and is thus conditioned through the negative self-dissolution of intelligence. The self-dissolution of thought is resolution, and the immediate act is decision. The pure self-knowledge of self-thinking thought does not simply pass over into existence in a transition that, once it has happened, is immediately necessary. Nor does it simply reflect on the externality that is to be grounded in self-reflexive conditioning. Both moments are integrated in a single act. Pure personality resolutely decides to let a particular moment of its internal determinations have an independent and contingent existence externally. This is the structure of freedom.[8]

Because thought can anticipate that the resultant determinations will be in some way transparent to its comprehending capacity, it can think of the result as a totality—as nature. But this nature will be characterized by relations that are purely external—in which the various particular features have no inherent connection one to another. How these relations will develop on their own is something that thought can neither anticipate nor master. It has allowed pure contingency its legitimate sphere of operation.

The difficulty in this text of Hegel lies not simply in its density and compactness, but also in its generality. The move from pure logic to nature is described in such abstract terms that it is difficult to be certain of its concrete reference. But it is precisely this purely formal structure that is essential, for any illustration would limit the range of application.

The philosophical description of the move from pure thought to nature reproduces what is common to a number of different activities. It is characteristic of divine creation. But it also defines conscience when the beautiful soul deliberately commits itself to a fallible and finite act that will contrast sharply with its pure self-knowledge.[9] In both cases, the contingency of external relations is willingly accepted because the agent anticipates that whatever arrives can be incorporated into a new comprehensive totality.

A third illustration, however, is also possible. Pure thought can turn to the external nature that is already present, not as a finite limitation but as a totality to be comprehended by thought. In this case the move is not one of creation nor of action but rather one of pure reference and of immediate intuition. No longer is the act of referring simply thought as the category *individual;* it is actually performed by the thinking agent as pure consciousness. Intelligence acts when it opens itself to the reality that is independent of it in order to become aware of its immediate being.[10]

Philosophy can make this move with confidence because it has already become fully master of its method: the simultaneous process of differentiating and synthesizing. For even though the structure of that operation was articulated as the culmination of the logic, the very generality of its expression allows its extension beyond the realm of pure thought: the decisive act is but the most radical form of differentiating; the openness to the other in its totality its correlative synthesis. The internal structure of pure thought is isomorphic with the activity of free, self-conscious personality.

Thought discovers that the pure externality of nature lies in its spatial and temporal relations. Because it could not anticipate that space and time would be the explicit forms of externality, they are radically contingent. But as we have seen, what is in one sense contingent is, in another, necessary; because it is actually the case, contrary possibilities have been excluded.

Space is pure abstract externality. Its very immediacy reflects the abstractness of the pure beginning of understanding. At the same time, however, it retains characteristics that make it transparent to thought. It is universal and continuous; it has internal distinctions between three dimensions that result in a four-fold structure: the immediate beginning of the point; its negation as a line; the negation of that negation as a plane; and finally the reconstituted immediate in three-dimensional totality.[11] Just as understanding retains in a static distortion all of the dynamic moments of conceptual thought,[12] so space, even though indifferent, unmediating externality, embodies the same basic elements.

But space is not all. For the negation that is already implicit in the relation between point, line and plane is also found external to space, existing for its own sake, as time. If space is reflected in the static isolation of understanding, time is mirrored in the negative transition of dialectic. Although abstract, external and (as isolated by philosophy) an ideal construct, it yet retains an inherent dynamic. As soon as it is, it ceases to be; and what is not comes to be. Time becomes external to itself. This double process reflects the conceptual transition called *becoming*.[13]

The external relations that characterize the world are spatial and temporal. But space and time schematically correspond to the immediacy of understanding and the immediacy of dialectical transitions. They represent the concept in the mode of pure externality. Therefore when external reflection brings together the material presented externally into a totality, it can use its criteria of identity and difference to determine what essentially characterizes the natural order. In the first instance this will produce the achievements of natural science. Then, when philosophy brings all the sciences together, it can recognize the essential ordering pattern by which one science presupposes and provides the ground for others.

(Since thought cannot anticipate what will be given in fact, Hegel's *Philosophy of Nature* remains bound to the conclusions of the science of his day. His healthy empirical refusal to impose on nature an *a priori* necessity makes this part of the *Encyclopaedia,* more than any other of his works, an historical curiosity. What would be required to revive it is not a reaffirmation of its explicit themes, but a new application of his methodological principles to the current achievements of natural science.)

While external reflection discovers essential identities and differences within the natural order when considered as a totality, the externality of nature has not itself comprehended this totality into an integrated individuality. Thought discovers, however, that there are finite beings in the natural world that are able to anticipate the future and remember the past, to recognize that space extends further than their direct awareness, and to integrate this broadened range into their immediate individuality. Although conditioned and limited by their geographical and historical setting, they can reflect on their environment, determine what appears to be essential, and self-consciously distinguish themselves from their context. Through this double activity of reference and self-reference, of consciousness and self-consciousness, they develop the capacity to integrate context and response within their finite individuality. Though their achievement is limited, and therefore relative, it embodies the reflective and individuating processes of speculative reason and conceptual understanding.[14]

The natural conditions of space, time, and finite conscious spirits, which are simply found to be present in the external world become the conditions for the phenomenological process of relative necessity that may lead to absolute knowledge.

Because the life of spirit is not only external but also developmental, it can be examined philosophically under two distinct perspectives. The first considers the various forms of spiritual existence as givens, simply presented to intelligence, to be organized into a conceptual totality by means of a distinguishable philosophical science. To this extent the philosophy of spirit reproduces the analytic structure of the philosophy of nature. The second, however, can consider the developmental structure—how each remembered temporal transition generates a new integration in the life of spirit, which leads in turn to the anticipation of an act that will both develop and disrupt what is already achieved. The philosophy of history discovers in the temporal process the pattern of increasingly determinate complexity that characterizes the system of pure thought. Because the integration that results is not imposed on the subject matter from outside but is discovered to be inherent in the actual development of spirit in its politics, art, religion and philosophy, this historical analysis has priority over the purely formal.[15]

When pure thought decides to reflect on the givens of the external world, it discovers not only space, time and self-conscious life but also political history, art, religion and philosophy. Since in the latter phenomena externality and internality are integrated into a single perspective, thought is able to comprehend the totality of the universe. For a fully comprehensive philosophy is but the most complete integration of the triple movement, in which the externality of *difference* and the internality of *synthesis* are grounded in a single disjunctive *individuality*.

The method, then, is not simply an atemporal logical idea. It equally characterizes the temporal process—the negative dialectic of passing away, the positive reflection of organic life, and their integration in spiritual memory and anticipation. But these two processes—the one logical, the other temporal—do not stand outside each other, simply sharing a common structure. They are conjoined by a double movement from logic to time and from time to logic. In the first, self-conscious integrated internality decides to commit itself to the contingencies of externality. In the second, the contingency of time dissolves into the pure self-knowledge of self-forgiving conscience to produce the absolute knowledge of philosophy. The generality of the method acquires its most radical and concrete form in the disjunction of these two transitions: from pure thought to pure externality and from experienced temporality to pure self-contemplation. It is as one moment of this complex yet simple totality that the logical operations of pure intelligence acquire their ultimate and complete justification. All relativism has been transcended, for spirit knows itself absolutely as that which can integrate both internal and external relations.

> *The Absolute is the Spirit*—this is the supreme definition of the Absolute. To find this definition and to grasp its meaning and content was, we may say, the ultimate objective of all education and all philosophy: towards this point all religion and science was directed, and on the basis of this drive alone can the history of the world be conceptually comprehended.[16]

This absolute spiritual reality cannot pretend to know *a priori* and in detail all there is to know. As we have seen, the advance of the natural sciences will show that there are other ways in which nature must be philosophically comprehended; developing history will produce new events, both radically more destructive and radically more creative than anything known previously; further reflection will make distinctions and clarifications that will render more rigorous the science of logic.[17] When Hegel says, then, "I could not pretend that the method I follow in this system of logic—or rather which this system in its own self follows—is not capable of greater completeness, of much elaboration in detail," he is not making a ritual disclaimer, with a modesty that is immediately vitiated by the claim to "the only true method."[18] Rather, he is affirming a constituent characteristic of that method. For its differentiating moment will continually introduce and discover radically new contingencies, even as its synthesizing moment will incorporate them into a more comprehensive unity. And since the method integrates both moments it is modified in the process of each new development. In other words, the method generates its own incompleteness in the process of its elaboration.

At the end of the third edition of the *Encyclopaedia* Hegel stated this explicitly. He took three paragraphs that had concluded the first edition, but were left out of the second, and reinstated them. In reintroducing them, however, he changed them.

In the first edition of 1816, the culmination has philosophy, as the spiritual achievement of pure knowledge, collapse into a simple individuality, dissolve the *appearance* of immediacy and of arbitrary presuppositions, and thereby return to the beginning of the logic. Then Hegel shows how a syllogism initially constitutes this appearance by passing from logic through nature to spirit, how this appearance is dissolved in another syllogism in which spirit reflects on nature as a presupposition to determine what is logical, and how this second appearance is in turn dissolved in the *idea* of philosophy. In other words, the suggestion is that the final three syllogisms are a recapitulation of the system.

In 1830, just as Hegel was beginning his revision of the *Logic* and a year before he died, the context of the final syllogisms changed. The return of the beginning does not *dissolve* the appearance, but the logic *rises out of* the appearance of inherent immediacy into its pure principle.[19] While once again the syllogisms constitute the appearance, Hegel introduces the final three paragraphs with a significant, new sentence: "It is this appearance which next gives the ground for further development."[20] The three syllogisms, then, do not simply review the externality in decision and the internality in reflection from the Olympian heights of a philosophy already achieved. Instead they show how pure philosophy will appear in the future and how this appearance will be transformed until pure philosophy is again reconstituted.

In its first appearance, logic will be the premise, nature the middle term, and spirit the result. This syllogism not only has the structure of the first figure, in which the determinate *particularity* of external nature mediates between logic's *universality* and spirit's *individuality*; but it also has the developmental pattern of the *syllogisms of a being*—an immediate transition from logic to its other, nature, and on to the other of both, spirit.

Since this first structure is called a science, the transitive movement is not a simple natural process. It presupposes philosophy's comprehensive achievement. Yet because the transition is immediate and necessary, both in the sense of what actually is the case and in the sense of being conditioned by the initiating impulse, the full freedom of self-controlled knowledge will be found only at one limiting extreme—the simplicity of pure logic. In other words, the initial development beyond Hegel takes place scientifically when the pure, integrated knowledge of self and world becomes the ground of a freely initiated natural event, radically conditioned by the contingency of space, time, and externality. Pure thought can neither control nor anticipate completely what will follow naturally from this freedom. Because of its self-knowledge, however, it can be confident that there will be some kind of spiritual integration of the novelties that natural contingency will introduce.[21]

The first appearance is dissolved into a second in which spirit is the middle term, nature a presupposition, and the pure thought of logic is the result. Here the second figure—*particular* through *individual* to *universal*—is integrated with the structure of *reflective syllogisms* in which denoted presuppositions become the basis for positing what is essential.

If the first syllogism represents the science of action—of differentiating and distinguishing—the second involves the science of reflective cognition—of bringing together into a totality. Spirit synthesizes what is externally presented in the natural order, including all the contingencies of historical events, in order to discern in them their logical principles.

This science is subjective cognition, the finite conclusions of reflection on an alien nature. Conditioned by natural and historical contingencies, its theoretical conclusions are affirmed on the basis of a relative necessity. And freedom is simply a goal to be achieved.[22]

The third syllogism completes the cycle. Not only does the *universal* of logical thought referentially differentiate the *individual* spirit from the *particular* nature, but it self-referentially identifies the synthesizing of one with the differentiating of the other. In this way it constitutes them as disjunctive moments of a comprehensive, dynamic individuality. The only addition made by the pure thought of philosophy to the contradictory sciences of free action and of conditioned cognition is to integrate the two in one operation.[23]

The idea of philosophy is that these three syllogisms will characterize all future developments just as they have all earlier ones. This triple structure, and this triple structure alone rises above all temporal contingency and is eternally absolute; for it has continued, and will continue, to hold true for all time.[24] In the last analysis, this one true method is the only absolute in Hegel's system.

In Chapter XII we noted how the circle of three types of necessity circulated through the logic at a number of different levels. Now that we have moved beyond pure thought to its relation with an external world two larger circles have been identified. The logic of immediate internal relations has been disjunctively conjoined with the relative necessity of external nature in the life of the spirit that culminates in genuine philosophy. And the immediate move of resolute decision contrasts with the conditioned reflection of subjective cognition as manifestations of self-knowing reason. In it are united: the concept or heart of the matter that progresses and develops; this development, active as cognition; and the eternal, inherently self-contained idea that, as absolute spirit, activates, engenders and enjoys itself.[25]

Neither Hegel's system nor the Hegelian philosopher stands outside of this completeness.[26] Any temporal achievement of pure self-knowledge includes a comprehension of its own limiting conditions and an anticipation of its demise. The destructive, yet creative, process that is the essential idea of the whole universe is known to be the inherent dynamic of one's own life. Far from being the arbitrary hypothesis of a presumptuous German, then, the absolute philosophy can be affirmed only because everything has been shown to be, and is experienced as, relative—except relativity itself.

15

Conclusion

One question remains concerning the scientific necessity of Hegel's philosophy, at the same time the most pressing and the most disquieting: Does its necessity encompass us as well? Are we who come after, whether philosophers or not, inevitably caught up into the dynamic spiral of the only true method, such that we have no option but to become implicit Hegelians?

In asking that question we introduce a distinction between the thought of Hegel and ourselves, contrasting one to the other. No longer, then, is his logic the inherent dynamic rhythm of intelligence, which has conjoined all contingency and relativism in the universality of pure thought; it becomes a peculiar construction of an eccentric individual. Nor is his philosophy a legitimate effort to comprehend the heart of the matter in nature and history, but a formal schematism imposed on an alien content.

Considered thus, abstract and subjective, the philosophy of Hegel is false even according to its own criteria. Therefore all criticisms of Hegelian thought are justified. By making it the object of detached and external reflection Popper and Russell, Findlay and Mure have falsified it; and each refutation or censure is only an analytic consequence of this initial presupposition.

Nevertheless the dialectic of time continues. The particular language and detailed argument used by Hegel have become but the expression of a past time, concretely located in a specific culture and historical epoch. But the criticisms become equally outworn. Just as the distance between commentator and system enables the latter to become an object of critical rejection, so a greater distance allows a more radical dialectic in which every criticism and refutation is shown to presuppose and posit that which it rejects, so that both can be integrated into a comprehensive perspective. The process of criticism itself simply confirms the one absolute that Hegel does not leave open to question—the method.[1] For it begins with the moment of pure difference, of active transition, of becoming other. But it inevitably pushes on to the complementary moments of reflection and comprehension.

Here, indeed, is the most devilish implication of Hegel's thought. It cannot be avoided. There is no freedom to agree or disagree. For both developments are already comprehended and anticipated in the final three paragraphs of the *Encyclopaedia*. Disagreement is the inevitable first response but the implicit agreement inevitably shows itself. Paradoxically enough, the only absolute rejection of his philosophy is the passionate commitment of dogmatic devotees who refuse to examine critically the details of his argument, but proclaim them in misbegotten piety as the definitive statement of all wisdom.

This devilish necessity is transformed into free opportunity when it ceases to be regarded as a restricting fetter, but is acknowledged to be the inherent structure of all human life, and therefore of all human philosophy. Its dynamic rhythm moves through the three syllogisms of action, of reflection, and of comprehension. When the student follows Hegel to this point of complete self-knowledge, he has achieved that level of freedom from which a genuinely new initiative can be undertaken.[2]

Such a new initiative is not easy. Noël poses the difficulty very succinctly: "As a result there is only one way to refute a system of logic in the sense that Hegel understood this word: it is to do it over again; it is to formulate a more profound and more comprehensive one, which contains the first and surpasses it. Outside of that, outside of a total remaking of the system when the conserved elements and the modifications penetrate each other in a new synthesis, criticism is reduced to being cavilling about details."[3]

A systematic transformation could come about, however, by reorganizing the three syllogistic movements that make up the essential structure of all spiritual existence into a different pattern. Instead of considering pure philosophic wisdom to be the essential idea which manifests itself in action and reflection, the innovator can substitute one of the latter two processes as the ultimate ground of the universal dynamic.

In the first place the pure act of natural externality may be the integrating concrete reality that generates on the one hand conditioned reflection, on the other, abstract universality. Under this schema, the first appearance of truth comes when spirit's reflection on natural events produces an immediate theoretical certainty; the second when pure thought submits itself to the conditions of nature and spirit in order to articulate their essential characteristics. The culminating achievement occurs, however, when a pure act concentrates scientific principles and immediate certainty into a particular event.

Examples of this alternative in post-Hegelian thought are Marx and Kierkegaard. For Marx, immediate reflection results only in ideology; disciplined thought that recognizes the integration of action and reflection produces philosophy or science; but the culmination is achieved in a particular revolutionary act when the truth becomes concretely embodied in an historical event, whether the revolution itself or the integrated synthetic culture of a classless society. For Kierkegaard, on the other hand, immediate reflection produces the aesthetic response of individual feeling; disciplined thought results in ethics and philosophy; the truth, to which philosophy can only point, is the particular instant when eternity and time—universal and individual—are one in the immediate paradoxes of incarnation and faith.

In the second alternative, the final achievement is the individual integration of reflective spirit, when the eternal verities of thought are combined with the radical contingencies of time. Then the immediate activity of spirit is to search dispassionately for what is eternal and unchangeable; in reaction it discovers the brute facticity of nature, discovering that man is essentially conditioned by time, by finitude, by suffering. When these two are combined in one reflective insight pure truth is achieved.

Heidegger moves from the immediate eternity of being to the radical contingencies of time. These are grasped in their truth only at the individual crisis of dread, or *Angst,* when spirit concentrates its reflection into one existential intuition. Similarly Nietzsche takes the penchant of man for stability in life, morals and thought together with the natural dissolution of all stable forms into a fluid vitality to ground the prophecy of the superman, who will crystallize the powerful forces of natural reality into a disciplined spiritual existence.[4]

Both of these alternative paths proclaim the demise of philosophy. No longer can it make a claim to truth—not even to the one true method. Rather it is a relative, transitory condition leading to something else, whether immediate act or spiritual individuality, which alone reveals the ultimate integration of the universe.

A paradox remains, however, for these alternative paths have been developed through a process of thinking that comprehends both the Hegelian synthesis and its options. In proclaiming revolution or faith, dread or the superman as *the truth,* the opponents of Hegel have only reconfirmed in practice the thesis that they have pretended to dismiss. For recognition of the truth is the dynamic action of comprehensive intelligence.

To be sure, they endeavour to avoid this implication, but do not always succeed. Marx urges the proletariat to immediate action, but has to appeal theoretically to a dynamic synthesis in the concept of a classless society, and ends his life writing scientific studies of political economy. Kierkegaard has the unbelieving philosopher, Johannes Climacus, simply point to faith as a pure hypothesis that cannot ultimately be comprehended; yet the paradox of faith can be theoretically described—even though negatively—and in the *Sickness unto Death* and the late Christian discourses is communicated in the universal structure of disciplined thought. When Nietzsche admits that even his proposal is only an interpretation, he affirms implicitly the absolute claim that all things are relative—that the synthetic totality is radically differentiated. And Heidegger, although he never completed *Sein und Zeit,* devoted himself to philosophical reflection on language.

Since even the compromise that each of the three alternatives has a relative validity within a comprehensive perspective would only reaffirm the Hegelian claim, we are left with a final uncertainty—one that cannot be resolved philosophically without begging the question: Is there only one true logical and scientific method after all?

Footnotes

Note on References Used

Because a commentary is useful only if there is a clear reference to the basic text, I have provided the page references to the two English translations of both *Phenomenology* and *Science of Logic* as well as to the Hoffmeister and Lasson editions of the German original. These are indicated by (Baillie), (Miller) and *Phän* for the *Phenomenology,* by (Miller) JS and WL for the *Logic.* The translation on which any citation is based is mentioned first.

With the *Encyclopaedia* material the problem is both simpler and more complicated. It is simpler because one can use the paragraph numbering, common to all editions. It is more complicated because the English translations of Wallace and Miller (*The Logic of Hegel, The Philosophy of Nature,* and *The Philosophy of Mind)* do not distinguish between the paragraph, and Hegel's *Remarks* on it. This confusion has hampered anglophone Hegel scholars for generations, and I do not understand why the recent edition did not rectify it. Only the lecture material, called *Zusätze* or *Additions,* is indicated by a smaller typeface. The English reader is advised that, in general, only the first paragraph under each number is the basic text of the *Encyclopaedia.* Anything else is a clarifying remark added by Hegel. Footnote references to *Enz* will therefore not only specify which volume of the English translation is applicable, but will also distinguish between the *Remarks* and the *Additions,* following the conventions used by Knox in his translation of the *Philosophy of Right.*

Occasionally I have referred to other German editions: JE signifies the

Jubiläumsausgabe edited by Glockner; (Suhrkamp), the paper-bound edition published by Suhrkamp in 1970; and HGW, the new critical edition being published by Meiner. ETW signifies Knox and Kroner's translation of *Hegel's Early Theological Writings.*

Since few anglophone readers are at ease in French and German, I have provided all quotations from secondary sources in English. Unless a published ET is cited, all translations are my own.

Preface

1. *Science of Logic* (Miller) 58, WL I 40, JS I 69.
2. (Miller) 54, WL I 36, JS I 65.

Chapter I
Introduction

1. J.N. Findlay, "Comment on Weil's 'The Hegelian Dialectic'," in *The Legacy of Hegel,* ed. O'Malley et al., (The Hague: Nijhoff, 1973), 69.
2. C. Taylor, *Hegel,* (Cambridge, CUP: 1975), 348.
3. J. M. E. McTaggart, *A Commentary on Hegel's Logic,* (New York: Russell & Russell, 1964), 5.
4. G. R. G. Mure, *A Study of Hegel's Logic,* (Oxford: Clarendon: 1950), 354.
5. B. Russell, *History of Western Philosophy,* (London: Allen & Unwin, 1961), 715.
6. K. Popper, *The Open Society and its Enemies,* Vol. II: *The High Tide of Prophecy: Hegel, Marx and the Aftermath,* (London: Routledge & Kegan Paul, 1966), 40.
7. Hegel himself makes this point: "Objective Logic takes the place of the former *metaphysics* considered as the scientific reconstruction of the world, which was to be built of *thoughts* alone. . .Logic, however, considers these forms detached from such substrata [as Soul, World, God], from the subjects of *representation*; it considers their nature and value in and for themselves." JS I 74f (revised), WL I 46f, (Miller) 63f.
8. See the articles by Caponigri and Lauer in *Hegel and the History of Philosophy,* ed. O'Malley et al., (The Hague: Nijhoff, 1974), 1-46.

Chapter II
Representations and Thoughts

1. *Enz (Logic)* §20 Remark. I have replaced Wallace's "conception" with "representation." For a justification of the conventions I have followed in translating Hegel's vocabulary into English see Chapter 3.
2. "Theoretical Mind" *Enz (Philosophy of Mind),* §455-§468. Justification for using the psychology to interpret the logic may be found in Hegel's introduction to the *Encyclopaedia.* The first paragraphs (§19ff) in the "Science of Logic" provide a preliminary discussion of the relation beween pure thought, sense, and representation. Also in one of Hegel's aborted beginnings for his 1808 course in philosophy at the Nürnberg secondary

school he notes that "an introduction to philosophy has to consider above all the different constitutions and activities of spirit through which it passes in order to arrive at a science. . . .The theory of spirit considers spirit according to the different species of its consciousness and *according to the different species of its activity*. The former can be called the theory of consciousness, the latter the theory of the soul." (*Nürnberger Schriften, Werke* IV, Suhrkamp, 73) [my italics]. Although he did not outline the theory of the soul in his notes, the theory of consciousness reproduces motifs from the Phenomenology. "Activities of the soul" would correspond to the functions analyzed later in the "Psychology." Encouraged by this text, I will consider the various constituents of intelligence as functions or operations rather than faculties.

3. The word "intuition" is derived from the latin *verb* "intueor, -eri." Therefore it refers not to a some*thing* but to an act. Throughout the analysis, Hegel is not talking about *faculties* but about functions and operations.

4. This is not the sensible intuition of Kant, as suggested by Mure: "Hegel: How, and How Far, is Philosophy Possible?" in F.G. Weiss, ed. (The Hague: Nijhoff, 1974) 8. As we shall see, that stage is already transcended because intuition presupposes the phenomenology of understanding. This is rather a type of intellectual intuition in which the intellect is productive in the same way as the object: "in which the producing agent is one and the same with the produced." See Schelling, *System of Transcendental Idealism* (Charlottesville: University of Virginia, 1978) 27, and the Addition to *Enz (Philosophy of Mind)* §477. Simple sensation has already been considered in the phenomenology of sense certainty. However the validity of Kant's claim that spatial and temporal relations are subjectively determined is shown to rest in the process of attention brought *to* intellectual intuition.

5. Hegel wrote two Phenomenologies. In the *Encyclopaedia (Philosophy of Mind)* §413-§431 he limits himself to the double problem mentioned here, and moves on to the intellectual activity of intuition in the following chapter on Psychology. The larger *Phenomenology of Mind* takes the movement much further into the activities of Reason, of Spirit, of Religion and of Knowledge. A remark on §25 of *Enz (Logic)* suggests why the exposition in *Phenomenology of Mind* became much more intricate.

6. Kant's "rule" corresponds to Hegel's "law." *Enz (Philosophy of Mind)* §422.

7. See *Critique of Pure Reason*, B245-6. (revised) "This rule, that determines something in accordance with the temporal succession is: in what precedes the event is to be found the condition under which an event invariably and necessarily follows. The principle of sufficient reason is thus the ground of possible experience, that is, of objective knowledge of appearances in respect of their relation in the order of time."

8. This argument is a fairly creative interpretation of the Hegelian text in *Enz (Philosophy of Mind)* §§422-3, relying more explicitly than he does on the argument in Kant. Hegel's discussion portrays the dynamic in more general terms. Wallace names this section "The Intellect" although its parallel in *Phenomenology* is called "Understanding."

9. *Enz (Philosophy of Mind)* §435 Addition.

10. Note the distinction between the act of synthesis and the act of integrating the synthesis into a unity—often overlooked by Hegel interpreters. In Hegel's analyses they are always two distinct stages in a process. In this he carries on the distinction made by Kant in the transcendental deduction between the *synthesis* of imagination and the *unity* of apperception. The Kantian unity of the I = I forms part of the problematic of the chapter on Phenomenology in the *Encyclopaedia*. For the purposes of this commentary I have

simply presupposed that context. See, however, K. Dusing, *Das Problem der Subjektivität in Hegels Logik* (Bonn: Bouvier, 1976).

11. Hegel's German: "*sein dumpfes Weben in sich*" (Wallace, "inarticulate embryonic life") §466. To characterize immediacy is always difficult. One may use a *via negationis,* denying complexity; or one may rely on metaphors which point to the immediate moment. Neither provides that objective clarity which reflective understanding expects. See D. Henrich, "Anfang und Methode der Logik," *Hegel-Studien,* Beiheft I (Bonn: Bouvier, 1964) 19-35.

12. *Enz (Philosophy of Mind)* §447.

13. In his psychology, Hegel is not tracing an experiential development as in the larger *Phenomenology.* He is isolating various intellectual functions, and introducing each when its basic necessary conditions are present. These functions will continue to operate in more complex settings—attention is constitutive of all conscious acts just as representation can be of impressions, of abstractions or of names, etc.

14. The preceding analysis is a commentary in *Enz (Philosophy of Mind)* §§446-450—the section on intuition. The "union of union and disunion" is a key phrase found in Hegel's *Early Theological Writings* (New York: Harper, 1961) 312, and repeated as "the identity of identity and nonidentity" in *The Difference Between Fichte's and Schelling's System of Philosophy* (Albany: SUNY, 1972) 156.

15. See the Addition to §448: "But things are in truth themselves spatial and temporal; this double form of asunderness is not one-sidedly given to them by our intuition, but has been originally imparted to them by the intrinsically infinite mind, by the creative eternal Idea."

16. Hegel's world *"Bild"* has been translated by Wallace as "image." But such vocabulary appears to limit the sphere of reference to sight. John Locke's term "impression" expands the range by including the sensation of touch.

17. Evidence for this comment regarding similarity of content is found in the Addition to §451 on recollection: "Here the represented content is still the same as in intuition; in the latter it receives its verification, just as, conversely, the content of intuition verifies itself in my representation. We have, therefore, at this stage a content which is not only intuitively perceived in its immediacy, but is at the same time recollected, inwardized, posited as mine." See also §455, Remark: "Abstraction, which occurs in the representing activity by which general representations are produced, . . .is frequently explained as a collapsing—of many similar images into one another—and is to be thus made intelligible. If this collapsing together be not mere chance and without principle, a force of attraction in like images, or something of the sort, must be assumed, which at the same time would have the negative power of rubbing off dissimilar elements against each other. This force is really intelligence itself." (revised)

18. The German "*Vorstellung,*" of course, does not allow this pun; but on the other hand it is equally impossible to reproduce in English Hegel's puns on "*Vorstellung*"—"placing before" and on "*Erinnerung*"—internalizing *and* remembering. Wallace's translation of the latter as "recollection," however, does catch other associations.

19. This sentence is my reworking of the sentence translated by Wallace as: "Intelligence is thus the force which can give forth its property, and dispense with external intuitions for its existence in it." (§454)

20. Kant (*Critique of Judgement* §76) drew a sharp distinction between the actualities of intuition and the possibilities of thought. Hegel here is arguing that this distinction is not absolute within the creative dynamic of intelligence. It can transform actualities into

possibilities, and through imagination, memory and thought, transform possibilities into actualities. The last five paragraphs are a commentary on §452-§454, the section on "Recollection."

21. See *Enz (Philosophy of Mind)* §465 and the Remark to §457 (revised): "Only with phantasy does intelligence cease to be the vague abyss and relating universal [of the subconscious], but becomes an individual—a concrete subject that is related to itself not only as a relating universal but also as a being."

22. Notice here that to the *synthesis* of phantasy is added the *unity* of the sign.

23. This marks the end of the commentary on §455-§460, the section on "Imagination."

24. Hegel calls this process the negation of negation.

25. Hegel himself refers to mechanical learning in relation to the study of foreign languages. See "On Classical Studies" ETW 328, JE III 241. Compare the Addition to §461 "When we hear or see a word from a foreign language, its meaning becomes present to our mind; but it does not follow that the converse is true, that we can produce for our ideas the corresponding word-signs in that language. We learn to speak and write a language later than we understand it." This passage suggests that the difficulty in understanding Hegel does not always lie in his referring to a strange and obscure reality, but rather in his discerning intellectual operations so familiar that they have been forgotten.

26. Hoffmeister (ed.) *Dokumente zu Hegels Entwicklung,* 50. The rest of the quotation is significant for the next transition to thought: "[The words] are already in our possession as forms, according to which we model our ideas, which have ready their determinate compass and limitation, and which provide the relations according to which we are in the habit of seeing all things."

27. Because T. Bodammer (*Hegels Deutung der Sprache,* Hamburg: Meiner, 1969, p. 65) confuses synthesis and unity, the only move open after the synthesis of memory is a falling apart of meaning and name in mechanical memory. He is not able, therefore, to provide a convincing explanation for Hegel's reference in §464 to "thought which no longer has meaning."

The preceding discussion is a commentary on §461-§464, the section on "Memory."

28. "Thus intelligence strips the object of the form of contingency, grasps its rational nature and posits it as subjective; and conversely, it at the same time develops the subjectivity into the form of objective rationality. Thus our knowing, which was at first abstract and formal, becomes a knowing that is filled with a true content and is therefore objective." *Enz (Philosophy of Mind)* §445 Addition.

29. §465. Wallace has simply ignored "—für sich;" which I have freely translated in the final phrase. Hegel wants to argue that thought not only reproduces its own true nature, but also what is implicit in the experience of all nature and history; logic is equally a metaphysics. The justification for that claim, however, will not be considered until Chapter 13.

30. Wallace uses "comprehend or understand" where we use "conceive." But our use retains the parallel between concept and conceive which is in the German. Wallace translates the noun as "notion."

31. The logical structure of this process will be explicated in Part IV. Since §468 is concerned with the transition to "Mind Practical" it is not of direct concern to a study of Hegel's *logic.* We have thus completed the commentary of §465-§467, the rest of the section on "Thinking."

32. §447.

33. Thus Wallace misleads when, in translating *"Vorstellung"* he puts "picture thinking" parallel to "conception" *Enz (Logic)* §20, Remark. *Eine Vorstellung* can also be *ein*

Gedachtes or *ein Gedankending*. Wallace unfortunately is not consistent. In *Enz (Philosophy of Mind)* §451 he uses "representation."

34. Compare Lebrun, *La patience du concept*, 89 "It is the persistence of a distinction between the representing and the represented (and it does not really matter whether one imagines them confused together or split apart) that characterizes the representative mode of thinking."

35. *Science of Logic* (Miller) 53 (revised), WL I 35, JS I 64.

Chapter III
Problems of Language

1. G.R.G. Mure in *A Study of Hegel's Logic* (Oxford: Clarendon, 1950) leaves the philosopher at the level of reproductive memory where "the conjunction of. . . .meaning with the reality as name is still an (external) synthesis." [*Enz (Philosophy of Mind)* §463] He writes: "Every philosophical thought is an incomplete synthesis of language with thought. It can never quite pass from meaning to truth, from reference to an object to utter self-identification with its object." (p.22) Because he fails to distinguish the relation word-meaning from that of word-thought, he misses the move, mediated by mechanical memory, in which the synthesis of word and meaning is collapsed into a unity. Since a surd of inexpressible intellectual activity remains, Mure's philosopher becomes a poet: "It follows that a philosopher, when his soul discourses with himself and even more so when he talks or writes for the benefit of others, must continually remodel, adjust, and expand his language, and that nevertheless he can never quite succeed in expressing all he means even to himself, because meaning falls always short of truth." (p.23) But this means that *Logic* simply expresses Hegel's own insight and not the inherent necessity in the subject matter itself. Whether or not this is what Hegel actually did, it is not what he intended to do.

2. *Enz (Philosophy of Mind)* §462 Addition (revised). See also in the Preface to the second edition of the *Science of Logic*: "Into all that becomes something inward for men, a representation as such, into all that he makes his own, language has penetrated, and everything that he has transformed into language and expresses in it contains a category—concealed, mixed with other forms, or clearly determined as such, so much is logic his natural element, indeed his own peculiar nature." (Miller) 39 (revised), WL I 9-10, JS I 39-40.

3. *Enz (Philosophy of Mind)* §461. This tension between private and public language partially reflects the contrast between psychological association and logical validity central to the attack on psychologism in Husserl and Frege.

4. This position is explored phenomenologically in "The Law of the Heart, and the Frenzy of Self-Conceit." *Phän* 266-274, (Baillie) 390-400, (Miller) 221-228. When the individual claims the right to define the meaning of the signs according to his own intellectual insight, he is confronted by the perversity of others who do not acknowledge the same specific meanings. (In the proceedings of the Hegel Society of America for 1978 is a version of this chapter that explores more fully the related texts from the *Phenomenology*.)

5. *Science of Logic* (Miller) 32, WL I 10, JS I 40.

6. *Hegel's Science of Logic* (Miller) 107, WL I 94, JS I 119f.

7. *Hegel's Science of Logic* (Miller) 389, WL II 3, JS II 15.

8. *Enz (Logic)* §166 Remark.

9. In addition the linguistic similarity between *Gedächtnis* (memory) and *Gedanken* (thought) helps to bridge the transition from representation to conceptual thought. These examples could be endlessly multiplied. For example the interplay between the internal, subconscious activity of intelligence and its explicit reality is expressed by the two terms "das Seiende" (what is) and "das Seinige" (its own). See A. Koyré, "Note sur la langue et la terminologie hégéliennes" in *Études d'histoire de la pensée philosophique* (Paris: Gallimard, 1971) 209-211. Koyré's argument that on Hegel's own principles the concrete language of German is an essential component of dialectical thought is profoundly convincing, even though I want to claim that it is only a part of the total picture.

10. *Briefe von und an Hegel* (Hamburg: Meiner 1952) I, #55, p. 99f. ET. in W. Kaufmann, *Hegel, A Reinterpretation,* (Garden City: Doubleday, 1966) 316.

11. *Lectures on the History of Philosophy,* III 114, JE XIX 218.

12. *Briefe,* I, #152 p. 299 (my translation).

13. *Lectures on the History of Philosophy,* III 150 (revised), JE XIX 257. See also "On Classical Studies": "The intimacy which characterizes the possession of our own language is lacking in the knowledge we possess in a foreign language only. Such a knowledge is separated from us by a barrier which prevents it from genuinely coming home to our mind." ETW 322, JE III 234. Compare this text from the Jena period: "To fasten down concepts a means is available that fulfills its ends in part; but that can also be more dangerous than the evil of a complete lack of concepts—namely philosophical terminology—words constructed with this end in view out of foreign languages, particularly Latin and Greek. . . .Concepts that we represent by foreign words appear to have an alien character and do not belong exclusively and immediately to ourselves. The elements of things do not appear to be the current concepts with which we regularly converse and occupy ourselves, in which the most ordinary man expresses himself. . . .However that which is intrinsic must not have this alien character for us, and we must not make it appear so by means of an alien terminology. But we must maintain the conviction that the spirit itself is present everywhere and that it articulates its forms in our immediate vernacular. . . .This strange terminology, which is used in part superfluously, in part speciously, becomes however a major evil in that it makes concepts which are in themselves dynamic into something fixed and permanent. In this way the spirit and the life inherent in the subject matter disappear, and philosophy degenerates into an empty formalism which is easy neither to appropriate nor to articulate. To those who do not understand this terminology, however, it appears to be very difficult and deep. What is most devilish about such terminology is precisely this: it is in fact very easy to master it. Indeed, it is all the easier to speak with it because I can allow myself to utter all possible inanities and trivialities—at least as long as I do not become ashamed of myself for speaking to people in a language which they do not understand." K. Rosenkranz, *Georg Wilhelm Friedrich Hegels Leben* (Darmstadt: WB, 1971) 183-4 (my translation).

14. G. R. G. Mure, *A Study of Hegel's Logic,* 23. In the Addition to *Enz (Philosophy of Mind)* §462, however, Hegel said: "What is ineffable is in truth only something obscure, fermenting, something which gains clarity only when it is able to put itself into words."

15. Fetscher points to the critical nature of this question for Hegel's whole endeavour: "Any articulation of logic necessarily makes use of language, indeed a determinate and specific language which can in no way stake a claim to absolute and universal validity. Thus the problem of the productive imagination and of language is the critical point on which the whole Hegelian system and the question of its legitimacy depends." *Hegels Lehre vom Menschen,* (Stuttgart: Fromann, 1970).

16. This is the claim of Gadamer: "It is the real power of the German language and not the schematic precision of. . . .artificially formulated concepts. . . .which breathes life into Hegel's philosophy. . . .The speculative power lying in the connotation of the German words and the range of meaning extending from them in so many directions is completely unable to penetrate the cloak of [a] foreign language." "Thus it does not appear coincidental to me that Hegel's acute analysis and dialectical deduction of categories is always most convincing where he appends a historical derivation of the word." H.G. Gadamer, *Hegel's Dialectic,* (New Haven: Yale, 1976) 112, 93. A similar point is made by Baillie, *The Origin and Significance of Hegel's Logic,* (London: Macmillan, 1901) 278: "Language, again, enabled Hegel in no slight degree to discover the categories—so much so that in some cases the analysis seems not logical but etymological, and the interpretation of a notion the mere recording of its current or historical signification. . . .And Hegel regarded the uncorrupted Teutonic of his own mother tongue as peculiarly adapted to reveal those ultimate conceptions which he sought." Baillie, however, immediately adds: "At the same time he renounced any affectation of purism, any supposition that the German language was the only authorized medium for the communication of absolute truth."

17. Hegel was aware of this difficulty. In a review of a book of von Humboldt on the Bhagavad-Gita, written at Berlin, he wrote: "It certainly conflicts with the actual state of affairs to demand that an expression in the language of a people which has a character and culture distinctly contrasting with ours (when such expressions are not immediately sense objects like sun, sea, tree, rose, etc. but concern spiritual matters) be reproduced by an expression in our language that corresponds to it in every detail. A word in our language represents for us our specific representations of such things, and just on that account not those of other people who have not only another language but other representations." JE XX 75. See also in "On Classical Studies" ETW 326f., JE III 239: "The language is the musical element, the element of intimacy that fades away in the translation; it is the fine fragrance which makes possible the reader's sympathetic enjoyment of the ancient work and without which that work tastes like Rhine wine that has lost its flavour."

18. HGW VI, Fragment 20 and 22. Also reprinted in *Frühe politische Systeme* (Frankfurt: Ullstein, 1974) pp. 291-335.

19. The others are work and family. In a curious effort to create a pun, Hegel writes "name" (*Namen*) with an "h" *('Nahmen')*. In this way it became the same as the imperfect, indicative plural of the verb "to take" (*nehmen*). In the name, consciousness *takes* the sign which is otherwise only a thing and makes it its own. (See, HGW VI 288).

20. HGW VI 318 (my translation and italics); Ullstein ed. 330.

21. HGW VI, 312-315.

22. Bodammer notes the contrast between individual sign-making and the use of public conventions (*Hegels Deutung der Sprach*; Hamburg: Meiner, 1969, 41). While he turns to the Jena material of 1803-4 for clarification, he misses the significance of recognition. Indeed, Glockner did not regard this latter concept to be of sufficient importance to include it in the *Hegel Lexicon.* (Hegel's term, *"Anerkennen"* can be translated "acknowledge" or "recognize." In the previous chapter we used "recognition" to translate *"Wiedererkennen"*—a term that stresses the element of knowing *again*).

23. *Enz (Philosophy of Mind)* §432.

24. *Enz (Philosophy of Mind)* §432 Addition.

25. HGW VI 308-9. Because the intellectual function of sign-making fantasy has not yet been analyzed, the *Encyclopaedia* discussion of "self-consciousness recognitive" can only be

of the life and death struggle. On the other hand, because recognition is presupposed, the transition in the Psychology from imagination to memory is possible. In the previous chapter the struggle for recognition was implicit as a moment in the dynamic of submission as a necessary condition for intuition.

26. *Phenomenology* (Baillie) 229, *Phän* 141, (Miller) 111.

27. See the first paragraph, *Phenomenology* (Baillie) 229, *Phän* 141 (Miller) 111, #178. Except for one short paragraph on p. 230 (142 and 112, #183) which I have included with its predecessor, each of the following paragraphs corresponds to a paragraph in Hegel's text. I acknowledge with thanks the contribution of a number of students whose essays on this text have helped me clarify this exposition.

28. *Phenomenology* (Baillie) 231, *Phän* 143, (Miller) 112. This concludes the *exposition de texte.*

29. See *Enz (Philosophy of Mind)* §458 Remark, and *(Logic)* §145 Addition.

30. I use the term "ineffable" to suggest that the meaning cannot be expressed in a *common* language. This does not prevent the individual from creating a sign to represent it. But he cannot use this sign to distinguish his ideas objectively from those of others without thereby transforming it into a public vehicle of common meaning. This would mean that the ineffable becomes effable.

31. "Here again we see language as the existence of Spirit." *Phenomenology,* (Miller) 395, (Baillie) 660, *Phän* 458. Hegel provides his own extended phenomenological exposition of this process in the chapters on "The Law of the Heart," "Spirit in self-estrangement," and "Spirit certain of itself." Notice that the process of recognition is repeated— once with regard to the common sign, the second, with regard to meaning. This precedes the integration of sign and meaning in mechanical memory.

32. See here the perceptive discussion of Hyppolite, *Logique et Existence* (Paris: PUF, 1961) 25f.

33. In defending the learning of ancient languages, Hegel said: "The substance of Nature and Spirit must have confronted us, must have taken the shape of something alien to us, before it can become our object." "On Classical Studies," ETW 327, JE III 240.

34. "Grammatical learning of an *ancient* language affords the advantage of necessarily implying a continous and sustained activity of reason. In speaking our mother tongue, unreflective habit leads us to speak grammatically; but with an ancient language it is otherwise and we have to keep in view the significance which the intellect has given to the parts of speech and call to our aid the rules of their combination. Therefore a perpetual operation of subsuming the particular under the general and of specifying the general has to take place, and it is just in this that the activity of reason consists. Strict grammatical study is accordingly one of the most universal and noble forms of intellectual education." "On Classical Studies" ETW 330, JE III 242f. On the study of other languages as an instrument in education see Bodammer, 174-179.

35. In the review of von Humboldt's book, JE XX 75.

36. *Science of Logic* (Miller) 57, (revised) WL I 39, JS I 68. Compare Hegel's confession to Niethammer in 1812: "One concluding comment is missing, however, which I did not add because I am not completely in agreement with myself—namely that perhaps all philosophical instruction in secondary schools could be seen as superfluous, that study of the ancients is most appropriate for students at that level, and in essence the valid introduction to philosophy." *Briefe von und an Hegel* I 211, p. 418-9 (also JE III 302).

37. *Science of Logic* (Miller) 708 (revised) WL II 357, JS II 346f. Bodammer, in explaining this passage (p. 236ff) sees the logical science as the abstraction of thought from the verbal

expression. As abstract it is independent of cultural determination. On our analysis, how-ever, thought can be absolute not as abstractly isolated from language but because, through the mediating influence of alien grammars, it becomes fully self-conscious in the use of its own language. The vernacular does not disappear; it is simply rendered more precise.

38. This position is brilliantly maintained by G. Lebrun, *La Patience du Concept* (Paris: Gallimand, 1972). See, for example, p.341 "From that we perhaps catch a glimpse of what will secure the originality of the Concept when compared with the types of know-ledge and with the methods Hegel criticizes: at the outset, the firm resolution never to sub-mit language to the jurisdiction of an appeal that may be external to it, and never to reco-ver from the 'things said' any other necessity than the necessity they incorporate in that they are 'said'."

39. This explains why the same Hegel who rejoiced in the speculative capacity of German could, when the occasion demanded it, appropriate a word from Latin: "For a seeming that has withdrawn into itself and so is estranged from its immediacy, we have the foreign word, Reflexion." *Science of Logic* (Miller) 399, WL II 13, JS II 25. We can now see that Gadamer's claims regarding German language (above note 16) are unfounded. Hegel's philosophy is not convincing because of its etymological arguments. Rather the etymological arguments are convincing because they illustrate the inherent philosophical and logical necessity of thought. Gadamer has assumed (p.63) that instinct is not only subconscious but unerring. Hegel by contrast points out that the subconscious is bede-villed by arbitrary contingency, and only by explicitly bringing its activity to conscious-ness is one able to set the various movements and moments in context and thus grasp their necessity. "The broad distinction between the instinctive act and the intelligent and free act is that the latter is performed with an awareness of what is being done." *Science of Logic* (Miller) 37, WL I 16, JS I 45. On this discussion compare M. Clark. *Logic and System* (The Hague: Nijhoff, 1971) 24-5.

40. It could still be the case that "truth is that kind of error without which a certain species of living being cannot exist." (F. Nietzsche, *The Will to Power,* §493). We will outline Hegel's response to that more serious challenge in Chapter 13.

41. Bodammer notes Hegel's preference for German and Greek as languages for philosophy in contrast to Chinese and Latin. *Hegels Deutung der Sprache,* 155.

42. More than one German-speaking student of Hegel's thought has commented that the foreigner has often the advantage in comprehending that philosophy simply because the latter is not as involved in the contingent representational associations which common life attaches to the various terms.
There is a difference between the task of the translator and that of the interpreter. The former is tied much more directly to the original German, and must try to retain as much as possible its specific associations. The latter is freer to move into more idiomatic speech and, in reconstructing the thought, leave the specific Germanisms behind. Bodammer discusses what Hegel himself says concerning translation in *Hegels Deutung der Sprache,* 161-165.

43. In this I take issue with John Findlay when he says: "I want to say very strongly that I think there is a tradition in these matters which oughtn't to be lightly disturbed. I've been reading Hegelian works all my life, and I think that there have been conventions set up. Of course they must be abandoned if they are grossly unsuitable; but I think that we should keep them if they are not grossly unsuitable." "Round-table Discussion on Problems of Translating Hegel," in *The Legacy of Hegel* (ed. O'Malley, et. al) (The

Hague: Nijhoff, 1973) 254. See also his Foreword to *Hegel: A Re-Examination,* p.77, "My quoted passages have in almost all cases been translated afresh, and I have tried to use verbal and sentence-structure resembling the German, and employing hyphenated Saxon compounds. I do not myself feel that Hegeliansm accords lucidly with Latinity." It may be that this formalism with regard to Hegel's language is closely related to Findlay's surrender of necessity with regard to Hegel's thought.

44. Revisions are always indicated in footnotes.

45. *Science of Logic* (JS) I 39f (revised), WL I 10, (Miller) 31.

Chapter IV
Being

1. *Science of Logic* (Miller) 50, WL I 31, JS I 60.

2. See (Miller) 68, WL I 53, JS I 80. For Hegel there is no absolute beginning. In an organic whole each part conditions, and is conditioned by, all others. None is primary. The same, suggests Hegel, is true of the universe. There is no primitive reality. Within the totality each beginning has its justifying conditions in other parts of the whole. It in turn conditions and modifies these other parts. Thus the beginning of the logic will be justified extralogically—psychologically, phenomenologically, or historically. But in due course the logic itself will be shown to be the condition for history, for the experience of nature, and for the appearance of intelligence. This model of explanation was suggested in Kant's *Critique of Teleological Judgement.*

3. JS I 81 (revised), WL I 53f, (Miller) 69.

4. For ease of comprehension, any category that becomes the content of thought will be in italics, whereas in reflective discussion about the intellectual process it will be in normal script. The reader, however, is reminded that the category is a sign for an intellectual process. It should also be noted that frequently, in the reflective discussion, terms will be used that will be defined precisely only later.

5. Certainly there are important differences, but to express them intelligence will use negation along with more determinate categories: *a being, reality, existence, actuality, object,* etc.

6. This section considers the question "With what must the Science Begin?" (Miller) 67-78, WL I 51-64, JS I 79-90, but does so following the approach proposed in the First Part. On the question of the beginning, see. D. Henrich, *"Anfang und Methode der Logik"* Hegel *Studien, Beiheft* I (Bonn: Bouvier, 1964) 19-35.

7. While Hegel appeals to both intuition and thought in this argument, he ignores representation. In a Remark he notes that representation gives *being* a determinate character and thus fails to take account of the thought's purity.

8. (Miller) 82, WL I 66f, JS I 94.

9. Compare *Phenomenology* (Miller) p. 19: "...Spirit is this power only by looking the negative in the face, and tarrying with it. This tarrying with the negative is the magical power that converts it into being." *Phän,* 30 and (Baillie) 93.

10. *Nothing* is neither a simple "no"—a spontaneous *act* of the I as intelligence, nor "nonbeing" (both of which are suggested by van der Meulen, *Hegel, die gebrochene Mitte,* 48f). Both interpretations involve reference to another: that which is denied, or *being.* *Nothing* however is taken in its simple immediacy as a concept. "We are concerned first of all not with the form of opposition (with the form, that is, also of *relation*) but with the

abstract, immediate negation: nothing, purely on its own account, negation devoid of any relations." (Miller) 83, WL I 68, JS I 95. Only because it will not remain independent in such simple immediacy does thought come to realize that it is inevitably a function of a relation. (Denial is considered as *difference* in Chapter 7; nothing becomes *non-being* when it becomes the contrary of *being* within the perspective of *becoming* or *a being*.)

11. By applying Leibniz's principle of the identity of indiscernibles, Hegel can say that the result is the unity of *being* and *nothing*. There is nothing thought can discern which could distinguish them.

12. See *Enz (Logic)* §87, Addition: "Hence the distinction between the two is only meant to be; it is a quite nominal distinction, which is at the same time no distinction."

13. ". . .for [Hegel] as probably for Heraclitus, the mediator between these opposed terms is the thinking itself—not a 'third' thing, but the two only taken in their unity." Fleischmann, *La science universelle*, (Paris: Plon, 1968) 69. (Fleischmann catches this dynamic quality of thought by using the infinitive *le penser* as noun in contrast to the participle *la pensée*.) Because *becoming* refers to the actual movement of thinking itself, and not simply to an abstracted common feature it is the "first concrete thought" *Enz (Logic)* §88, Addition. This derivation of the category *becoming* shows that it is not strictly temporal, but that it reflects the intellectual process of relating—of judging and inferring. While that process may happen in time, its significance is atemporal. Therefore it makes sense to talk about an atemporal becoming.

14. Because they can appeal only to intuition to justify the logical transition English commentators on Hegel fail to recognize that such transitions are grounded in the intellectual acts of relating that simply arise from the earlier concepts. This leads Taylor, for example, to such selective judgements as "The derivation of Becoming here is not as solid as that of *Dasein*. This is the first but not the last place in the *Logic* where Hegel will go beyond what is directly established by his argument, because he sees in the relation of concepts a suggestion of his ontology." *Hegel,* 233. In this he follows McTaggart, *Commentary,* 17ff. Similarly Findlay *(Hegel, A Re-examination,* 148) says that the logic is not deductive but ignores the question of what makes deduction "intuitively self-evident," and therefore valid. When one's intuition fails, one attributes the failure to Hegel rather than searching in thinking itself for the ground that will mediate the development.

15. Before all true Hegelians erupt, I will allow that this word will not suffice to translate *aufheben* literally, but it does have a number of nice associations that capture the process signified. Among others OED lists these: decompose, die, put an end to, annul, refute, make a solution, solve, resolve, absorb, liquify, release, set free.

16. Notice again the distinction between synthesis and unity. The identity is implicit in the synthesis of *becoming,* but only as the moments are explicitly related and shown to be one, single act of thought does it become integrated into a unity.

17. *Becoming* as a logical process is atemporal; therefore when thought returns to *being* it is not a new thought, but the same as the original. A logical process, therefore, can be circular, although a temporal one cannot. See my article "Concept and Time in Hegel," *Dialogue* XII, 409. It is important to draw this distinction because it explains why illustrations from temporal experience often misrepresent the logical argument, even though the logical terms may be used to *explain* experience.

18. This circle becomes all the more vicious when understanding refuses to recognize it and acts as if it has avoided all problems. Thought is then condemned never to become master of its own operation.

19. The possibility of this resolution to a perennial problem of translating Hegel was suggested by Tillich's: "What is that which is not a special being or a group of beings. . . .but rather something which is always thought implicitly, and sometimes explicitly, if something is said to *be*?" *Systematic Theology* (Chicago: U of C, 1951) I 163. This translation in no way captures all the associations and uses of *Dasein,* particularly those exploited by Heidegger. But the usual "determinate being" is a phrase much too complex, including a meaning more developed. It is significant, for example, to learn that *"a being* is determinate being" but a simple tautology when one says *"determinate being* is determinate being." See WL I 91. (Note the circumlocution Miller is forced to use: "In considering determinate being the emphasis falls on its determinate character." 108; JS omits the sentence altogether.) The whole structure of determination is yet to be made explicit.

20. The following discussion is based on Hegel's prefatory comments in the *Encyclopedia (Logic)* §§79-82.

21. See *Enz (Logic)* §80: "Thought, as *Understanding*, sticks to fixity of characters and their distinctness from one another: every such limited abstract it treats as having a subsistence and being of its own."

   And the *Addition:* "That Philosophy never can get on without the understanding hardly calls for special remarks. . . .Its foremost requirement is that every thought shall be grasped in its full precision, and nothing allowed to remain vague and indefinite."

   Since Descartes, the terms "clear" and "precise" have been used to describe this act. Hegel notes that this vocabulary refers to a subjective or psychological process not to a logical category. (See WL II 254, JS II 247f, (Miller) 613.) *Understanding,* however, is a psychological term, and we will continue to use these adjectives when we wish to indicate what the understanding is attempting to achieve.

22. The move from *identity* through *contradiction* to *ground* is explicitly considered in Book II of the Logic. See below Part III.

23. *Enz (Logic)* §81: "In the Dialectical Stage these finite characterizations or formulae supersede themselves, and pass into their opposites." In the Remark Hegel adds: "But in its true and proper character, Dialectic is the very nature and essence of everything predicated by mere understanding—the law of things and of the finite as a whole. . . .By Dialectic is meant the indwelling tendency outwards by which the one-sidedness and limitation of the predicates of understanding is seen in its true light, and shown to be the negation of them." This movement corresponds to the activity called "judging" in the psychology (*Enz [Philosophy of Mind]* §467). The justification of this correspondence will have to wait until Chapter 10.

24. See *Enz (Logic)* §88 Remark (1): "So far the deduction of their unity is completely analytical: indeed the whole progress of philosophising in every case, if it be a methodical, that is to say a necessary, progress, merely renders explicit what is implicit in a notion."

25. See *Enz (Logic)* §82: "The Speculative stage, or stage of Positive Reason, apprehends the unity of terms (propositions) in their opposition—the affirmative, which is involved in their disintegration and in their transition." This corresponds to the third moment of inference and reasoning in *Enz (Philosophy of Mind)* §467.

26. Because the third moment cancels the isolation of the first, the fourth inverts the significance of the second. The initial synthesis of speculation may be a bare conjunction. (See WL II 227, JS II 223, Miller 589). Its validity needs to be demonstrated by showing it to be inherent. Thus the fourth and fifth moments are necessary.

Chapter V
A Being

1. Like *being, a being* is a feature common to all determinations of intelligence and there-fore serves as a basis upon which the subconscious can relate terms. But it is more deter-minate. The distinguishing moment will become explicit, not as *nothing*, but as *quality*, as *determination*, as *limit*. This second moment is always relative to the term it defines. However the first and third categories of every logical movement—the simple concept and its speculative integration—apply to all ideas and things and can therefore be used abso-lutely. See *Enz (Logic)* §85.
2. In *becoming, being* and *nothing* were shown to be contraries and not independent cate-gories. Therefore the second category changes its sense and can be called *non-being*.
3. Notice the distinction between reflection on a logical process in which the logician recalls the earlier moments and anticipates their significance and the necessity inherent in the process of understanding, dialectic and speculation that considers only the determinate connotation of the categories themselves. In the 1812 edition of the *Logic,* Hegel had not clearly drawn this distinction. He appears to use external reflection to justify introducing the thought of *not a being* into *a being*. (HGW XI, 60) In the edition of 1831 he explicitly rejected such a procedure. (See Miller 110, WL I 96f, JS I 122) By that time Hegel used the "meta-logical" stance "to elucidate or indicate in advance the course which will be exhi-bited in the development itself." It may be that this clarification in procedure required the reorganization of the argument in the second edition.
4. Notice that through this reasoning the earlier moment of *non-being* begins to become explicit in the new category of *a being*. An important theme of Hegel's is derived from Spinoza: All determination is negation. See JS I 125, WL I 100, (Miller) 113.
5. Difficult to translate is Hegel's sentence: "Das Dasein ist Daseiendes." The gerund is transformed into a gerundive, with adjectival concretizing force. But there are no ge-rundives in English. Miller's solution "Determinate being is a determinate being" misses the moments of activity contained in the verbal form. The gerundive is important for Hegel, however, because it renders explicit the determining *act*.
6. *Something* is the first negation of negation. *Becoming* anticipated this move, but neither pure *being* nor pure *nothing* was sufficiently determinate to be defined as an opposite of the other. Therefore there is no explicit negation or contrast to be negated. Hegel does anticipate the later statement in the transition to *a being:* "Their vanishing [is]. . . .the vanishing of the vanishing itself." (Miller) 106, WL I 93, JS I 119.
7. The German word *Veränderung* is etymologically related to other *Andere*. Compare the English *alteration,* with its root in the Latin *alter*.
8. Van der Meulen's profound analysis of Hegel's logic (*Hegel, Die Gebrochene Mitte,* [Hamburg: Meiner, 1958]) fails to recognize this ambiguity. Because he thinks there are only *four* movements in the method he moves directly from synthesis to new immediate unity. But it is in testing the synthesis to see if it does in fact invert the dialectic that the dif-ference in the final stage becomes apparent.
9. We have modified Hegel's argument here. He suggests focusing simply on "otherness." The phrase "to be other," however, contains the dynamic movement which has become the object of speculative reflection. At times Hegel uses *Anderssein* in this sense.

We here move into a difficult passage because the category named is also the activity it undergoes. But the complexity of the prose cannot be helped. The reader will have to try to get the various moments as clear as his mind's ability to abstract with precision allows him. I am afraid that this is but the first of a number of such passages. They get particularly cumbersome in the doctrine of Essence.

10. Hegel's term: "Sein-für-Anderes," or "Being-for-others."

11. Notice how the connotation of *something* changes as thought works out its implications. What may appear superficially to be a "family" of meanings is shown on reflection to be moments in a systematic development of thought.

12. Difficult to catch in translation is the difference between *an sich,* in itself and *an ihm* with respect to it. "Determinate" is to suggest the inherent state (*an sich);* "determined" the element of motion (*an ihm*). My colleague, David Kettler, has commented on the parallel to Spinoza's *natura naturans* and *natura naturata.*

13. The word translated here "determination" is the same as that translated by "vocation" in Fichte's *Vocation of Man.*

14. There is certainly something arbitrary about the use of English words here. The terms could be interchanged, since *constitution* sometimes refers to what is implicit and inherent, whereas *determination* is what is determined by another. However, I follow Miller's usage. Johnston and Struthers' *modification* suggests process more than determinateness. David Kettler has drawn my attention to the root *Stimme* (voice) of *Bestimmung* (determination) and the root *Schaffen* (to create) of *Beschaffenheit* (constitution).

15. The use of the possessive pronoun or of the plural with "being" indicates that we are translating *Dasein* (a being) and not *Sein* (pure being).

16. Hegel compares this move to the transition from *nothing* to *being.* In that earlier logical transition, however, the move resulted from thinking the concept; it was to that extent subjective. Here, the concept of *limited being* itself requires that the limitation or negation of the finite be perpetual. Its *becoming nothing* is its very *being.*

17. (Miller) 132, revised. The German is not as explicit about our role: "Wenn es wäre, so sollte es nicht bloss *sein.*" See JS I 145.

18. If the finite ceases to be, period, it also ceases to be *finite.*

19. Notice that this infinite progress is different from that which appeared at the end of the section on *finite.* There attention was paid simply to the process of *going beyond,* as such. The new term was ANOTHER finite. Here there is a restless movement BACK AND FORTH from the effort to think *infinite* clearly to the thought of *finite.*

20. Note that the term "define" is derived from the Latin *de* and *finis:* "from the limit." To define a concept is to render it finite.

21. *Science of Logic* (Miller) 147 (revised), WL I 136, JS I 160.

22. In the *Encyclopaedia Logic,* Hegel shortens this whole analysis. Infinite progress, as it appears at the end of the section on *The Finite,* implicitly contains the true infinite. The two concepts, however, are simply *something* and *other,* not *finite* and *infinite.* Other becomes *something; something* becomes *other.* The closed circle implicit in the earlier discussion of *being other* is the basis for the transition. The larger logic isolates more precisely the distinct moments of the thought process, and thus clarifies more categories: *determination,* and *constitution,* the contrast between *limit* and *limitation,* etc. In this section one sees a significant modification in the details of Hegel's argument as one moves from the first edition of the *Logic,* through the three editions of the *Encyclopaedia* to the final edition of the *Logic.* A useful commentary on the logic of *finite* and *infinite* can be found in F.H. Bradley's *Ethical Studies* (Oxford: Oxford U.P., 1927) 75ff.

23. Unlike *quality,* however, the negation is not simply implicit. It has become explicit, and in due course transcended. Hegel notes an implication of this: It is the isolated, finite con-

cept that is "simply ideal" in contrast to reality. And this isolation of a thing which makes it finite is a construction of thought.

24. Hegel's word is *Fürsichsein,* often translated "Being-for-self." Sartre's use of *pour soi* has suggested that "being for self" is being conscious of oneself. But although Hegel uses consciousness to illustrate this concept, the illustration is much more complex than anything that has yet appeared in the logic. Sartre (and others) have confused *Für sich* with *für es.* The latter term is used in the *Phenomenology* for the moment of consciousness and certainty. To prevent such a confusion, then, I propose *being for its own sake.* This captures the representations, "general ideas," or images Hegel cites in *Science of Logic* (Miller) 157f, WL I 147f, JS I 170f.

25. E Fleischmann, *La Science Universelle,* 85. The failure to recognize this context in using understanding alone results in abstract idealism. (See Miller 154ff, WL I 145ff, JS I 168f.) For an isolated concept is finite—it is defined by its limits. But finite terms can be rendered precise only if thought goes beyond those limits and makes clear what the concept is not as well as what it is. This means that a category must be distinguished from those that ought to be similar, and identified with others that ought to be different. This intellectual dynamic, which integrates distinctions and relations in a comprehensive context, is what Hegel calls the true infinite. When separated from this context by understanding, concepts become abstract and ideal; they lose the setting that establishes their reality. A logical empiricism, then, that uses formalized symbols to represent the world "labours under a delusion when it supposes that, while analyzing the objects, it leaves them as they were; it really transforms the concrete into an abstract." [*Enz (Logic)*§38 Addition (revised)] Compare also Lebrun, *La patience du concept,* 76: "Rather than for errors of fact, [the understanding] is responsible for an ideology. By isolating 'thoughts' and stringing them together like simple objects of acquaintance it gives credit to the idea that knowledge is a 'subjective' strategy." Only by exploiting the full network of the intellectual dynamic can thought hope to use logic to comprehend the complex structure of reality.

Chapter VI
Seeming

1. See, for example, *Science of Logic* (Miller) 110, WL II 96f, JS I 122. This difference between what thought thinks and how it is understood by the logician is comparable to that between the "for it" and the "for us" of the *Phenomenology of Spirit,* but as we shall see in this chapter it progressively disappears as thinking thought incorporates more and more explicitly the intellectual activity of the logician into its concepts.

2. *Science of Logic* (Miller) 389, WL II 3, JS II 15. Hegel uses another German pun to make the same point: the immediacy of being is "inwardized, recollected" into the process of reflection. As noted above in Chapter 2, note 18, the German *Erinnerung* has both senses: internalizing and remembering. Here the process referred to is atemporal and logical; in the psychological act of recollection it is temporal and developmental. The logical sense is independent of, and thus logically prior to, the temporal application.

3. *An-und-fürsichsein* (Miller: Being-in-and-for-itself).

4. The Hindu term *maya* expresses much of what is involved in this concept. Miller uses the term "Illusory Being," which lays too much stress on its negative unreality. Wallace (*Enz [Logic]* §112) employs a longer phrase "A seeming or reflected light." The simple term "show" proposed by Johnston and Struthers retains much of the sense of the German, *Schein,* even though it lacks the aspects of "lustre" or "shine." Hegel has another pun

with *Unwesen,* which Miller has translated "non-essence," but equally means "disorder," "excess" or "monster." I have translated this as "nonentity." It should read with the stress on the second syllable.

5. *Essence* will certainly develop a more complex meaning. But at this primitive stage of its appearance in the logical process only these two characteristics can be applied. As we shall see, the movement of thought produces a number of different meanings for *essence* (and also for *form* and *ground*) which, when isolated, appear to be diverse with only a family resemblance. Hegel's self-reflective consideration of the intellectual processes shows how they may be intrinsically related.

6. It is this fact—remaining self-identical through negation—that distinguishes it from *a being.* The latter concept *changes* in the intellectual activity and becomes *other.*

7. This explains why "illusory being" is so unsatisfactory as a sign for its meaning. The Hindu term *maya* does involve this double "flickering" character. In itself it is illusory, but when seen as *maya,* thought has already penetrated behind to its positive essence.

8. Notice how the categories articulated are applied to the very process of articulation. This contributes to the complexity of the dialectical discussion in "Essence."

9. See the comment Hegel made in his lectures: "This word 'reflection' is originally applied, when a ray of light in a straight line impinges upon the surface of a mirror and is thrown back from it. Here we have a doubling—first, something immediate, a being, and secondly something mediated or posited. The same takes place when we reflect, or think back upon, an object." *Enz (Logic)* §112, Addition (revised).

10. Compare the Addition to *Enz (Logic)* §111 (revised): "In *essence* transition [or passing over] is no longer present but only reference. In *being* the form of referring is purely a matter of our reflection; in *essence,* however, the referring is its own determination. In the sphere of *being* when *something* becomes *another,* the *something* has vanished. Not so in *essence:* here we have no genuine other, but only diversity, reference of one to *its* other. Transition in *essence* is therefore at the same time no transition, for in passing over from what is diverse into what is diverse, the diverse does not vanish: what are diverse remain in their relation." The language of reflection that had to be introduced metalogically in the last part now comes into its own. Determinations like "identity," "difference," "reflection," "contradiction," and "essential" are not simply used, but become defined.

11. At this point "not" has not yet been defined, much less "negativity." Reflection, then, simply takes its starting point as not valid in itself. The nature of this invalidity will become more explicit as we proceed. This imprecise generality of the terms makes it difficult to clarify this definition of *reflection* with more exactitude. What will become explicit as we proceed through the doctrine of essence, however, is how this "not" becomes more radically defined as "external to" or indeed "excluded from." Reflection is the ability to make distinctions—even to distinguish from its own activity. It thereby ignores its own responsibility. Gradually, however, the integrating perspective will begin to become evident.

12. Hegel's title for this section is "Positing Reflection," but he also uses the term "absolute reflection," that is reflection in itself apart from all relations to anything else. Since the term "absolute" generates associations to some kind of incomprehensible metaphysical entity, I use instead the term "reflection as such."

13. This pun is specifically English. Indeed *positive* will only be defined later.

14. The German: *Setzen* and *Voraussetzen* expresses the close relation between positing and presupposing.

15. See Chapter 14, below. It will be important in making that move, however, to recognize

that logic, as an independent discipline, already has the tools with which it can think about things that are external to it.

16. (Miller) 407; WL I 21f, and JS II 33.

17. The *essentials* were expressed in the tradition as the so-called laws of thought. Aristotle identified identity, non-contradiction and excluded middle as the criteria thought must use to reflect coherently. But he also insisted that they were essential characteristics of real entities. The two realms are different from each other, yet related; and it is this double structure that enabled Aristotelianism to discern the essence of the real world.

Chapter VII
The Essentials

1. The German text here is somewhat confusing. The first paragraph is marked by a "1." But there is no "2" before Remark 1 on Abstract Identity. "2" appears only after the first paragraph of the Remark. Miller inserts a "2" before the second paragraph of "Identity" and appears to assume that the first Remark continues right through to the second. Labarrière and Jarczyk (*Science de la Logique: La Doctrine de l'Essence*, p. 39 n21) rightly point out that Remark 1 is interjected between the two main parts of the section and that the "2" (Miller, p. 412) which appears to begin its second paragraph in fact takes up the basic text again. This interpretation has been followed in the critical edition (HGW XI 261). Lasson confuses matters even further by beginning Remark 1 one sentence too soon. (In JS the "Observation" ends conveniently at the bottom of page 38, and "2" begins at page 39.) There is much in this second volume that cries out for the critical revision underway when Hegel died. The first edition was written while he exercised a full-time occupation as teacher and rector of the gymnasium at Nürnberg, and he was not at all content with its published form. See *Hegel Briefe*, §198, 393 and O. Poggeler, "Nachwort zu Entwicklungs-geschichte von Hegels Logik," *Hegelstudien* (Bonn: Bouvier, 1963) II 47-70.

2. Or absolute difference.

3. The pun in English (and French) on "difference" and "indifference," although relevant to the discussion, cannot be expressed in the original German. On the other hand German relates diversity *"Ver-schiedenheit"* and difference *"Unterschied."* Diversity is *difference* pushed to its limit. See Léonard, *Commentaire Littéral*, 157n1.

4. In the two previous determinations of reflection, dialectic introduced the self-reflexive moment. In *diversity,* however, it finds the self-reflexivity already implicit in the concept as isolated by understanding. As we shall see, this will lead ultimately to a dissolution of the pure externality of reflection as a "third."

5. Making a subtle distinction, Hegel moves from talking about "the positive and the negative" to "the positive and negative." The latter phrase is consistently made subject of a *singular* verb. In this way he designates the relation rather than the terms related. Miller and JS miss this. On p. 425, Miller translates: "The determinations which constitute the positive and negative consist in the fact that the positive and [?] negative are. . . .absolute moments of opposition." While the first "the positive and negative" is an exact translation, Hegel has another "the" where I have inserted [?]. Similarly on p. 426 Miller writes: "But, thirdly, the positive and negative are only something posited. . ." where Hegel has "the positive and negative is." JS translates the two passages as: "The determinations which constitute Positive and Negative consist then in this, that Positive and

Negative are, first, absolute moments of Opposition." (II 52) and "But thirdly, Positive and Negative are not only a posited term." (53) Labarrière and Jarczyk also miss the point by always inserting "le" before "negatif" and using plural verbs. To avoid confusion I use positive-and-negative as the singular term.

6. In this sentence I have tried to capture the sense of "Jedes ist an ihm selbst positiv and negativ." The translators have approximated *an ihm* to *an sich*. But the non-reflexive pronoun suggests that the determinations are brought to it. See above in Chapter 5, note 12.

7. I follow Miller and the critical edition (HGW XI 275) in replacing *Negative* here with *Positive*.

8. As we have seen, this would be the concept *being other*.

9. Important to note here is how the reflective effort to maintain distinctions breaks down and intelligence reverts to the simple process of becoming.

10. *Excluding reflection* is as contradictory as *positive* or *negative*. Rather than being an independent conceptual object, however, it is the dynamic relation of thought. This is why it can posit and exclude at the same time. This structure was already anticipated in the essential relation *positive-and-negative*.

11. The three exclusions need to be clearly distinguished: First, the exclusion of *positive* from *negative* and vice versa; second, the exclusion of that first exclusion from the intellectual activity of reflection; third, the intellectual activity that performs the second exclusion.

12. Therefore English sometimes uses "reason" for this concept: "What is the reason for this paradox?" we ask. Compare here the following quotations: "This systematic dissolution of the contradictions against which the philosophical understanding collides: that is the Concept." Lebrun, *La patience du concept*, 374. "It is, then. . . .to avoid logical contradiction that the dialectical process gets under way and follows through to its term." Grégoire, *Études hégéliennes,* 62 (see the whole study "L'universelle Contradiction" pp. 51-139). "In fact so far is the dialectic from denying the law of contradiction, that it is especially based on it. The contradictions are the cause of the dialectical process." McTaggart, *Studies,* 9. "The removal of contradiction is rather the process of realising the complete truth than the indication of falsehood, for contradiction is not so much error as the mode of manifesting the truth." Baillie, *Origin and Significance,* 228.

Chapter VIII
Ground

1. In the three sections of *ground as such,* ground is the self-identical first as *essence,* then as *matter,* finally as *grounding relation*. The move to determinate ground, however, has introduced a difference into the content of *ground*. That difference will be examined in the subsequent section. See *Enz (Logic)* §127 Add. "We must be careful, when we say that the ground is the unity of identity and difference, not to understand by this unity an abstract identity. To avoid this misconception we may say that the ground, besides being their unity, is also the difference of identity and difference."

2. The bare *difference* of formal ground has become explicit as *diversity*.

3. That is *an und für sich*.

4. The opposition that developed in complete ground has now become a contradiction.

5. See here Chapter 5.

6. Hegel points out that the concept *relatively unconditioned* can also lead into an infinite regress, since each condition is limited and finite, and thus presupposes another which conditions it. This infinite regress cannot fully explicate the grounding process, for it

always leaves an ungrounded surd. A complete explanation takes all the moments and shows how they mutually imply and ground each other. This organic model was anticipated in Kant's *Critique of Teleological Judgement*.

7. I use this phrase to express the German *Sache*. Neither "thing" (which equally translates *Ding* later in Book II) nor the "fact" (of Miller and JS) is adequate to capture the double sense of essential totality.

8. Notice how, once again, the constituent categories are applied self-reflexively to their own inter-relationship. This generates the final collapse into immediacy.

9. In Heidegger and Sartre *existence* signifies a determinate, and hence self-conscious individuality that is absolutely immediate and hence irreducible to anything else. Neither is it generated out of something else that would represent its essence. For Hegel, however, not only physical existence, but also consciousness is the result of a process or becoming, so that any individual existence inevitably contains an inherent reference to a persisting natural and cultural totality. What is immediate is simply the indeterminate universality of pure being.

10. See *Enz (Logic)* §114 Rem (and also §162 Rem). This concern for a parallel scheme does not completely work, however, for the paragraphs on *existence* do not match the more developed complexity of those on *a being*.

11. Similarly *ground* reproduces reflectively the constituent moments of *being for its own sake*.

12. This is why the second book is still part of "The Objective Logic." Even though the role of the subject has been brought to consciousness, it cancels itself in order to think the object.

13. As we have seen, it is this self-reflexive structure that complicates the discussion of this section.

14. See *The Science of Logic* (Miller) 391, WL II 6, JS II 17.

15. Recall as well the points where reflection thought of itself as an external third.

Chapter IX
Conceiving

1. The use of "comprehension" to refer to this third book of the *Logic* is suggested by Fleischmann in *La Science Universelle*, 59: "Indeed, the word 'comprehension' is perhaps the best translation yet for *Begriff*, for at this level it is a question of developing the objective world from the very notion of the knowing subject and of showing that it is actually contained and included therein." Many of the English translators have preferred the term "notion" to translate the German *Begriff* because it has connotations of the Greek *nous*. It is inadequate, however, because it has no correlate verb form, and therefore does not easily represent the dynamic intellectual process that is to be signified. The French have generally preferred *concept* and *concevoir*, and this relation can easily be maintained in the English *concept* and *conceive*.

2. Part of the incomprehensibility of the earlier "objective logic" is that Hegel discusses the concepts without reference to this context of the thinking dynamic. In this way he endeavours to reproduce the way intelligence does in fact clarify its terms and move on to other terms. The necessity of the development is thus inherent, and not the product of comprehensive totality, and the descriptions of the movement become very dense. See the Remark to *Enz (Logic)* §162: "The preceding logical categories. . .demonstrate that they are *concepts* in their transition [their dialectical moment] and in their return to themselves

and totality. But they are only *determinate* concepts, concepts inherently, or what is the same thing concepts *for us.*" (revised, my italics) A commentary can take more liberty as long as the relative unimportance of the interpretative perspective is recognized.

3. (Miller) 54, WL I 36, JS I 65.

4. "It is Aristotle who has best elaborated the structure of thinking as pure act, being itself its own substratum." E. Fleischmann, *La Science Universelle*, 233. Aristotle's term *energeia* does not translate easily into the English "energy."

5. Compare *Phenomenology* (Baillie) 118f (revised). [*Phän* 49f, (Miller) 37 and (Kaufmann) 92]: "Since the concept is the very self of the object, manifesting itself as *its becoming*, it is not a quiescent subject, passively supporting accidents: it is a self-determining active concept which takes up its determinations and makes them its own. In the course of this process that inert passive subject loses its solid ground; it enters into the different constituents and pervades the content; instead of remaining in inert antithesis to determinateness of content, it constitutes, in fact, its very specificity: i.e. the content as differentiated along with the process of bringing it about." The philosophical counterpart to this all-pervasive universality is romanticism.

6. Many commentators want to argue that, for Hegel, the *universal concept* simply includes the other two concepts. One wonders why, then, the succeeding two sections are necessary. On our interpretation, dialectic has shown only that *any* universal concept is not purely universal. The implications of this are yet to be explored.

7. This is why the subjunctive is the proper mood to express the process.

8. It is the basic connotation that makes the effort to determine natural species so unsatisfying intellectually. A contingent diversity is external to the unity of conceptual thought, and their relation is only a matter of external reflection. The concern of science is to think through this diversity to the limit of explicit opposition so that an immanent relation can be recognized.

9. Hegel here adds a number of explanatory comments concerning the application of these categories to nature. Since these do not concern the process of pure thought in itself, we pass them by.

10. Any effort to introduce the latter is dismissed as "psychologism" when this stage of thought becomes the basis of a formal theory. See, for example, Carnap's *The Logical Syntax of Language,* and Frege's *The Foundations of Arithmetic.*

11. Compare *Phenomenology,* (Baillie) 93 [*Phän* 29, (Miller) 18f, Kaufmann 50]: "The action of separating the elements is the exercise of the force of understanding, the most astonishing and greatest of all powers, or rather the absolute power. The circle, which is self-enclosed and at rest, and *qua* substance, holds its own moments, is an immediate relation, the immediate, continuous relation of elements with their unity, and hence arouses no sense of wonderment. But that an accident as such, when cut loose from its containing circumference,—that which is bound and held by something else and actual only by being converted with it,—should obtain an existence all its own, gain freedom and independence on its own account—this is the portentous power of the negative; it is the energy of thought, of pure ego. Death, as we may call that unreality, is the most terrible thing, and to keep and hold fast what is dead demands the greatest force of all. . .The life of mind is not one that shuns death, and keeps clear of destruction; it endures death, and in death maintains its being." The whole paragraph is a powerful commentary on this section.

12. Compare here *Science of Logic* (Miller) 601, WL II 219, JS II 234, as well as the second §138 and the final part of the Remark to §139 in the first edition of the *Encyclopaedia.* (JE

VI 115 & 118). Since this edition of the *Encyclopaedia* was published within a year of the final book of the larger logic, it can be read as a specific commentary on some of the transitions. In the second and third editions he added a significant Remark to §164 (parallel to §113 in the first edition): "Universality, particularity, and individuality are, taken in the abstract, the same as identity, difference, and ground."

13. Hegel here is able to use the determinations that were generated when thought clarified the concept *being for its own sake* [(Miller), 157-184, WL I 147-176, JS I 170-197] as well as those that follow from the reflective contrast between *this* and its *material* [(Miller) 492-494, WL II 114-117, JS II 120-123].

14. (Miller) 620 (revised), WL II 263, JS II 256. Notice that Hegel here identifies the abstract universal of a denotative set by means of the psychological vocabulary of representation. The process here, which is neither signifying nor symbolic imagination, is bare association.

15. This absolute exclusion found expression in symbolic logic in Russell's paradoxes of self-reference that required the theory of types.

16. There is a play on words in the German. "Its return into itself is therefore the absolute original partition (ursprüngliche Teilung) of itself, or, in other words, it is posited as judgement (Urteil)." (Miller) 622, WL II 264, JS II 257.

Chapter X
Judging

1. It is clear that I am taking the contrary position to Marcuse, in *Hegels Ontologie*, 141: "It is scarcely necessary to stress that the Hegelian theory of judgement is concerned with the judgement not as a form of judgement or cognition nor as a logical figure, but as a fundamental phenomenon of being itself. . ."

2. Because the judgement form entails certain criteria concerning its application, one cannot use the same illustrative content for all. Each set of judgements has its own appropriate range of examples. See Van der Meulen, *Hegel, die gebrochen Mitte*, 5: "If we want to provide examples, we will have to provide a different example for the logical content in each different figure of the syllogism. This is a question not of the empirical content of the example, but exclusively of the logical form, which is, however, the logical form of *this* content, belongs to it, and is not introduced in any way externally."

3. Only external reflection can indicate that "a" must be an existing individual in contrast to a category of thought "Q." "a" could equally be a definite description and "Q" could be a name.

4. Since symbolic logic lacks a distinct copula, only the latter alternative is applicable.

5. A more appropriate term would be "indefinite judgement." Boethius, however, translated Aristotle's *áoristos* by the Latin *infinitus* and it became the term enshrined by tradition. This type of judgement is implicit in the discussion of category words in Carnap and Ryle. Pap makes explicit the need for two types of negation in "Types and Meaninglessness," *Mind*, LXIX (1960) 41-54.

6. The adjective "true" is here appropriate because it refers to the correspondence between the form of judgement and its implicit criteria, as well as the coherence of their combination.

7. Hegel's illustration of crime shows how the two negations can be abstractly isolated from each other in unreflective action. *Enz. (Logic)* §80 Addition points out that the isolation of understanding, which cannot be maintained within the comprehensive context of pure

thought, is unavoidable when thought moves into the bare externality of space and time through action.

8. At this point we elaborate on Hegel's transition, incorporating material from the introduction to the succeeding section.

9. With this speculative conclusion it is recognized that the symbol "∿" is not appropriate for the simple *judgement of a being*. It will find its place later in the *judgement of necessary relation*.

10. See (Miller) 643, WL II 286, JS II 279: "The universal is no longer an *abstract* universality or a *single property*, but is posited as a universal that has gathered itself together into a unity through the relation of distinct terms; or, regarding it from the point of view of the content of various determinations in general, as the *taking together* of various properties and existences."

11. See here the discussion of Existence in Book II, (Miller) 481-498, WL II 102-122, JS II 109-127.

12. Symbolic logic has introduced tools to distinguish clearly between inherence and subsumption—a distinction not made explicit in the formal logic of Hegel's day. There is an interesting "found pun" between "essential" and "ε". The validity of the pun will be demonstrated only as we proceed.

13. These pronouns could equally be adjectives, but at this point the subject has been determined neither qualitatively nor essentially. Therefore there is no noun or category to specify it more precisely.

14. Dialectic makes explicit the transitions that were involved in the earlier logic of simple becoming. The reference to the *limitation* inherent in *some* generates an *ought* that passes over to something *other*.

Hegel illustrates this point with reference to the use of the indefinite pronoun as an adjective, modifying the noun "man" (or "animal"). By calling the whole expression ("some men") the subject he misleads, for the important point in this discussion is not the relation between "some" and the universal concept in one of the terms of the judgement, but rather their relation in a judgement as such. (This is why the predicate is irrelevant to his discussion.) Any relation *between concepts* will become explicit only in the *judgement of necessary relation*. Hegel recognizes this when he writes: "This universality anticipates what results from the judgement of reflection." (Miller) 646 (revised), WL II 289, JS II 282. Miller obscures this stress by not breaking paragraphs after this sentence as in the original. This is a good example of how an empirical illustration can mislead because it does not isolate what is essential.

15. It is important to note that the sense of totality, suggested by (x), is not involved at this point in the logical development. That will appear only when we move beyond the particularity of judging to the comprehensive universality of inferring.

16. (Miller) 648, WL II 291, JS II 284.

17. (Miller) 649 (revised), WL II 292, JS II 286.

18. Notice how the comprehensive dynamic of conceptual thought reappears, but now as explicitly determinate. The abstracted isolation of *positive judgement* gradually gives way to a more comprehensive intellectual perspective. Notice also how the *identity* and *difference* of the *judgement of a being* that passed over to the *diversity* of the *judgement of reflection* now become the *opposition* of the *judgement of necessity*.

In the same way that the *infinite judgement* turns out to be no judgement at all, and thus acquires no significant place in symbolic logic except in the definition of a category, so the *universal judgement* (ϕx)xεC or {a,b,c, . . .n} xεC has disappeared from view except in the definition of a denotative set.

19. It may appear strange that I propose *conjunction* as the relation involved in the *categorical judgement*. Recent logical theory has proposed instead an *hypothesis* using the universal quantifier: (x)(Qx⊃Rx). But this form uses the absolutely universal quantifier, a symbol that has not yet been required or defined. Since universality has been defined relative to a denotative class, all that can be symbolically expressed is an intersection of classes. It is because this form expresses a universality but without a necessary relation that logic is forced to move on to hypothesis. In other words, the proposal of modern logic reflects the conclusion of Hegel's analysis: The truth of the *categorical judgement* is the *hypothetical*.

20. We have already indicated this symbolically in using "p" and "q" and the "." of conjunction. In other words it is becoming clearer that p and q are not simply the terms of a judgement but have the characteristic of becoming judgements on their own. Complete independence, however, will become explicit only in *disjunctive judgement*, just as the complete definition of a denotative class becomes explicit only with the *universal judgement*.

21. Only with the move to *assertoric judgement* does the *reference* of p and q become relevant, not to an indicated individual, but to what is the case. It should be noted that as yet there has been no definition of the rule of double negation. Therefore the implication that p could be false even though the relation is true is not yet explicit. That will follow from the succeeding discussion.

22. Note that we have used only transformation rules, not inferential syllogisms.

23. In q($\bar{\text{p}}$ v p), q is the universal, p and $\bar{\text{p}}$ are the particulars.

24. The German "sowohl als" is better translated "as well as" than "both-and". (Miller) *Both-and* asserts positive conjunction, which is too strong.

25. The interpretation of "v" as "and/or" maintains the same two relations. What are commonly called contrary and contradictory *concepts* are in fact *disjunctive judgements*. A concept is thought as having *contrary* implications insofar as the latter are simply thought as diverse: the *difference* in *either/or* is externally related to the *identity*. It is thought as *contradictory* when its implications exclude each other.

26. Hegel illustrates this by showing that the statement: "Colours are light as well as/or dark" follows from the conceptual structure more precisely than "Colours are either red or orange or. . ." The latter lists determinate differences that are not *immediately* relevant to the inherent structure of the concept "colour."

27. The fact that the relation expressed is an identity and a difference at the same time makes it into a contradictory concept. There is no external universal from whose perspective the two terms can be seen to be contraries. While the *judgements of necessity* explored the structures of *opposition*, the *judgements of conceptual thought* will involve *contradiction*.

28. Because of the self-contradictory character of ($\sim$p.$\sim\sim$p) the symbols p, q, etc. are more clearly defined. For $\sim$($\sim$p.$\sim\sim$p) can be transformed to pv$\sim$p — the full-fledged definition of a proposition as either true or false. This corresponds to the definition of a denotative class as including both those individuals indicated and those not indicated; and of a predicated quality as allowing change within a categorical range. Each definition introduces a new universal concept: Q & $\bar{\text{Q}}$ initially defines *class*; ($\exists$x & $\bar{\exists}$x), or ϕx, *proposition*; pv$\sim$p, *assertion*. We have now moved beyond propositional forms of expressions to statements.

29. (Miller) 657f, WL II 302, JS II 294.
30. Hegel distinguishes between the evaluation expressed in the judgement and that implicitly contained in the act of assertion. The former can itself be stated: (p is correct, q is good); the latter cannot. In this way he distinguishes between the distinct evaluative aspect involved in *asserting* "p is true" and the evaluation it asserts. This is why the evaluation asserted need not be restricted to truth or falsity.
31. Note how the three sets of evaluative predicates assess its individuality, its universality, and its particularity.
32. One could say that the subject expresses the universal and the predicate assesses its individuality; or that the subject refers to an individual and the predicate evaluates its comprehensive universality.
33. This paradox is the object of Kant's analysis in the *Critique of Aesthetic Judgement*.
34. In one, "Some S is P" entails "Some S is not P"; in the other, the assertion of the relation leaves the being of the terms problematic.
35. For *constitution* see above in Chapter 5, and in (Miller) 122f, WL I 110ff, JS I 135ff. This dialectic reflects the paradoxical relation between sense and reference that generated Frege's discussion in "On Sense and Reference" (See Geach and Black, eds. *Translations from the Philosophical Writings of Gottlob Frege,* (Oxford, 1962)), as well as Russell's difficulties with definite descriptions (see "On Denoting" in *Logic and Knowledge* (London & New York, 1956)).
36. See the discussion of this concept in Chapter 8.
37. Hegel here follows the path later taken by Frege: the paradoxical contradiction between sense and reference leads to an effort to do away with psychological subjectivity by appealing to a purely logical reference. Rather than stopping at this point, however, he will proceed to develop its paradoxical implications.
38. Note here how the reflection that cancels the negative contrasts of essence to return to the simple transition of being is not the only operation of comprehensive thought. The latter also cancels the simple identity of being, to constitute the negative contrasts of essence. Both are fundamental to its operation.
39. Notice that there are really four terms here: the individual, the particular determining conditions, the universal grounding relation in the subject, and the comprehensive essence that is the predicate. There are three relations expressed—the determining and the grounding are to justify the comprehending. Distinct judgements use the first three terms to express the three relations. The total set of three judgements articulates the fourth term.

    There is a double reference for this discussion. On the one hand it refers to the subject of the judgement and its evaluative predicate; on the other it refers to judgement as an assertion and the act of asserting it. In the latter case, the act of assertion must itself be justified by specifying what are its determining conditions. Both are possible because the form of the judgement can be used self-referentially with respect to its own operations in judging.
40. ϕa expresses the determining conditions; $\phi < C$ is the grounding relation; $a\varepsilon C$ is the simple essence.
41. In other words one moves beyond *contradiction* to *ground*.
42. We are not involved here with empirical reference. But because this very same dynamic relation holds between the appearances of a thing and the thing itself, the rigorous use of judgement will lead to a full comprehension of an object. See Hegel's discussion of understanding in *Phenomenology*, and in *Enz. (Philosophy of Mind)* §§422-3.

43. With *necessary judgement* the inherent integrity of the content—the intellectual process—has been clearly established. But this unity has not acquired an appropriate form. Note that the contrast here between content and form makes the whole analysis of syllogism purely formal. This limitation has replaced the earlier one of the finite subjectivity of the judging act.

44. It is always a delight to find plays on words that are English, but that yet receive a very precise definition by developing them within the rigour of Hegel's analysis. Thus we have been able to draw a contrast between self-reflexive operations and self-reference as analogous to the contrast between simple reflection and pure reference. And we here discover that *in-ference* might very well refer to an act of *referring into* oneself in which the distinction between the self as subjective agent and the self as object (suggested by the prefix "re-") is dissolved.

Chapter XI
Inferring

1. This distinction is not retained in German, which uses *der Schluss* for both. Compare the comment of Fleischmann, 266: "It is evident that the term 'syllogism' is the worst possible translation for the German word *Schluss,* which does not signify the well-known scholastic technique for reaching a conclusion, but rather the 'issue,' the 'unification,' the 'reconciliation' of the artificial distinctions of the understanding."

2. This is the interpretation of Aristotle.

3. The analysis of Boolean algebra.

4. This makes clear why these syllogisms are those of *a being*. The process of inference is nothing else than a determinate becoming—the type of transition characteristic of the doctrine of *being*.

5. Compare the comment from Hegel's lectures: "In this syllogism conceptual thought is at the very height of self-estrangement. " *Enz. (Logic)* §183 Addition (revised).

6. Hegel's *second figure* is Arisotle's third. The reason for this change follows from the preceding speculative analysis; but it will also have a more comprehensive implication in the system as a whole. This change does reflect the fact, however, that the primary characterization of the figures is the role of the middle term as *particular, individual* or *universal,* not its relative position to the subject and the predicate in the premises. The latter is derived, not basic.

7. This syllogism underlies any empirical effort to determine species. Under the genus "bird" for example, one can only know what are the particular species by finding individuals that embody them.

8. This introduces an important new perspective into the concept of class. Previously C was defined as Q & Q̄. Now, however, C and Q are external to each other: there is nothing in C which would indicate that Q is a particular species, nor is there anything in Q which would implicitly refer to the genus. The simple transition of thought that appeared in the dialectic of *negative judgement* is dismissed as arbitrary, contingent and individual. Thus classes can be specified only denotatively.

9. There are a number of illustrations for Hegel's *second figure:* not only the third figure of Aristotle, but also the tendency of ordinary thought to claim that two qualities that happen at the same time are profoundly associated. Notice how pure abstraction is mediated by the individuating operations of conceptual thought. This syllogism, then, self-referentially represents the process analysed in Chapter IX as *individuating.*

10. Compare van der Meulen, *Hegel, der gebrochene Mitte,* 77: "It was a magnificent thought of Hegel's to take this side of a possible, but purely logical and essentially meaningless, quantification and 'logification' of inference whose prototype and epitome is the fourth figure and in one and the same result of the formal process of inference to oppose it to the true aspect that contains the valid logical progression."

11. See (Miller) 684, WL II 330, JS II 322: "The defect of the *formal syllogism,* therefore, does not lie in the form of the syllogism—on the contrary this is the form of rationality—but in the fact that the form appears only as an *abstract* form, therefore isolated from conceptual thought."

12. With the move to *inference* the dialogue between Hegel's analysis and contemporary symbolism takes on a different character. The precision of the symbols represents in sharper detail the structures of *inference,* even as their formalism hides more completely its grounding dynamic. There is, then, no absolute correspondence between Hegel's argument and current discussions. Nevertheless by bringing the two together in an effort to determine what is in fact essential and what is contingent in both, we can extend the philosophy of logic.

13. The use of ϕ here, rather than the Q of the original definition of C, reflects the fact that ϕ is determinate and therefore particular. Q became determinate but was originally abstract. As we shall see ϕ becomes an abstracted universal in a reverse process in this discussion.

14. This is why $\phi \times C$ is a reciprocal relation.

15. Notice that in rejecting the definition of C as $\phi \& \phi$, all that is left is the denotative definition of $\{a, b, c, \ldots, n\}\ x\varepsilon C$ or $(\phi x)x\varepsilon C$ — a purely denotative definition. The use of pure denotation to define a category is the result of inference.

16. *Enz (Philosophy of Mind)* §456.

17. This is the *fourth figure* in Hegel's analyis—in effect simply one part of the synthetic argument of speculative reason with regard to the *third.* Note the pun on *equality*: the *quality* has been left aside (*ex-*).

18. The reference to phantasy in the previous paragraph was not irrelevant, however. Because speculative reason discovers that inference is an operation that might be pure phantasy or subjective imagination, it seeks to signify the operation in an objective symbol.

19. As previously expressed under categorical judgement. Since neither operation is purely abstract, the relation between a class and its members is not the one of nominalism. The members of a class are conceptually identified by means of denotation and differentiated from the members of its complementary class. These essential determinations are not derived from the non-conceptual act of pure reference, but from the double dynamic of identifying and differentiating intelligence.

20. "All green things are pleasant; this is a green thing; therefore this is pleasant." Just as the subject of the *judgements of reflection,* Hegel's illustrations introduce an independent conceptual content into the middle term. The independence of the content becomes explicit only below when the precision of modern symbolism is used to clarify what is involved.

21. Strangely, Hegel's text at this point refers to the *major* premise, in which the *individual* is related to the *universal.* This was not the problem in the second figure. There are other indications that this section needs the revision of the second edition. The 2. does not initiate the dialectical problematic but simply extends the definition of the syllogism. The subsequent discussion of *analogy* as well leaves much to be desired for clarity and effectiveness.

22. Hegel also refers to the role of this syllogism in *experience*. In contrast to bare perception, where each sensation is an independent individual, experience differentiates within the total range of past sensations, and thus identifies the individuals that have common characteristics. Experience, in contrast to immediate intuition (symbolized in the *second figure* of the *formal syllogism*), is thus a generalizing process. As noted above, the dialectical problems do not become developed until '3.' in the German text. For clarity, then, I have inserted '2.' where Hegel has '3.', and put '3.' at the beginning of the next paragraph.

23. In Mill's discussion of induction (*A System of Logic* III 3) this presupposition is rendered explicit: "We must first observe that there is a principle implied in the very statement of what induction is; an assumption with regard to the course of nature and the order of the universe, namely, that there are such things in nature as parallel cases; that what happens once will, under a sufficient degree of similarity of circumstances, happen again, and not only again, but as often as the same circumstances occur." Mill's methods, based on agreement and difference, recognize that identification and differentiation are both involved, but he does not consider what justifies the synthesis of the two. It was this latter question that exercised Whewell, and later Peirce, and becomes explicit below in the discussion of *analogy*.

24. Compare a comment from Hegel's lectures: "In the experimental sciences, analogy deservedly occupies a high place and has led to results of the highest importance. Analogy is the instinct of reason, creating an anticipation that this or that characteristic, which experience has discovered, has its roots in the inner nature or kind of an object, and arguing on the faith of that anticipation." *Enz (Logic)* §190, Add. In this lecture material Hegel provides examples that are more intuitively compelling than the one he gives in the larger logic, although he does refer to the analogical inference that the moon has inhabitants to show how it embodies the fundamental weakness in analogy. (It is worth noting that with such terms as 'instinct,' 'anticipation,' 'faith,' the cited two sentences could have come from a text of C. S. Peirce on abduction.)

25. The arbitrariness of the conjunction is made explicit in lower functional calculus, for example, where the criteria for universal generalization (*induction*) and particular instantiation (*analogy*) are specified only in the meta-logical perspective. In the empirical sciences either a criterion of randomness is required, resulting only in possibility, or some kind of conceptual connection must be established between the phenomena correlated. The appropriate kind of conceptual connection will be specified in the third part of this chapter.

26. Referring to an analysis previously developed (Miller) 555-7, WL II 185-8; JS II 188-191) Hegel calls it the substance that grounds its accidental manifestations.

27. Hegel adds a paragraph here to show that *condition/conditioned* is a more general, and thus more adequate, representation of the inherent meaning of the *hypothetical judgement* than either *cause/effect* or *ground/grounded*. The existence of a *condition* is indifferent to the fact that the result appears (that is, it might not be sufficient) and avoids the restrictive limitation of *cause* or *ground*. In addition, *condition* can refer equally well to both sides of the other relations: In some sense an *effect* conditions its *cause*; and what is *grounded* conditions its *ground*. A *hypothetical judgement* is often used to move from effect or what is grounded as antecedent to the cause or ground as consequent.

28. Hegel has not used numbers in this section; we have introduced them to clarify the structure of the discussion.

29. See *Phen.* (Baillie) 105, (Miller) 27, (Kaufmann) 70, and *Phän.* 39: "The truth is thus the

bacchanalian revel, where not a member is sober; and because every member no sooner becomes detached than it *eo ipso* collapses straight away, the revel is just as much a state of transparent, unbroken calm."

30. It needs to be stressed that we are still in the confines of the logic. We have reached the definition of the *concept* of *objectivity*. Hegel has not here deduced the world independent of all thought. He has only shown that thinking itself is objective. See the Addition to *Enz (Logic)* §192: "Both of them, subjectivity as well as objectivity, are certainly thoughts—even specific thoughts: which must show themselves founded on the universal and self-determining thought. This has been done—at least for subjectivity." But the concept of subjectivity itself "breaks through its own barriers and opens out into objectivity by means of the syllogism."

   For this reason, in the first edition of the *Encyclopaedia,* Hegel explicitly refers to the whole development as being the itinerary of the syllogisms of *understanding* (JE VI §138 [the second § with this number], Bourgeois §140, p. 255.)

31. If the act of assertion was a *particular* determination in *categorical inference,* it is here shown to be an *individual* contingency.

32. Since pv~p could be symbolized as C+C̃ we have here the explicit definition of absolute universality that could be symbolized as (*x*) or as the class 1. This symbolism is required if either class algebra or the lower functional calculus is to advance to determinate assertions. But it is so general that it lacks any determinate content. Therefore it is subject to the same ambiguity as the disjunctive syllogism.

Chapter XII
The Necessity of Hegel's Logic

1. (Miller) 541-553, WL II 169-183, JS II 173-186. For a detailed commentary see in *Art and Logic in Hegel's Philosophy,* ed., Steinkraus, Schmitz and O'Malley (New York: Humanities, 1980) "The Category of Contingency in the Hegelian Logic" by G. DiGiovanni, and my "The Necessity of Contingency."

2. In "Hegel's Theory of the Concept" (*Art and Logic in Hegel's Philosophy)* Merold Westphal identifies individuality and self-determination.

3. Does each of these nine sections also incorporate the full circle of the three types of necessity? The movements from *being* to *a being,* and from *a being* to *a being for its own sake* were complete units. However in the second and third books we found that thought did not collapse into a single individual concept until the end of a much more complex development involving three distinct discussions. In addition the variation in the internal divisions in these sections suggests that they may not manifest a uniform structure.

4. *The Open Society and its Enemies* II 40; *History of Western Philosophy,* 715.

5. Mure, *A Study,* 354; Taylor, *Hegel,* 348; and Findlay, *Hegel,* 74: "A study of Hegel's dialectical practice will show, further, that in spite of anything he may *say* regarding their necessary, scientific character, his transitions are only necessary and inevitable in the rather indefinite sense in which there is necessity and inevitability in a work of art." As Findlay himself notes on page 354 of the second edition, a third reading shows that the necessity of the whole is not indefinite, but is determined by the dialectical method (which involves a disjunctive relation between immediate and relative necessity).

6. "It is only after profounder acquaintance with the other sciences that logic ceases to be for subjective spirit a merely abstract universal and reveals itself as the universal which embraces within itself the wealth of the particular—just as the same proverb, in the

mouth of a youth who understands it quite well, does not possess the wide range of meaning which it has in the mind of a man with the experience of a lifetime behind him, for whom the meaning is expressed in all its powers." *Science of Logic* (Miller) 58, WL I 40, JS I 69.

7. Compare *Phenomenology* (Baillie) 83 (revised), (Miller) 11, (Kaufmann) 32, *Phän* 21: "This horrified rejection of mediation, however, arises in fact from want of acquaintance with its nature, and with the nature of absolute knowledge itself. For mediating is nothing but self-identity that moves itself; or in other words, it is self-reflexive, the moment of the I that is for its own sake. It is pure negativity, or, reduced to its utmost abstraction, *simply becoming.*"

8. The *Phenomenology,* the *Science of Logic,* and the *Encyclopaedia* are three of the four systematic statements published by Hegel while he was alive. Since the fourth, the *Philosophy of Right,* is an elaboration of a sub-section of the *Encyclopaedia,* the subsequent two chapters will review the fundamental principles that underlie the system as a whole.

Chapter XIII
The Logic as Metaphysics

1. *Die Sache an sich selbst*; Miller: "The object in its own self," JS: "The Thing in itself."
2. (Miller) 49f (revised), WL I 30f, JS I, 60. The last phrase (after "veil") translates *an und für sich selbst.*
3. (Miller) 63, WL I 46, JS I, 74; Compare *Enz (Logic)* §24. "Logic therefore coincides with Metaphysics, the science of things set and held in thoughts,—thoughts accredited able to express the essential reality of things."
4. Is there a limitation in Hegel's actual achievement in the fact that he knew only languages from the Indo-European family? Although he discussed the written character of Chinese in *Enz (Philosophy of Mind)* §459 he has not considered its grammatical structure, any more than that of Semitic Hebrew and Arabic, etc. While this wider context might significantly modify the details of his logical discussion, he would maintain that it would not touch its essential method.
5. (Miller) 54, 50; WL I 36, 31; JS I 65, 60.
6. See Hegel's letter to Schelling, Bamberg, May 1807 (I, #95, 161ff); E.T. Kaufmann, *Hegel* 323: "Regarding the greater deformity of the later parts, be considerate also because I finished the editing around midnight before the battle of Jena."
7. E.L. Fackenheim's *The Religious Dimension of Hegel's Thought* (Bloomington & London: 1967) is an extended discussion of the conditions necessary for absolute knowledge.
8. *Ansichsein.*
9. *Fürsichsein.*
10. *Wie er an und für sich ist. Phen* (Baillie) 793f (revised), (Miller) 482f, *Phän* 553.
11. See *Phenomenology* (Baillie) 96 (revised), (Miller) 21, (Kaufmann) 56, *Phän* 32: "Experience is the name for this very process by which the immediate, the unexperienced and the abstract, either sensed or simply thought, alienates itself and then returns to itself out of this alienation; only then is it set forth as it actually is in truth and becomes the possession of consciousness."
12. See *Phen* (Baillie) 791, (Miller) 480, *Phän* 551.
13. They are thus abstractions from his or her concrete actual life. See *Phen* (Baillie) 459, (Miller) 264, *Phän* 314: "Spirit is the self-supporting absolutely real ultimate being. All the previous modes of consciousness are abstractions from it: they are constituted by the

fact that spirit analyzes itself, distinguishes its moments, and halts at each individual mode in turn." In the *Encyclopaedia,* where Hegel is concerned simply to show the analytical structures of human subjectivity, this level is sufficient for his purposes, and leads immediately to the psychology of intelligence and will. In *Phenomenology of Spirit,* however, the question is a matter of knowledge, in which the individual subject must become integrated with other subjects and with the world that is independent of all subjectivity. Therefore he proceeds to the chapters on *Spirit* and *Religion.* See in this respect his interesting remark to *Enz (Logic)* §25.

14. *Phen* (Baillie) 791, (Miller) 481, *Phän* 551. Chapter VI on Spirit is thus not a full-fledged philosophy of history. It considers only those cultures that have passed beyond any religious submission to an alien fate, destiny, or God, and are certain that they, as cultures, embody the whole truth: Greece, Rome, the Renaissance, and the modern world. This certainty becomes expressed in its literature, which explains why *Antigone* and *Le Neveu de Rameau* assume such an important role in this section.

15. See *Phen* (Baillie) 793, (Miller) 482, *Phän* 552.

16. The allusion to Lessing's monograph is intentional.

17. It is this self-awareness of human limitation as such that enables Hegel to resist all Feuerbachian interpretations in which the reductionism of Hegel's early writings is taken as the norm for interpreting his later texts on religion. W. Kaufmann misses this important point; see his *Hegel* 271-275.

18. The statement of these beliefs is detailed by Hegel in the chapter on Revealed Religion, *Phen* (Baillie) 767ff, (Miller) 465ff, *Phän* 535ff. Compare as well §§564-571 in *Enz (Philosophy of Mind).*

19. It is in collapsing these two into one that Hegel distances himself from Christian orthodoxy, although he could find justification in John 20:22.

20. See Lebrun, *La patience du concept,* 33: "If the Christian community does not yet *think* the history it recalls, it lives rather than contemplates it."

21. "I do not accept the authority of popes and councils, for they have contradicted each other—my conscience is captive to the Word of God. I cannot and I will not recant anything, for to go against conscience is neither right nor safe. God help me. Amen." R.H. Bainton, *Here I Stand, A life of Martin Luther,* (New York: Mentor, 1959) 144.

22. See W. Pauch, tr. *Luther: Lecture on Romans* (London: SCM, 1961) 127. "Now can we say that he is perfectly righteous? No; but he is at the same time both a sinner and righteous, a sinner in fact but righteous by virtue of the reckoning and certain promise of God that he will redeem him from sin in order, in the end, to make him perfectly whole and sound." The Lutheran doctrine of *simul peccator et justus* is essential for Hegel. When Luther stresses the *simul,* he transcends the relativism of all earlier Christian confessions. Hegel moves beyond Luther by recognizing that it is the assurance of the promise of God as present, and of the reconciliation as not future but already achieved, that grounds the authority of Luther's self-confidence.

23. Iwand, for example, in his *Rechtfertigungslehre und Christusglaube* (Munchen: Kaiser, 1966) can define the relation only in negative terms.

24. This third and critical constituting moment is developed in *Phen* (Baillie) 794-798, (Miller) 482-486, *Phän* 553-556.

25. *Phen* (Baillie) 798 (revised), (Miller) 486, *Phän* 556. Once again the number of the verb is important. Hegel takes the compound subject *Die Natur, Momente und Bewegung dieses Wissens* and uses it as the subject of a singular verb, which then becomes captured in the singular *it* is I. Note that the three constituents correspond to *essence, conditions* and

grounding *relation*, the three constituents of the *heart of the matter* (as equally, do beautiful soul, experience and revealed religion). The concrete nature of *this* I means that I will inevitably articulate my universal knowledge using the particular language of my own culture. The individuality of this integration in the Hegelian use of language is stressed by A. Koyré. "Note sur la langue et la terminologie hégéliennes" and provides a necessary corrective to the main thrust of Chapter 3 above.

26. In other words *Phen* (Baillie) 798f, (Miller) 486, and *Phän* 556f contain the answer to the perennially vexing problem of "we the philosophers" in *Phenomenology*. What "we" introduce is this criterion of what is essential in the dynamic process. Other than this, "we" can say nothing *a priori* concerning how it will develop. That will be affected by the contingency of geographical and historical setting, and by the negative, "sinful" act of arbitrary limitation.

27. (Miller) 50, WL I 31, JS I 60. Compare Fleischmann, 21: "According to Hegel, the task of pure thought presupposes the long education of history on the part of the individual humanity; and the abstract notions of the logic flow from concrete experience, from deceptions and from human error." And Hyppolite, *Studies on Marx and Hegel*, 169: "In the strict sense of the term, the *Logic* is a rigorous poetic of Being which unfolds through the agency and mediation of man. It is the manifestation of a universal self-consciousness in the singular consciousness of the philosopher. It is the Idea which is manifest in human judgement and not simply its arbitrary or subjective creation." Hegel makes the same point in the *Logic* (Miller) 588 (revised), WL II 226, JS II 222: "Abstract thinking is not to be regarded as a mere setting aside of the sensuous material, the reality of which is not thereby impaired; rather it is the dissolving and reduction of that material as mere phenomenal appearance to the essential, which is manifested only in conceptual thought." See also *Phen* (Baillie) 97, (Miller) 21f, *Phän* 33.

28. Fleischmann, 32.

29. Fleischmann, 24.

30. This interpretation is advanced by Kojève and Rosen. "This absolute Knowledge, being the *last* moment of Time—that is a moment without a *Future*—is no longer a temporal moment." *Introduction to the Reading of Hegel*, (New York and London: Basic, 1964) 148; "Once the truth is revealed, nothing fundamental can change." Rosen, "Hegel and Historicism," *CLIO*, VII 1 (1977) 41.

31. *Phen.* (Baillie) 800 (revised), (Miller) 487, *Phän* 558.

Chapter XIV
Thought and Action

1. (Miller) 824-844, WL II 483-506, JS II 466-486. Hegel's text makes a number of detours to relate this discussion to earlier transitions in the logic and to more common opinions. To isolate the pure method, we have not incorporated these remarks into our commentary.

2. Hegel has only 1 and 2 numbered in the text, indicating the pure beginning and the first difference. Thereafter he surrenders any effort to enumerate, noting that numbers abstract and petrify a process and are therefore in some sense contingent. See (Miller) 836, WL II 497f, JS II 478f.

3. (Miller) 838, WL II 500, JS II 480.

4. The comprehensive, individual thrust can be identified as the *positive-and-negative*. See Chapter VII.

5. (Miller) 842 (revised), WL II 504, JS II 485.

6. Therefore those like Schelling (*Werke* I 10: 154, 212f, and II 3 89) who protest that this move is not adequately comprehended logically fail to notice the radical novelty of this move. It is its illogicality that takes seriously the reality of the material order. See, for example, Baillie, *The Origin and Significance of Hegel's Logic,* 316-7. Findlay discusses this point at 268f. This discussion is based on the final paragraph of the *Logic* (Miller) 843f, WL II 505f, JS II 485f.

7. Recall *Enz (Logic)* §85.

8. The individuation of free action is an act of understanding, for "understanding is as indispensable in practice as it is in theory. Character is an essential in conduct, and a man of character is an understanding man, who in that capacity has definite ends in view and undeviatingly pursues them." *Enz (Logic)* §80, Addition.

9. Compare as well, in the more limited context of the psychology, the transition from intelligence to will (*Enz [Mind]* §468). When Mure laments the fact that "the logician, however firmly he conceives finitude within and not without the activity of Spirit, cannot display in finite thinking the whole movement of spirit's issue and return upon itself," *(A Study of Hegel's Logic,* 43f) he overlooks the fact that this very failure of the logician is but one component of the whole movement, and is thus not alien to it.

10. It is interesting to notice a difference between the first and the second editions of "With What Must the Science Begin?" In 1812 the sentence read: "Thus at the *end* of the development of pure knowing, spirit will freely externalize itself, and abandon itself to the shape of an immediate consciousness, as consciousness of a being that stands opposed to it as an other." HGW XI 35. In 1831 it was changed to: "Thus in still greater measure the absolute spirit which reveals itself as the concrete and final supreme truth of all being is known at the *end* of the development as freely externalizing itself, abandoning itself to the shape of an *immediate* being—deciding to create a world. . ." (Miller) 71 (revised), WL I 55f, JS I 83. What originally was to be the simple release into the immediacy of pure reference was transformed into a reference to the divine decision to create. Compare here (Miller) 592, WL II 230f, JS II 226f.

11. See *Enz (Nature)* §§254-256, and L.S. Stepelevich, "The Hegelian Conception of Space," *Nature and System* I (1979), 111-126.

12. Recall the analysis of abstract universality and pure individuality in Chapter 9.

13. *Enz (Nature)* §§257-9. See my article, "Concept and Time in Hegel," *Dialogue* XII 3 (September 1973), 403-422.

14. The reflective or speculative moment is already present in living beings. When Hegel calls the individual reality *spirit* he does not want to refer simply to mind as distinguished from body. (This is why the common English translation for *Geist* is inadequate.) Rather spirit integrates a natural life, including all its mechanical, chemical and biological determinations, through a new type of activity that can specifically react to itself in order to control both itself and its world.

15. These two perspectives correspond to *The Philosophy of Mind,* of *Enz.* and the *Phenomenology,* although the four series of lectures on history, art, religion and philosophy are also relevant to the historical discipline. Would the *Philosophy of Nature* also benefit from a philosophical history of natural science?

16. *Enz. (Mind)* §384 Remark (revised).

17. Indeed, because the passage of time will expand the range and the nature of experience (the interaction of self and world), new intellectual processes may become differentiated that result in new categories and new logical transitions—"For two thousand years of

continuous working on the part of spirit must have supplied it with a higher consciousness of its thinking and of what is genuinely essential in its very self." WL I 33, JS I 62, (Miller) 51.

18. (Miller) 54, WL II 36, JS I 65.

19. "...die Seite der Erscheinung...ist aufgehoben...." (JE VI 474) is replaced by "...dass es...hiemit aus der Erscheinung ...sich erhoben hat." (*Enz.* [*Philosophy of Mind*] §574).

20. §575. See on this, Fulda, *Das Problem einer Einleitung,* 288. It is this sentence, deliberately introduced at the end of his life into the final section of his one systematic statement that provides convincing evidence that Hegel did not think that the history of philosophy had ended with his system, despite Kojève's assertion: "We know that for Hegel this end of history is marked by the coming of Science in the form of a Book." *Introduction to the Reading of Hegel,* 148.

21. Since pure self-knowledge presupposes the concrete actuality of political action and cultural reflection, philosophy comes on the scene only after spirit has achieved a level of coherent life. It leads immediately to the sharp decisiveness of a disruptive act, which destroys the integration already achieved. Since all action generates unexpected contingency, philosophy cannot determine with *a priori* certitude how one ought to act. That is left to the initiative of responsible, but pure, freedom. See here the Introduction to the *Philosophy of History* translated by R. S. Hartmann in *Reason in History* (Indianapolis and New York: 1953) 87-95; and the Preface to the *Philosophy of Right* (Oxford: 1942) 12f. In his doctoral dissertation Marx rendered explicit this implication of Hegel's philosophy of history. See K. Löwith *From Hegel to Nietzsche,* (New York: 1967) 89-101.

27. The explicit references to freedom here and in the previous paragraph are additions of the third edition.

23. With this, the end of our short commentary of §§575-577. Compare from Hegel's lecture material the interesting addition to *Enz. (Logic)* §187.

24. Klaus Hedwig has drawn my attention to the interesting contrast between the *concept* of philosophy (§574) and the *idea* of philosophy in §577. According to our interpretation, Hegel's system has established the absolute principle (*Begriff)* of philosophy; its complete achievement is yet to come. Compare Lebrun, *La patience du concept,* 410: "Anti-Hegelianism in principle is no longer, then, solely what one supposes: the rejection of a devouring absolute. It denotes the uneasiness with not being able to locate the absolute otherwise than by recommencing the discourse, the concern to safeguard a closed beginning."

25. *Enz. (Mind)* §577.

26. Despite the accusation of Kierkegaard that "most systematizers. . .do not live in their own enormous systematic buildings," *Journal,* ed. Dru (New York: Harper, 1959) 98.

Chapter XV
Conclusion

1. This, even Popper grudgingly allows. "I am quite prepared to admit that this is not a bad description of the way in which a critical discussion, and therefore also scientific thought, may sometimes progress. For all criticism consists in pointing out some contradictions or discrepancies, and scientific progress consists largely in the elimination of contradictions wherever we find them." But because Popper does not distinguish between relative and absolute necessity he assumes that because for Hegel contradictions are relatively

unavoidable and desirable they are not to be eliminated at all. See *The Open Society,* II 39.

2. Hegel writes in *Enz (Logic)* §13 (revised): "The philosophy that is the latest birth of time is the result of all the philosophies that have preceded it and must include the principles of all; and so if, on other grounds, it deserves the title of philosophy, it will be the most developed, richest, and most concrete of all"; thus he spelled out the criteria not only for his own system, but for those of his successors.

3. G. Noël, *La logique de Hegel,* 2nd ed., 112.

4. The same model can be seen in Buddhism. The logical cosmology of Hindu thought is confronted with the painful suffering of human existence, to be then integrated into the paradoxical achievement of Nirvana—the pure reflection of the will not to will, of the non-existing existence. The three categories of Peirce's pragmatism also reflect this pattern.

Bibliography

Primary Sources

Fichtes Werke. ed. I.H. Fichte. Berlin: Gruyter, 1971.

Fichte, J.G. *Science Of Knowledge.* ed. & tr. P. Heath and J. Lachs. New York: Appleton-Century-Crofts, 1970.

Dokumente zu Hegels Entwicklung. ed. J. Hoffmeister. Stuttgart: Fromann, 1974.

Briefe von und an Hegel. ed. J. Hoffmeister. Hamburg: Meiner, 1952.

Hegel, G.W.F. *Sämtliche Werke, Jubiläumsausgabe in zwanzig Bänden.* ed. H. Glockner. 4. Ausgabe. Stuttgart: Fromann, 1968.

Hegel, G.W.F. *Werke in zwanzig Bänden.* Frankfurt a/M: Suhrkamp, 1970.

Hegel, G.W.F. *Gesammelte Werke.* Hamburg: Meiner, 1968.

Hegel, G.W.F. *Jenenser Logik, Metaphysik und Naturphilosophie.* ed. G. Lasson. Hamburg: Meiner, 1967.

Hegel, G.W.F. *Jenaer Realphilosophie.* ed. J. Hoffmeister. Hamburg: Meiner, 1969.

Hegel, G.W.F. *Phänomenologie des Geistes.* ed. J. Hoffmeister. Hamburg: Meiner, 1952.

The Phenomenology of Mind. tr. J.B. Baillie. London: Allen & Unwin & New York: Macmillan, 1955.

Phenomenology of Spirit. tr. A.V. Miller. Oxford: Clarendon, 1977.

La Phenomenologie de l'Esprit. tr. J. Hyppolite. Paris: Aubier, 1941.

Hegel: Texts and Commentary. tr. W. Kaufmann. Garden City: Doubleday, 1966.

Hegel, G.W.F. *Wissenschaft der Logik.* ed. G. Lasson. Hamburg: Meiner, 1967.

Hegel's Science of Logic. tr. W.H. Johnston & L.G. Struthers. London: Allen & Unwin & New York: Macmillan, 1951.

Hegel's Science of Logic. tr. A.V. Miller. London: Allen & Unwin & New York: Humanities, 1969.

Science de la Logique. tr. P.J. Labarrière et G. Jarczyk. Paris: Aubier, 1972 & 1976.

Hegel, G.W.F. *Enzyklopädie der philosophischen Wissenschaften im Grundrisse (1830).* ed. F. Nicolin & O. Pöggeler. Hamburg: Meiner, 1959.

The Logic of Hegel. tr. W. Wallace. Oxford, 1950.

Encyclopédie des Sciences Philosophiques, I, La Science de la Logique. tr. B. Bourgeois. Paris: Vrin, 1970.

Hegel's Philosophy of Mind. tr. W. Wallace & A.V. Miller. Oxford: Clarendon, 1971.

Hegel, G.W.F. *On Christianity: Early Theological Writings.* tr. T.M. Knox & R. Kroner. New York: Harper, 1961.

Hegel, G.W.F. *Lectures in the History of Philosophy.* tr. E.S. Haldane & F.H. Simpson. London: Kegan Paul, Trench, Trubner, 1895.

Kant, Immanuel, *Kritik der reinen Vernunft.* [Band 3 & 4 of *Immanuel Kant Werke in zehn Bänden*] Darmstadt: Wissenschaftliche Buchgesellschaft, 1968.

Immanuel Kant's Critique of Pure Reason. tr. N.K. Kemp Smith. London: Macmillan, 1953.

Schelling, F.W.J. *Ausgewählte Werke.* Darmstadt: Wissenschaftliche Buchgesellschaft, 1966-68.

Secondary Sources
(a) Monographs

Baillie, J.B. *The Origin and Significance of Hegel's Logic.* London: Macmillan, 1901.

Bloch, E. *Subjekt-Objekt, Erläuterungen zu Hegel.* Frankfurt a/M: Suhrkamp, 1962.

Bodammer, T. *Hegels Deutung der Sprache; Interpretation zu Hegels Äusserungen über die Sprache.* Hamburg: Meiner, 1969.

Caird, E. *Hegel.* Edinburgh & London: Blackwood, 1903.

Clark, M. *Logic and System, A Study of the Transition from "Vorstellung" to Thought in the Philosophy of Hegel.* The Hague: Nijhoff, 1971.

Cook, D. J. *Language in the Philosophy of Hegel*. The Hague & Paris: Mouton, 1973.

Croce, B. *Saggio Sullo Hegel*. Bari: Gius, Laterza & Figli, 1948. [*Ciò che è vivo e ciò che è morto della filosofia di Hegel*. pp. 1-204.]

What is Living and what is Dead in the Philosophy of Hegel. tr. D. Ainslie. London: Macmillan, 1915.

D'Hondt, Jacques. *Hegel, Philosophe de l'Histoire vivante*. Paris: PUF, 1966.

Düsing, K. *Das Problem der Sujektivität in Hegels Logik*. Bonn: Bouvier, 1976.

Eley, Lothar. *Hegels Wissenschaft der Logik, Leitfaden und Kommentar*. München: Fink, 1976.

Fackenheim, E.L. *The Religious Dimension in Hegel's Thought*. Bloomington & London: Indiana U.P., 1967.

Fetscher, I. *Hegels Lehre vom Menschen*. Stuttgart-Bad Cannstatt: Fromann, 1970.

Findlay, J.N. *Hegel, A Re-examination*. London: Allen & Unwin & New York: Humanities, 1958.

Fleischmann, E.J. *La Science universelle ou la Logique de Hegel*. Paris: Plon, 1968.

Fulda, H.F. *Das Problem einer Einleitung in Hegels Wissenschaft der Logik*. Frankfurt a/M: Klostermann, 1965.

Gadamer, H.-G. *Hegels Dialektik, Fünf hermeneutische Studien*. Tübingen: Mohr, 1971.

Hegel's Dialectic, Five Hermeneutical Studies. tr. P. Christopher Smith. New Haven & London: Yale, 1976.

Garaudy, R. *La Pensée de Hegel*. Paris: Bordas, 1966.

Grègoire, F. *Études hégéliennes, les points capitaux du système*. Louvain: PUL & Paris: Beatrice-Nauwelaerts, 1958.

Harris, W.T. *Hegel's Logic*. Chicago: Griggs, 1890.

Hyppolite, Jean. *Genèse et Structure de la Phénomenologie de l'Esprit de Hegel*. Paris: Aubier, 1946.

Hyppolite, Jean. *Logique et Existence, Essai sur la Logique de Hegel*. Paris: PUF, 1961.

Hyppolite, Jean. *Studies on Marx and Hegel*. tr. J. O'Neill. London: Heinemann, 1969.

Kaufmann, W. *Hegel, A Reinterpretation*. Garden City: Doubleday, 1966.

Kojève, A. *Introduction to the Reading of Hegel*. ed. A. Bloom. tr. J.H. Nichols, Jr. New York & London: Basic, 1969.

Kroner, R. *Von Kant bis Hegel*. 2. Auflage. Tübingen: Mohr, 1961.

Lakebrink, B. *Studien zur Metaphysik Hegels*. Freiberg: Rombach, 1969.

Lebrun, G. *La Patience du Concept*. Paris: Gallimard, 1972.

Leisegang, H. *Denkformen*. 2nd. ed. Berlin: de Gruyter, 1951.

Léonard, A. *Commentaire literale de la Logique de Hegel*. Paris: Vrin, 1974.

Marcuse, H. *Hegels Ontologie und die Theorie der Geschichtlichkeit*. Frankfurt a/M: Klostermann, 1968.

Marcuse, H. *Reason and Revolution: Hegel and the Rise of Social Theory*. 2nd ed. New York: Humanities, 1954.

Marx, W. *Hegels Theorie logischer Vermittlung*. Stuttgart-Bad Cannstatt: Fromann, 1972.

McTaggart, J.M.E. *A Commentary on Hegel's Logic*. New York: Russell & Russell, 1964.

McTaggart, J.M.E. *Studies in the Hegelian Dialectic*. 2nd ed. New York: Russell & Russell, 1964.

van der Meulen, J. *Hegel, die gebrochene Mitte*. Hamburg: Meiner, 1958.

Mure, G.R.G. *An Introduction to Hegel*. Oxford: Clarendon, 1940.

Mure, G.R.G. *A Study of Hegel's Logic*. Oxford: Clarendon, 1950.

Noël, G. *La Logique de Hegel*. Paris: Vrin, 1967.

Rosenkranz, K. *Georg Wilhelm Friedrich Hegels Leben*. Darmstadt: Wissenschaftliche Buchgesellschaft, 1971.

Sarlemijn, A. *Hegel's Dialectic*. Tr. P. Kirschenmann. Dordrecht & Boston: Reidel, 1975.

Stace, W.T. *The Philosophy of Hegel: A Systematic Exposition*. New York: Dover, 1955.

Stirling, J.H. *The Secret of Hegel, being the Hegelian System in Origin, Principle, Form and Matter*. Dubuque: Wm. C. Brown, nd. Reprint of Edinburgh: Oliver & Boyd; London: Simkin, Marshall; New York: Putnam's, 1898.

Taylor, C. *Hegel*. Cambridge: Cambridge U.P., 1975.

Wallace, W. *Prolegomena to the Study of Hegel's Philosophy and especially of his Logic*. Oxford: Clarendon, 1894.

(b) Articles
i. Anthologies

D'Hondt, J. ed. *Hegel et la Pensée Moderne*. Paris: PUF, 1970.

Fetscher, I. ed. *Hegel in der Sicht der neueren Forschung*. Darmstadt: Wissenschaftliche Buchgesellschaft, 1973.

MacIntyre, A. ed. *Hegel, A Collection of Critical Essays.* Garden City: Doubleday, 1972.

Methais, P. ed. *Hegel et Marx, La politique et la réel.* Poitiers: Faculté des Lettres et Sciences Humaines, 1970.

O'Malley, J.J., K.W. Algozin, et al. eds. *The Legacy of Hegel.* The Hague: Nijhoff, 1973.

O'Malley, J.J., K.W. Algozin, et al, eds. *Hegel and the History of Philosophy.* The Hague: Nijhoff, 1974.

Steinkraus, W., K. Schmitz & J.J. O'Malley, eds. *Art and Logic in Hegel's Philosophy.* New York: Humanities, 1980.

Weiss, F.G. ed. *Beyond Epistemology, New Studies in the Philosophy of Hegel.* The Hague: Nijhoff, 1974.

ii. Individual Articles

Burbidge, J. "Concept and Time in Hegel," *Dialogue,* XII (1973), 403-422.

Dove, K. "Hegel and Creativity," *The Owl of Minerva,* IX, 4 (June 1978), 5-10.

Fleischmann, E.J. "Objektive und Subjektive Logik bei Hegel," *Hegelstudien,* Beiheft 1 (1964), 45–54.

Fulda, H.F. "Über den spekulativen Anfang," in *Subjektivität und Metaphysik, Festschrift für Wolfgang Cramer.* Frankfurt a/M: Klostermann, 1966, 109-127.

Henrich, D. "Anfang und Methode der Logik" *Hegelstudien,* Beiheft 1 (1964), 19-35.

Koyré, A. "Note sure la langue et la terminologie hégéliennes," in *Études d'histoire de la pensée philosophique.* Paris: Gallimard, 1971.

Mueller, G.E. "The Hegel Legend of 'Thesis-Antithesis-Synthesis'," *Journal of the History of Ideas,* XIX (1958), 411-414.

Pöggeler, O. "Fragmente aus einer Hegelschen Logik mit einem Nachwort zur Entwicklungsgeschichte von Hegels Logik," *Hegelstudien,* 2 (1963), 19-70.

Rosen, S. "Hegel and Historicism," *CLIO,* VII, 1, (1977) 35-52.

Stepelevich, L.S. "The Hegelian Conception of Space," *Nature and System,* I, (1979), 111-126.

Surber, J.P. "Review of *Language in the Philosophy of Hegel,* by D. J. Cook," *Owl of Minerva,* VIII, 1, (1976) 1-4.

Index of Names

Index of Concepts

Some terms are central to the explication of the logic and are used throughout the study. For these, major references are indicated, but *"and throughout"* is added to indicate their more general use.